KOSHER KETTLE™

International Adventures
in
Jewish Cooking

Edited by
Sybil Ruth Kaplan

Five Star Publications
Chandler, Arizona

First Printing, June 1996
Second Printing, August 1996

Library of Congress Cataloging-in-Publication Data

Kosher Kettle: International Adventures in Jewish Cooking / edited by Sybil Ruth Kaplan.
     p.   cm.
  Includes index.
  ISBN 1-877749-19-2 (perfect bound, paper, layflat binding)
  1. Cookery, Jewish. 2. Kosher food. I. Kaplan, Sybil Ruth, 1938-
TX724.K643 1996
641.5′676--dc20   96-11791
                                      CIP

Edited by Sybil Ruth Kaplan
Cover design and interior illustrations by Lynlie Hermann
Typesetting, layout, and book design by Toni Smith

Table of Contents

Special Thanks to...

Sybil Ruth Kaplan for doing an incredible job gathering, editing, and contributing to this cookbook. Even though our relationship has transpired over the phone, fax, and mail, her essence is felt in every transaction along the way. Sybil has been and continues to be an inspiration.

Lynlie Hermann for creating the cover design and interior illustrations, and for always going beyond the call of duty.

Toni Smith for doing a great job in typesetting this book.

Ellen Weiner for helping to get recipes contributed and for maintaining a positive approach to every endeavor she is asked to tackle.

Mary E. Hawkins who helped get **Kosher Kettle** off the ground and into flight.

Barry Kaplan, whose quiet talents helped contribute to this cookbook.

Nellie Foster for contributing and testing some of the **Kosher Kettle** recipes.

Dalia Carmel for contributing so many of her wonderful kosher recipes.

KitchenAid for contributing two mixers to allow the testing of many of the recipes found in **Kosher Kettle**. KitchenAid makes life in the kitchen so much easier.

Quaker Oats Company, Empire Kosher Poultry Company, Hagafen Cellars, Kedem Royal Wine Corporation, **The Aleph-Bet of Jewish Cooking** for contributing to this cookbook.

To each **Kosher Kettle** contributor from around the world who allowed us to enter into their kitchens and homes by sharing their kosher recipes. My goal in publishing this cookbook was to show how we share a common bond and how it unites us and binds us. I was pleased to see how kosher cooking varied around the globe.

To each person who has purchased this cookbook, you have not only added international kosher recipes to your home, you have contributed to MAZON: A Jewish Response to Hunger. We are cognizant of the hungry as we gather around our tables. I want to build this concern into **Kosher Kettle**. No kettle should be without, no kettle empty. Therefore, Five Star Publications is going to donate 3% of every **Kosher Kettle** sold to MAZON: A Jewish Response to Hunger. I met MAZON during the High Holidays when Lorre Levy, a friend, indicated that she was going to contribute to MAZON the money she normally would have spent on the meals she gave up during her Yom Kippur fast. I agreed and did the same. I wanted to do more. I am normally not one to set New Year's resolutions, but that year was different. I made a resolution to do more for those that had less. I wasn't sure how I was going to do it...but I intended to do something. We can make a difference! The difference for me started with Lorre Levy telling me about MAZON and continues with you. No one should have to go to bed hungry or wake up hungry. Hence, our commitment of 3% to MAZON. Your purchase of **Kosher Kettle**: Consider it a *mitzvah*.

Linda Foster Radke, Publisher

Foreword

by Joan Nathan

Kosher Kettle: International Adventures in Jewish Cooking is a collection of recipes from around the world.

I met Sybil Ruth Kaplan 20 years ago in Jerusalem while she was writing her first cookbook, **Wonders of a Wonder Pot**. A "wonder pot" was a marvelous invention created in Israel to help cooks with baking before they had ovens. Like her inventiveness with the wonder pot, Sybil has done it again, this time compiling her own kosher recipes with those of over 75 contributors.

In addition, I was delighted to see that she has included so many of Dalia Carmel's kosher recipes. Dalia, a food hobbyist, has been an invaluable help to food writers like myself throughout the years.

Joan Nathan is the author of **Jewish Cooking in America**, winner of the 1994 Julia Child Award for Best Cookbook of the Year and the 1994 James Beard Award for Food of the Americas. Her other books include **The Children's Jewish Holiday Kitchen, The Jewish Holiday Kitchen, American Folklife Cookbook** and **The Flavor of Jerusalem**.

Ms. Nathan was also the senior producer of *Passover: Traditions of Freedom*, a one-hour documentary sponsored by Maryland Public Television, and winner of a Silver Award at the 1994 Houston International Film Festival and the highest Chris Award, in the Religion & Philosophy division of the 1994 Columbus International Film Festival.

In addition, Ms. Nathan lectures around the country and is a frequent contributor to *The New York Times, Los Angeles Times Syndicate, Food Arts Magazine* and *Hadassah Magazine*.

Introduction

The paragraph was interesting. It was late summer and I noticed it in one of the Jewish papers that comes into our home, announcing a cookbook being prepared and recipes needed.

That really sparked my interest because it had been about seven years since I had last helped compile and edit a cookbook. I jotted a quick letter off to the publisher in Chandler, Arizona, telling her I could supply her with whatever was lacking in her cookbook from my immense recipe files.

It didn't take long for Linda Radke to pick up the phone and call me. We clicked immediately. The more we talked, the more we realized we were absolutely on the same wavelength as far as cookbooks were concerned. Before long I was offering to go through my files and see what I could contribute.

My next letter yielded a list of 157 possibilities from people who had given my recipes over the years and who were from all kinds of ethnic backgrounds. By fall we had a deal, and I was going to actually compile and edit the cookbook. I was off and typing! Linda was busy soliciting recipes from around the world also, and it became great fun to talk on the phone and share experiences.

With each new idea, we saw again how closely we thought alike in the planning of the cookbook.

By December we had set our deadlines. January has been a difficult time, getting all the last-minute recipes in and getting the cookbook out of my hands and into the mail to Arizona. One tends to get a mother bird-baby bird attachment to the manuscript, and the more I looked at it, the more details I would think of to perfect.

It has really been a delightful fax/phone/letter experience for me to get to know Linda and to try to fulfill her dream with this project. When she asked me how I felt about three percent of the proceeds being donated to MAZON, the Jewish answer to hunger project, I was even more touched by the kind of person Linda must be.

Please note, the recipes have only been tested by the contributors, although the publisher, Linda Radke, and I have tested some in our own kitchens at random.

I hope readers will enjoy meeting the people who contributed the recipes for this book and will "read" the cookbook. Linda knew some of the people and was related to others; I knew some as my friends, relatives and acquaintances.

I want to thank Linda for having faith in me to let me try to fulfill her ideas with this **Kosher Kettle**.

I want to thank my friend, Marilyn, in Jerusalem, for helping me "track down" a number of my contributors in Israel.

I want to thank my daughters, Shara and Elissa, for listening to all my adventures as I gathered the recipes and readied the cookbook and to say how pleased I am that they, too, love cooking.

I want to thank my husband, Barry, for supporting my enthusiasm for this project by receiving the faxes in his office and transmitting messages to me, for listening to the stories and hearing about recipes, and for tasting some of the recipes as I was inspired to try new ones.

We hope everyone will be as excited to use this kosher international cookbook as we are to produce it.

Sybil Ruth Kaplan
January 1996

Basic Guidelines of *Kashrut*

Kashrut (keeping kosher) for many people is an intrinsic part of their daily living. It is not just a practice which our mothers and/or grandmothers followed, but it is a natural part of our lives today.

Keeping kosher is adhering to a commandment given to us by G-d. *Kashrut* is a matter of discipline which we impose upon ourselves so that we have an intimate connection to following a precept connected to our daily needs.

Open the Torah to Leviticus 11 and you can read all that one may eat and what one may not eat. The reason is clearly stated also--"For I am the Lord that brought you up out of the land of Egypt, to be your G-d; ye shall therefore be holy, for I am holy." Elaborations on which foods are fit are in other chapters, particularly Deuteronomy 14, as well as the Talmud and codes of Jewish law.

For those keeping kosher, foods are divided into three categories. These designations--meat, dairy and pareve--are also used on all of the recipes in this cookbook.

Meat

Meat (*basahr* in Hebrew, *fleishig* in Yiddish) consists of all meat, fowl and their byproducts. The book of Leviticus 11 explains the precise animals that one may eat and the rules. Basically, kosher meat must come from an animal that chews its cud and has split hooves. Cows, sheep and goats fall into this category.

The most common fowl which are kosher are domesticated chickens, Cornish hens, turkeys, ducks and geese.

All of these animals must be slaughtered by a *shochet*, a ritual slaughterer, who is trained in kosher slaughtering.

Today, it is fairly easy to purchase meat and fowl from a reputable kosher butcher which have already been kashered and thus this eliminates the time-consuming job which our foremothers had to soak and salt meat after slaughter.

Dairy

Any food which comes from milk is considered dairy (*chalavi* in Hebrew, *milchig* in Yiddish). Milk, butter, yogurt, dairy margarine, sour cream and cheeses are dairy. Dairy products must also come from a kosher animal and contain no non-kosher additives. A product which has the words caseinate, lactose or whey is a product which is dairy.

Pareve

Pareve foods are those which are neither meat nor dairy and contain neither meat nor dairy derivatives.

Fruit, vegetables, eggs, juices, fish, grains coffee, tea, soft drinks and pasta are among the foods which are pareve.

Kosher fish are those which have fins and scales. Among the kosher fish are anchovies, bass, carp, cod, flounder, grouper, haddock, hake, halibut, herring, mackerel, perch, pike, red snapper, salmon, sardines, St. Peter's fish (tilapia), trout, tuna, and whitefish. Fish roe from a kosher fish is also kosher. Swordfish and sturgeon have fins and scales but they fall off so Orthodox do not eat them and Conservative do.

Cheese made with rennet, an extract of the enzyme renin, are not considered kosher by Orthodox. Conservative no longer consider processed rennet an animal product.

Some products bear "non-dairy" in their names but unless the word "pareve" is written on the label accompanied by the ⓤ in a circle or other reputable kosher symbols, these products may not be totally without dairy derivatives.

How Do We Know It's Kosher?

Companies which produce processed foods usually have a rabbi on staff or readily available to act as overseer to make sure the foods are kosher. Many foods in today's supermarkets carry a D or P next to a symbol which means Dairy or Pareve although "P" can denote "kosher for Passover" as well. If a food is kosher for Passover, that is usually labeled as such.

More than 130 symbols are used to mark products that are kosher, but the five most widely accepted ones are:

Ⓤ inside a circle which means certified by the Union of Orthodox Congregations.

Ⓚ inside a circle which means certified by Organized Kashrut Laboratories of Brooklyn, New York.

The Hebrew letter Kuf with a K inside which means certified by Kosher Supervision Service of Teaneck, New Jersey.

a five-sided star with a K in the center which means certified by the Orthodox Jewish Council of Baltimore, Maryland.

a triangle with a K in the center which means certified by Rabbi Joseph Ralbag of New York City, New York.

Many manufacturers also use a plain K. This generally means the supervision of the production of that product is by a rabbi and is as reputable as that rabbi.

What Goes With What?

Meat and dairy foods are not cooked or eaten together. ("Thou shalt not seethe a kid in its mother's milk," Exodus 23:19). Traditions vary on how long one must wait, but in general, one must wait some brief time after eating dairy before eating meat.

When one eats meat, one must generally wait anywhere from three to six hours before eating dairy.

Setting Up the Kitchen

In order to have a kosher kitchen with the least amount of problems, it is recommended that one have separate cabinets for dairy dishes, silverware, cooking and bakeware and another set of cabinets for meat dishes, silverware, cooking and bakeware.

Drinking glasses and salad plates can be used for dairy meals and meat meals but it is necessary to wash them thoroughly after each use.

One may also want pareve cookware and bakeware.

In addition to these, one uses separate salt and pepper shakers, bread baskets or trays, dish racks, sponges, scouring pads, towels and tablecloths. Most people use some readily identifiable color code such as white or beige or sometimes blue for dairy and brown or red for meat.

Some people also mark on the inside of a drawer or cabinet whether the items contained therein are dairy or meat or pareve. If something is similar, such as knives or wooden spoons, one can mark those for meat with red nail polish on the end.

All of the above also applies to Passover when separate meat and dairy dishes, silverware, cookware and bakeware and drinking glasses must be used that are not used the rest of the year.

In the Kitchen

When one has two sinks, one can be designated dairy and one meat. If one has only one sink, then food and dishes must be put on meat or dairy racks and not in the sink directly. Separate categories of place mats or tablecloths should be set aside for use with meat or dairy. Color coding is easy for this also (e.g., light colors for dairy and dark colors for meat). Countertops can be set aside, one for dairy and one for meat, or a covering used for each.

Separate areas should be set aside in a freezer and refrigerator for meat and dairy.

Some people use the oven and broiler of a stove for meat and a separate toaster-oven broiler for dairy to avoid mixing. If the oven will be used for both dairy and meat, then foil can be placed under the pans for each use. Small appliances can be used for dairy and meat as long as separate attachments are used and there is a good cleaning after each use.

There are many intricacies to keeping kosher which cannot be elaborated upon here so, when in doubt, if you have a question, always consult your local rabbi.

Special thanks to Rabbi Herbert J. Mandl, my rabbi at Kehilath Israel Synagogue in Overland Park, Kansas, for looking over this article.

Sybil Kaplan

Beverages

Quick Cappuccino

Sybil Kaplan   Italian Style
Overland Park, Kansas   Yield: 4 Servings

1 cup milk   **3 tablespoons cocoa**
3 cups double-strength coffee   **2 teaspoons vanilla**
  (no-caffeine is okay)   **¼ cup brandy (optional)**

1. Place milk and coffee in a saucepan. Stir in cocoa and vanilla and heat.
2. Add brandy if using. Heat and serve.

Preparation and Cooking Time: 10 minutes

Note: Cappuccino is really an Italian coffee made with a creamy foam on top from steamed milk.

Quicker Cappuccino

Sybil Kaplan   Italian Style
Overland Park, Kansas   Yield: 4 Servings

3 cups water   **3 tablespoons cocoa**
1 cup milk   **¼ cup brandy or**
6 teaspoons instant coffee   **2 teaspoons vanilla**

1. Heat water and milk in a saucepan.
2. Add coffee and cocoa and heat.
3. Stir in brandy or vanilla.

Preparation and Cooking Time: 10 minutes

Mocha Cappuccino

Sybil Kaplan
Overland Park, Kansas

Italian Style
Yield: 4 Servings

1 cup milk
3 cups water
4 teaspoons chocolate chips
4 teaspoons instant coffee
¾ teaspoon vanilla

6 teaspoons sugar
½ teaspoon cinnamon
⅛ teaspoon allspice
1 teaspoon brandy extract

1. Place milk and water in a saucepan. Add chocolate chips and coffee when it begins to get warm.
2. Add vanilla, sugar, cinnamon, allspice and extract. Heat. Serve instantly.

Whipping cream on top makes a special presentation.

Preparation and Cooking Time: 10 to 15 minutes

Hana's Diet Milk Shake

Sybil Kaplan
Overland Park, Kansas   Yield: 1 Serving

*Hana and I met and became friends when her husband was the
aliyah shalich (emissary) in Chicago. We spent many hours together.
I practiced Hebrew with her and we exchanged recipes. I think she
made this up while in Chicago. She now lives with her husband,
Yehudah, and children Eyal and Sharon in Rishon l'Tzion, Israel.*

1 teaspoon instant coffee powder	**2 teaspoons sugar**
½ cup low-fat milk (2%)	**substitute**
½ cup water	**2 ice cubes**

1. Place all ingredients in a blender. Blend a few seconds.
   Pour into a glass.

Preparation and Cooking Time: Less than 5 minutes

Note: This recipe can be doubled or tripled for larger
quantities.

"And she opened a bottle of milk, and gave him
drink" *(Judges 4:19)*

My Egg Cream

Sybil Kaplan
Overland Park, Kansas   Yield: 1 Serving

A neighbor taught this to me when I lived in New York.

2 teaspoons chocolate syrup
⅓ glass milk
Seltzer

1. Place syrup in a glass. Stir in milk. Add seltzer to the top of the glass.

Variations: Use ⅓ glass milk, 1 teaspoon chocolate syrup, ⅓ glass seltzer and 1 banana, cut up.

Preparation and Cooking Time: Less than 5 minutes

Note: This New York City soda fountain drink was created in the 1930s and got its name from the froth on top, although it contains no eggs.

Melon Shake

Sybil Kaplan   Israel
Overland Park, Kansas   Yield: 1 to 2 Servings

*Many of Israel's hotels would have special food festivals and invite the press. Since I wrote a food column in Israel's only English language daily, **The Jerusalem Post**, I frequently learned new recipes created by the country's top chefs. This was given to me by the Jerusalem Hilton Hotel.*

1 8-ounce container sour cream
2 teaspoons honey
1 cup milk
½ melon, cut into pieces

1. Place all ingredients into a blender. Blend a few seconds until smooth.
2. Pour into tall glasses.

Preparation and Cooking Time: Less than 5 minutes

"...They shall eat your fruit and they shall drink your milk" *(Ezekiel 25:4)*

Tova's Hot Apple Punch
Punch Tapuchei Etz

Sybil Kaplan
Overland Park, Kansas

Israel
Yield: 4 Servings

Tova Weinberger was the wife of the Israel economic attaché in Chicago when we met. She gave me this recipe.

4 cups apple juice
½ cup sugar (optional)
2 cinnamon sticks
1 cup dry red wine
1 seedless orange,
  sliced and peeled

Whole cloves
¼ cup chocolate-orange
  liqueur, cognac or
  brandy (optional)

1. Place apple juice, sugar and cinnamon sticks in a pot. Add wine. Bring to a boil.
2. Stick cloves in orange slices and add to punch. Add liqueur, cognac or brandy. Serve hot.

This recipe can be doubled or tripled according to number of guests.

Preparation and Cooking Time: Approximately 15 minutes

Tova's Orange Punch
Punch Tapuzim

Sybil Kaplan
Overland Park, Kansas

Israel
Yield: 8 Servings

I met Tova Weinberger when she was living in Chicago as the wife of the economic attaché from Israel. She gave this recipe to me.

4 cups orange juice
1 cup sugar (optional)
3 cups dry white wine
3 cups strong tea

1 cup orange liqueur
   or orange-chocolate
   liqueur
10 whole cloves
2 seedless oranges,
   cut into slices

1. Place orange juice, sugar, and wine in a large pot. Add tea and liqueur and heat.
2. Stick cloves into orange slices. Drop into punch. Serve hot.

This recipe can be doubled or tripled according to number of guests.

Preparation and Cooking Time: Approximately 15 minutes

For punch, make an ice mold. Boil water, cool then pour into the bowl or mold. Let freeze solid. Arrange fruit pieces or mint leaves on ice, add ¼-inch cool, boiled water and let freeze again.
To use, dip mold in hot water and turn into punch bowl.

Hot Sangria

Sybil Kaplan
Overland Park, Kansas

Spanish Style
Yield: 8 to 10 Servings

I don't recall where I got this recipe, but I remember the reason I liked it was because of its color and because it was something different to serve in winter at parties because it was hot.

1 pink grapefruit, peeled, seeded and cut into pieces
4 cups dry red wine
3 cups apple juice
1 6-ounce can orange juice concentrate
1 small lemon, sliced
2 small oranges, sliced and seeded
2 tablespoons brown sugar

7 hours before serving:

1. In a large soup pot, combine grapefruit, red wine, apple juice, and orange juice. Let stand 6 hours.
2. Before serving: Add lemon slices, orange slices and sugar and heat. Serve hot.

Preparation and Cooking Time: Approximately 15 minutes

Note: Sangria is Spanish for "bleeding" because of the red color of the beverage made with red wine.

My Mulled Wine

Sybil Kaplan
Overland Park, Kansas   Yield: 16 Servings

I made this recipe up while living in Israel to serve for parties in winter.

1 quart red dry wine	**1 crushed nutmeg**
1½ cups sugar	**24 cloves**
4½ teaspoons lemon peel	**3 cinnamon sticks**
½ cup water	**Peel of one orange**
2 cups lemon juice	

1. Place all ingredients in a large pot.
2. Heat and serve warm.

Preparation and Cooking Time: 10 to 15 minutes

"And wine that maketh glad the heart of man"
(Psalms 104:15)

Pareve

Coffee Cordial

Sybil Kaplan
Overland Park, Kansas

Yield: 7 Cups

3 cups brown sugar
2 cups white sugar
4 cups water
½ cup instant coffee
 powder

2 ⅔ cups vodka
4 teaspoons vanilla

1. In a saucepan, combine brown sugar, white sugar and water. Bring to a boil. Reduce heat and simmer 5 minutes. Cool.
2. Add coffee powder, vodka and vanilla. Pour into a container with a tight-fitting lid. Let sit one week.

Preparation and Cooking Time: 10 minutes

Creme de Menthe Cordial

Sybil Kaplan
Overland Park, Kansas

Yield: 7 Cups

Someone gave this recipe to me when I lived in Israel, probably because it was cheaper than buying liqueur, or at least more creative.

6 cups sugar
4 cups water
2 lemons, thinly sliced
2 ⅔ cups vodka

1 teaspoon peppermint extract
Green food coloring
4 teaspoons vanilla

1. In a saucepan, combine, sugar, water and lemon slices. Bring to a boil. Reduce heat and simmer 5 minutes. Strain and cool.
2. Stir in vodka, peppermint extract, green food coloring and vanilla.

Pour into a container with a tight lid. Let sit one week.

Preparation and Cooking Time: Approximately 10 minutes

Russian Tea

Hilda Meth   Russia
Richmond, Virginia

I can't remember where I got this recipe but I've had it for years.

Peel of one orange
Peel of one lemon
2 cinnamon sticks
3 heaping tablespoons whole cloves
½ pound loose tea

1. Chop orange and lemon peel in a blender. Place in a mixing bowl.
2. Add cinnamon sticks and cloves to bowl. Mix in tea. Place contents in a jar with a lid. Keep in a dark place for a week.

Use a teapot or strainer, 1 teaspoon for each cup. Pour on boiling water. Let steep.

Preparation and Cooking Time: Approximately 5 minutes

Turkish Coffee
Cafe Turkit

Sybil Kaplan   Middle East Style
Overland Park, Kansas   Yield: 6 Servings

I don't recall where I got this recipe, but I have been making it for years.

2 cups boiling water
2 tablespoons instant demitasse-type coffee
2 teaspoons sugar
2 cardamon pods

1. Boil water in a pot. Add coffee, sugar and cardamon pods. Bring to a boil. Take off heat. Let settle.
2. Replace on heat and repeat letting coffee boil and removing from heat 5 times. Serve immediately.

Preparation and Cooking Time: 10 to 20 minutes

Note: Turkish coffee is very strong coffee cooked with sugar and water and allowed to cool between boilings. It is made in a special pot and served in demitasse-type cups.

Appetizers

Baked Cheese Sandwiches
Butterbrody s Syrom

Svetlana Sorkin
Overland Park, Kansas

Russia
Yield: 10 Servings

*I came from Penza in Central Russia and I got this recipe from my
mother who came from the Ukraine.*

20-30 slices white cocktail-size bread
8 ounces cheddar cheese, grated
3 garlic cloves, pressed
1 carrot, grated
1½ tablespoons mayonnaise

1. Preheat oven to 500° F.
2. In a bowl, mix grated cheese, garlic, carrot and
   mayonnaise.
3. Spread mixture on bread slices.
   When oven is hot, reduce heat to 325° F.
4. Meantime, place open-face sandwiches on a greased cookie
   sheet. Bake in oven 10-15 minutes until all cheese is
   melted.
   Try to put the sandwiches in the oven just as you reduce
   the heat.

Preparation and Cooking Time: Approximately 25 minutes

Note: Good for Shavuot or any special occasion or for
company.

Yehudit's Cheese Spread

Sybil Kaplan   Israel
Overland Park, Kansas   Yield: 4 Servings

Yehudit Yellin-Ginat is a well-known artist, specializing in collages and was especially known for those which depicted various Israeli ethnic groups such as Chassidim dancing, Yemenites and others. We met when she taught art at the teachers' college named for her grandfather and I learned many Israeli recipes, such as this one from her.

⅓ cup cream cheese	½ teaspoon salt
(low fat is fine)	¼ teaspoon paprika
1½ tablespoons low-fat	¼ teaspoon celery seed
sour cream	Pepper to taste
2 teaspoons onions, chopped	2 hard-boiled eggs

1. Combine cream cheese and sour cream with onions and spices.
2. Mash hard-boiled eggs and add. Blend well.

Great on crackers or pita chips or toasted bread!

Preparation and Cooking Time: Approximately 10 minutes

For whipped cream cheese, place an 8-ounce package of dry pot cheese, dry cottage cheese or farmer cheese in a blender or food processor. Whip on high 2 to 3 minutes.
Place in covered container and store in refrigerator.

Liptauer Cheese Spread
Korosot

Dalia Carmel
New York, New York

Hungary
Yield: 12 to 15 Servings

This recipe came from my home. My father was Hungarian, and he used to make this for special occasions.

2 8-ounce packages cream cheese	1 tablespoons paprika
1 4-ounce bar butter	2 tablespoons chives, chopped
1 8-ounce or less piece of Brindza cheese	1 teaspoon caraway seeds

1. In a food processor, combine cream cheese, butter, Brindza cheese, paprika, chives and caraway seeds. Mix well until all are blended. Refrigerate.

Serve with crackers. Enough for a party!

Preparation and Cooking Time: Approximately 10 minutes

To serve a dip, hollow out:
red pepper
green pepper
red cabbage
Cut off a very thin slice from the bottom so it will stand upright before filling with dip.

Olive Cheese Balls

Hilda Meth
Richmond, Virginia

Yield: 4 to 6 Servings

3 cups cheddar cheese, shredded	**1 cup flour**
½ cup soft unsalted butter or margarine	**¼ teaspoon salt**
	2 teaspoons dry mustard
	Pitted green olives

1. Preheat oven to 350° F.
2. In a mixing bowl, combine cheese and margarine. Add flour, salt and mustard. Blend into a thin dough.
3. Wrap each olive in dough or cut circles with a glass, place olive in center and close up.
4. Place on a greased cookie sheet. Bake in a 350° F preheated oven for 15-20 minutes. Serve immediately.

Preparation and Cooking Time: Approximately 20 minutes

"For the churning of milk bringeth forth curd"
(Proverbs 30:33)

Out-Of-This-World Mold

Sybil Kaplan
Overland Park, Kansas

Yield: 20 Servings

I have been making this for years and don't remember where I got it.

¼ cup cold water	1 cup cream cheese, cubed
1 envelope unflavored gelatin	¼ cup cheddar cheese,
1 cup boiling water	shredded
1 cup heavy cream	2 tablespoons blue cheese
2 tablespoons sugar	

1. Blend cold water and unflavored gelatin. Let stand a few minutes.
2. Add boiling water and mix on low speed until gelatin dissolves. Add heavy cream, sugar and blend at high.
3. Gradually add cream cheese, cheddar and blue cheeses. Mix until well blended. Pour into a greased 1-quart mold and chill.

Unmold and serve spread on crackers.

Preparation and Cooking Time: Approximately 10 to 15 minutes

Borrekas

Matilda Rosenberg   Greece
Overland Park, Kansas   Yield: 40 Pieces

I learned this from my mother, Alegre Tevet, who came from Drama, Greece. Borrekas are served for Shabbat breakfast or for a light lunch in many Sephardic homes. When I was a young girl growing up, Friday afternoons at our house would smell of freshly baked bread, and borrekas for a snack would be waiting for me on the table. There are various fillings for borrekas, but the cheese filling remains the most popular. My children love borrekas because they can be eaten with their hands. Borrekas can be frozen and reheated later.

10 medium-size potatoes	**2¼ cups cottage cheese**
2 cups oil	**2 cups grated Romano**
½ cup water	**or Parmesan cheese**
Pinch of salt	**7 eggs**
6 cups flour	**1 egg**
plus a generous handful	

1. Preheat oven to 350° F.
2. Peel potatoes. Place in a saucepan with water. Bring to a boil. Cook until soft. Drain. Mash and let cool.
3. Meantime, mix together in a bowl, oil, water, salt and flour. Knead dough with alternating scissors motion. Dough should resemble pie dough. Let rest.
4. To potatoes, add cottage cheese, Romano or Parmesan cheese, and 7 eggs. Blend.
5. Take a large walnut-size piece of dough and roll into a circle with a rolling pin. Fill with 1 large tablespoon filling. Fold in half and crimp edges as for a pie. Place half circle on ungreased cookie sheet. Continue until all dough is used.
6. Beat 1 egg. Brush each borreka with egg. Sprinkle with more Romano or Parmesan cheese. Bake in a 350° F oven for 45 minutes.

Preparation and Cooking Time: 1 to 1½ hours

Note: Borrekas are thought of as Turkish in origin but are found throughout the Middle East and are served as hors d' oeuvres or as a main course.

Dairy

Borrekas
(Sephardic)

Soly Mizrahi   Greece
Mission, Kansas   Yield: 3½ Dozen

*I was born in Cairo, Egypt, and learned this from my mother, who
was born in Larissa, Greece--and from my imagination. These are
good any time, especially on Shavuot. My grandchildren enjoy the
borrekas the most!*

Dough	Filling
4½ cups unbleached flour	1 egg, beaten
1 cup vegetable oil	5 ounces Parmesan cheese
1 cup water	or feta cheese
Dash of salt	8 ounces cream cheese
	1 egg, beaten
	Sesame seeds

1. Preheat oven to 350° F.
2. Stir with a wooden spoon flour, oil, water and salt in a
   bowl. Mix all together to form a soft dough.
3. Place the dough in a sheet (flat) and start kneading with
   your hands for about 10 minutes until the dough is ready.
   Cover with a dry towel and let stand for 15 minutes.
4. Cut the dough and form a ball about the size of an orange.
   With a rolling pin, flatten the dough to the size of a circle
   3 inches in diameter.
   Continue until all the dough is used and in circles.
5. Mix in a bowl the beaten egg, Parmesan cheese or feta
   cheese and cream cheese.
6. Place a teaspoon of the filling in the middle of each circle.
   Fold each to form a half moon. Press close the edges.
   Place a glass, 3 inches in diameter, on the top of each
   borreka and take off the excess dough. Pinch the edges
   firmly closed. Continue until all are filled and closed.

7. Line a shallow baking pan with foil (this makes for an easy cleanup). Beat egg in a bowl. Brush the top of each borreka with egg, then sprinkle with sesame seeds. Arrange borrekas around the pan. Bake in a 350° F oven for 35 minutes or until brown. Be careful not to burn them.

Preparation and Cooking Time: 1 to 1¼ hours

Dairy

Seafood Tartlets

Sandra Rothberg
Overland Park, Kansas

Yield: 32 Pieces

1 loaf thin sliced
  sandwich bread
6 tablespoons margarine, melted
1 cup mayonnaise
  (no cholesterol)
⅓ cup Parmesan cheese
⅓ cup Swiss cheese, grated

¼ cup onions, chopped
¼ teaspoon Worcestershire
  sauce
2 drops Tabasco sauce
4 ounces imitation crab
  meat, flaked
Paprika

1. Preheat oven to 400° F.
2. Roll bread slices thin with a rolling pin. Cut 2½-inch diameter rounds. Brush both sides of rounds with margarine.
3. Press bread rounds into muffin cups. Bake in a 400° F oven 10 minutes.
4. In a bowl, combine mayonnaise, cheeses, onion, and sauces. Blend.
5. Add seafood flakes. Spoon into baked tarts, sprinkle with paprika. Place under broiler and broil until golden and bubbly. Serve immediately.

For future use: Cool and freeze. When ready to serve, reheat in a 450° F oven 7-10 minutes.
Variations: Substitute ½ pound chopped, cooked mushrooms for the seafood.

Preparation and Cooking Time: Approximately 20 to 25 minutes

Note: For quick and easy tartlets, use puff pastry dough squares (eight to a package). Place filling on each square, roll up, wet end of square with water to seal, cut in six pieces. Place on greased cookie sheet, each tart on its end. Bake in a 400° F oven 15 minutes.

St. Peter's Fish Cocktail

Sybil Kaplan   Israel
Overland Park, Kansas   Yield: 4 Servings

I found this recipe in a booklet of recipes for St. Peter's Fish, "St. Peter's Fish from the Sea of Galilee" produced by Carmel Agrexco Agricultural Export Co. of Israel. It explains that tilapia is the name for St. Peter's fish.

1 pound 2 ounces tilapia, fried and cubed*	1 medium onion, sliced
	2 garlic cloves, crushed
¼ cup prepared piquant techina**	Salt and pepper to taste
	Mint leaves or
¾ cup yogurt	blanched almonds

1. Place fried and cubed fish in a mixing bowl. Add techina, yogurt, onion, garlic, salt and pepper. Mix lightly and set aside.
2. Divide into 4 and place in bowls. Garnish with mint leaves or almonds.

   * The fish can be cut into cubes, marinated in wine a few hours, drained and placed on paper towels. Then it can be dredged in flour and fried in a little oil until golden. Drain on paper towels before putting in a salad.
   ** Instead of techina, a piquant tomato sauce can be used. Place fish in serving dishes, heat sauce, add 2 tablespoon of gin to sauce and pour over fish before serving.

Preparation and Cooking Time: 2¼ hours

Note: Techina (tachine) is sesame seed paste.

Dairy

Hot Dip

Dalia Carmel
New York, New York   Yield: 10 to 20 Servings

I ate this at a party a few years ago and when I asked what was in it, they gave me the recipe orally, so I reconstructed it myself to use at parties.

1 can artichoke hearts	1 8-ounce package
1 can hearts of palm	cheddar cheese,
1 medium onion or	shredded
8 shallots	¾ cup Parmesan
2-3 garlic cloves or	cheese, grated
garlic powder to taste	1 cup mayonnaise
1 8-ounce package	Tabasco sauce to taste
mozzarella cheese,	3 tablespoons butter or
shredded	margarine, melted
	Cornflake crumbs

1. Preheat oven to 350° F.
2. In the food processor, chop artichoke hearts, hearts of palm, onion or shallots, garlic or garlic powder, medium fine to coarse. Empty into a bowl.
3. Mix in mozzarella cheese, cheddar cheese, Parmesan cheese, mayonnaise, and Tabasco sauce. Spread in a greased casserole and pat straight across.
4. Mix melted butter or margarine with enough cornflake crumbs to make a paste for spreading. Spread all over top surface. Bake in a 350° F oven for 35-40 minutes or until top is brown.
Serve with sturdy crackers or corn chips.

This can be refrigerated and reheated for a later use. It does not spoil fast.

Preparation and Cooking Time: 50 minutes

Vegetable Appetizer Pizza

Sybil Kaplan
Overland Park, Kansas   Yield: 8 to 10 Servings

Pizza dough   **4½ ounces black olives,**
1½ packages ranch dressing   **finely chopped**
¾ cup mayonnaise   **¼ cup broccoli,**
12 ounces cream cheese   **finely diced**
½ red pepper diced finely   **¼ cup cauliflower,**
1 green pepper, diced finely   **finely diced**

1. Preheat oven to 425° F.
2. Roll out pizza dough in rectangular shape. Place on a cookie sheet sprayed with no-stick cooking spray. Bake in a 425° F oven 20-25 minutes.
3. In the meantime, in a mixing bowl, mix dry ranch dressing, mayonnaise, and cream cheese. Add finely diced vegetables.
4. Spread cheese/vegetable mixture on baked pizza. Cut into slices to serve.

Preparation and Cooking Time: 35 to 45 minutes

Pareve

Chinese Fish Appetizer

Sybil Kaplan   Chinese Style
Overland Park, Kansas   Yield: 20 Fish Balls

While living in Israel in the 1970s I tasted this at a friend's house and thought it was so special I asked for the recipe and have had it ever since.

6 small potatoes, peeled and halved	1 tablespoon grated ginger root or ground ginger
Salt and pepper to taste	
¼ cup pareve margarine	4 tablespoons white dry vermouth
3 tablespoons non-dairy creamer or milk	2 eggs
4 tablespoons oil	½ cup flour
3 green onions, chopped	1½ cups bread crumbs
1 pound fish, chopped	Oil

1. Place potatoes in a saucepan of water, bring to a boil, reduce heat and simmer 25 minutes. Drain. Mash potatoes, add salt and pepper, margarine, milk or non-dairy creamer and mash until smooth.
2. Heat oil in frying pan. Sauté green onions 2 minutes. Place in a bowl.
3. Place fish and ginger in a bowl. Cover with vermouth so fish is completely covered. Fry fish in frying pan used for onions for 3 minutes. Place in bowl with green onions.
4. Add mashed potatoes to fish and 1 egg and mix. Form into oblong or round patties. Let stand 30 minutes.
5. Beat one egg in a dish; place flour in a second plate and bread crumbs in a third. Dip each patty first in flour, then in egg, then roll in bread crumbs. Add if you need more.
6. Heat oil in frying pan. Fry fish until completely brown and crispy on all sides. Drain on paper towels.

Serve with Chinese mustard or Duck sauce.

Preparation and Cooking Time: 1¼ hours

Mushroom Salad Tapas

Dalia Carmel   Spanish Style
New York, New York   Yield: 6 to 8 Servings

*In my reading cookbooks and reading magazines, I found this recipe
which I decided to try as an extra for a party. This is my version
after making it for about 10 to 15 years because it's a wonderful,
easy dish.*

¼ cup good olive oil	1 tablespoon parsley,
2 tablespoons lemon juice	minced
1 garlic clove, crushed	½ pound fresh
⅛ teaspoon pepper	mushrooms, sliced
½ teaspoon salt	1 red pepper, sliced thin
½ teaspoon cumin	into half rings

1. In a bowl, mix oil, lemon juice, garlic, pepper, salt, cumin
   and parsley.
2. Toss mushrooms and pepper rings into mixture. Let stand
   for a while to blend tastes, then serve.

Preparation and Cooking Time: Approximately 10 minutes

Note: Tapas are appetizers served in Spain, in restaurants and
bars.

Chinese Vegetarian "Shrimp" Balls

Sybil Kaplan
Overland Park, Kansas

Chinese Style
Yield: 10 to 12 Servings

2 pounds potatoes, peeled
Water
10 water chestnuts
1 carrot, minced
1 tablespoon green onions,
  minced
1 tablespoon white sweet wine
  or vermouth

2 teaspoons ginger root,
  minced
1½ teaspoons oil
Salt to taste
1 egg white, beaten
¼ cup cornstarch

1. Place potatoes in a saucepan with water. Bring to a boil, reduce heat and simmer 50 minutes. Drain. Mash to 3 cups, in a bowl.
2. Place water chestnuts in boiling water. Blanch 1 minute. Drain, rinse in cold water, add to potatoes and mash.
3. Add carrot, green onions, sweet wine or vermouth, ginger, oil and salt. Stir. Add egg white. Stir for 1 minute.
4. Add cornstarch and stir. Form into tablespoon-size balls. Place on a platter.
5. Heat oil in a pot. Deep-fry balls for 1½ minutes or until brown. Drain on paper towels. Return balls to oil and fry 30 seconds more. Drain well.

Preparation and Cooking Time: 1¼ hours

Gefilte Fish with Fried Onions
Farshirovannaya Riba Zharenym Lukom

Tamara Krasilnikova   Russia
Israel   Yield: 10 to 12 Servings

400 grams (14 ounces) onions   2 eggs
Vegetable oil   Salt and pepper to taste
200-250 grams (8 ounces)   2 carrots
  stale white bread   1 large beet
2 kilos (4½ pounds) fish   Sugar (optional)
3 garlic cloves

1. Finely chop all but one onion. Heat oil in soup pot. Add chopped onions and saute until golden.
2. Place bread in a bowl and soak in cold water.
3. Clean fish, cut into pieces, remove flesh and grind with bread, garlic and 1 whole onion.
4. Add all but 2 teaspoons fried onions to the fish mixture. Leave 2 teaspoons in pot. To fish, add eggs, salt and pepper and mix well. If mixture is too salty, add some sugar.
5. Fill fish skin with mixture. Slice carrots and beet and place on top of onions in pot. Place fish on top of all of this. Add salt and pepper. Cover fish with cold water. Bring to a boil. Cook for 2 hours. If too much water boils out, add cold water but not later than one hour before completion.

Preparation and Cooking Time: 2½ hours

Note: Reprinted with permission from **Aleph-Bet of Jewish Cooking**, published by Shvut Ami, the International Center for Soviet Jews, Jerusalem, Israel.

Pareve

Roe Caviar
Greek Tarama Dip

Soly Mizrahi   Greece
Mission, Kansas   Yield: 6 Servings

I've been making this for a long time--maybe 30 years. The original Greek recipe used the soft part of bread. In Egypt I knew what bread to use, but when I came here I couldn't find the right bread so I tried the mashed potatoes and it worked. S.M.

2¼ cups water	½ teaspoon lemon pepper
1 cup mashed potato flakes	1 teaspoon dry parsley
3 tablespoons tarama (caviar)	flakes
Juice of 1 lemon	1 tablespoon olive oil
1 teaspoon garlic, minced	12 black olives

1. Heat water in a saucepan. Add potato flakes and stir well.
2. Add tarama, lemon juice, garlic and lemon pepper and mix together. This will look like mayonnaise. Set in refrigerator for about ½ hour to cool.
3. Remove saucepan from refrigerator. Transfer to serving plate. Sprinkle parsley and olive oil on top. Garnish with olives.

Serve with pita or crackers.

Preparation and Cooking Time: 45 minutes

Greek Tuna-Avocado Spread

Sybil Kaplan
Overland Park, Kansas

Greece
Yield: 36 Crackers

1 tablespoon pareve
  chicken bouillon
2 tablespoons boiling water
2 tablespoons sweet pepper
  flakes
2 tablespoons water
½ cup mayonnaise
2 hard-boiled eggs,
  chopped

2 teaspoons mustard
½ teaspoon caraway seeds
⅛ teaspoon coriander
1 6½-ounce can tuna
  and liquid
1 avocado, peeled and
  mashed

1. Combine chicken bouillon and boiling water in one bowl.
2. Combine sweet pepper flakes and cold water in a second bowl then add to first bowl.
3. Blend mayonnaise with eggs in second bowl then add to bouillon mixture.
4. Stir in mustard, caraway seeds and coriander. Add tuna, liquid and avocado and blend. Chill at least 1 hour before serving.

Spread on crackers before serving.

Preparation and Cooking Time: 10 to 15 minutes

Egg-Garlic Sandwiches
Butterbrody s yaitsami i chesnokom

Svetlana Sorkin   Russia
Overland Park, Kansas   Yield: 10 Servings

My mother, who came from the Ukraine, gave this recipe to me.

20-30 slices white,   **3 green onions, minced**
  cocktail-size bread   **1 teaspoon fresh parsley,**
Oil   **minced**
1 whole head garlic,   **Salt and pepper to taste**
  all cloves pressed   **1 tablespoon mayonnaise**
10 hard-boiled eggs, minced **1 lemon, cut into slivers**
3 green onions, minced

1. Heat oil in a frying pan. Fry one side only of the bread slices. Put on a plate.
2. Rub crushed garlic on each bread slice, on the fried side.
3. Place minced egg in a bowl. Add onions, parsley, salt and pepper. Add mayonnaise and mix well.
4. Spread egg mixture on the fried garlic side of each slice of bread.

Garnish each slice with a lemon sliver.

Preparation and Cooking Time: 10 to 15 minutes

Mock Chopped Liver

Sybil Kaplan   Israel
Overland Park, Kansas   Yield: 4 To 6 Servings

When I lived in Israel, people were making this dish frequently, so I took the basic idea and elaborated on it.

Oil   2 hard-boiled eggs
1 onion, thinly minced   2 teaspoons pareve chicken
2 cups green beans,   soup powder
   cooked and minced   Salt and pepper (optional)

1. Heat oil in a frying pan. Fry onion until brown.
2. Mash green beans in a bowl with eggs. Add onions, chicken soup powder, salt and pepper.

   Serve on a lettuce leaf or on crackers.

Preparation and Cooking Time: 10 to 15 minutes

Dvora's Pareve Chopped Liver

Sybil Kaplan   Israel
Overland Park, Kansas   Yield: 6 To 8 Servings

Dvora and Rafi Arbisser were neighbors of mine in the Jerusalem neighborhood of Rehavia. They had moved to Israel from Texas, but he had been a religious school principal when I was growing up in Kansas City. She gave me this recipe.

3 medium eggplants	3 medium onions, chopped
2 eggs	3 hard-boiled eggs
Flour	Salt and pepper to taste
Oil	

1. Peel and slice eggplants. Place in a colander. Salt and let "sweat" a few hours. Pat dry.
2. Beat eggs in one bowl. Place flour in a second bowl. Heat oil in a frying pan.
3. Dip eggplant slices first in eggs then in flour. Fry in oil until brown. Drain on paper towels.
4. Heat oil in another frying pan. Fry two onions until limp.
5. Puree or chop eggplant with 1 raw onion. Add hard-boiled eggs. Add fried onion, salt and pepper.

Preparation and Cooking Time: 2½ hours (including "sweating")

Malka's Squash Appetizer Salad

Sybil Kaplan
Overland Park, Kansas

Israel
Yield: 6 Servings

Canadian-born Malka Nisan had come to live in Israel when I met her. She and her husband lived in Jerusalem where he taught political science and wrote articles. We often ate with them, and she gave me this recipe.

1½ pounds small squash	Salt to taste
Oil	Garlic powder to taste
1 large onion, chopped	2 teaspoons mayonnaise
3 hard-boiled eggs	2 teaspoons lemon juice

1. Peel squash and cut lengthwise. Heat oil in a frying pan. Add squash and cook until soft. Drain on paper towels.
2. Fry onion until brown. Add to squash and mash. Add eggs, salt, garlic powder, mayonnaise and lemon juice. Blend. Refrigerate until ready to serve.

For leftover cooked squash:
1. Fry onion until brown. Add squash and blend with eggs.
2. Add salt, garlic powder, mayonnaise and lemon juice and mix well.

Preparation and Cooking Time: 10 to 15 minutes

Breads

Corn Bread or Muffins

Sybil Kaplan
Overland Park, Kansas   Yield: 15 Muffins

I learned this from my mother, Rae Horowitz, and found it to be the best corn bread recipe around. She told me she had been making it more than 45 years and thought she had learned to make it right after she got married. She also told me her mother had made corn bread when she and her brothers were older.

1¼ cup flour	5 teaspoons baking powder
4 tablespoon sugar	1 egg
(or less if you like)	1 cup milk
½ teaspoon salt	2 tablespoons butter or
¾ cup corn meal	margarine

1. Preheat oven to 375° F.
2. In a mixing bowl, combine flour, sugar, salt, corn meal and baking powder.
3. Add egg, milk and butter or margarine and blend. Pour into a greased baking pan or spoon into greased muffin tins. Bake in a 375° F oven for 20 minutes.

Preparation and Cooking Time: 30 minutes

"He will also bless...thy corn and thy wine and thine" *(Deuteronomy 7:13)*

Grandma's White Bread

Sybil Kaplan
Overland Park, Kansas   Yield: 2 Loaves

While looking through the cookbook collection of my grandmother, Sade Lyon, which I inherited, this recipe came out, handwritten on the bottom of the Table of Contents page of a cookbook.

1 package yeast	2 tablespoons sugar
¼ cup water	2 teaspoons salt
2 cups milk, scalded	6¼ cups flour
1 tablespoon butter	

1. Preheat oven to 400° F.
2. Heat water in a saucepan until it is lukewarm, then dissolve yeast and set aside.
3. Place scalded milk in a mixing bowl. Add butter, sugar and salt. Gradually stir in 2 cups flour. Add yeast mixture and mix. Add remaining 4¼ cups flour and mix to a dough.
4. Put dough on a lightly floured surface and knead. Shape into two balls and place in two greased bowls. Cover and let rise in a warm place 2 to 2½ hours. Punch down and let rise again. Mold into two loaves. Place in two greased bread pans. Let rise until double in bulk. Let rest 10 minutes. Bake in a 400° F oven and bake for 35 minutes.

Preparation and Cooking Time: 6 hours

Jonnie's Monkey Bread

Barbara Gorodetzky
Kansas City, Missouri   Yield: 1 Loaf

*Jonnie is an old, dear friend of mine from Kentucky and she's the
one who made this and served it.*

1½ cups flour	⅓ cup margarine
3 packages yeast	1 egg
2 tablespoons sugar	2½ cups flour
1 teaspoon salt	¾ cup margarine, melted
1½ cups milk	

1. Preheat oven to 425° F.
2. In a bowl, mix 1½ cups flour with packages of yeast, sugar
   and salt. Set aside.
3. In a saucepan, heat the milk and ⅓ cup margarine. Pour
   over yeast mixture. Add the egg and then mix in the
   remainder of the flour to make a soft dough. Knead until
   well mixed.
4. Grease a bowl and add dough. Cover with a towel and let
   rise 30 minutes. Knead dough again. Divide dough in
   half. Roll to a rectangle. Cut each rectangle into ¾-inch
   strips. Cut each strip into 3-inch pieces.
5. Melt ¾ cup margarine. Dip each piece of dough into the
   margarine. Toss into a 10-inch tube pan. Cover and let
   rise 1 to 1½ hours. Bake in a 425° F oven 20 minutes.

Preparation and Cooking Time: 2 to 2½ hours

Walnut or Olive Bread

Barbara Gorodetzky
Kansas City, Missouri   Yield: 2 Loaves

*For this bread, I melded a couple of different recipes together and
this is what I came up with.*

2 packages yeast	1½ cups bread flour
2 tablespoons honey	3-3½ cups flour
½ cup warm water	1 cup walnuts, chopped
1½ cups warm milk	or 6 ounces black
2 tablespoons olive oil	olives, sliced
1½ teaspoons salt	

1. Preheat oven to 375°F.
2. Dissolve yeast and honey in a bowl with ½ cup warm
   water. Let sit 10 minutes.
3. Add warm milk, olive oil, salt and bread flour to make a
   sticky dough. Add the rest of the flour to make a firm
   dough.
4. Add either chopped walnuts or sliced olives. Knead, then
   place in a greased bowl and let rise until it is double in
   size.
5. Punch down the dough, knead again and divide into two.
   Form into two round loaves. Place on a greased baking
   sheet and let rise another 45 minutes. Cut slashes on the
   top of the breads with a sharp knife.
6. Bake in a 375°F oven for 30-35 minutes.

Preparation and Cooking Time: 2 to 2½ hours

Hana's Pita

Sybil Kaplan
Overland Park, Kansas

Middle Eastern
Yield: 12 Large Breads

When I lived in Chicago, Hana, of Yemenite background, and I conducted some cooking classes together and shared cooling ideas. This was a recipe she gave to me.

1 package dry yeast	**1 tablespoon and 2**
1 teaspoon sugar	**teaspoons sugar**
1 cup water, warm	**1 tablespoon salt**
8 cups flour	

1. Preheat oven to 475° F.
2. Place yeast and 1 teaspoon sugar in a small mixing bowl with 1 cup warm water. Let sit 5 minutes.
3. Place flour, rest of sugar and salt in a large mixing bowl. Add yeast and knead. Remove dough from bowl, oil bowl and return dough to bowl. Cover and let rise 1 hour.
4. Separate dough into 12 balls. Roll each flat. Let rise 5 to 10 minutes.
5. Place flattened dough balls on cookie sheet.
6. Bake in a 475° F oven 5 minutes. Turn each over. Bake 5 minutes more.

Preparation and Cooking Time: 1½ hours

Pareve

Aunt Lil's Bagels

Sybil Kaplan
Overland Park, Kansas   Yield: 48 Bagels

Aunt Lil is in her 90s and although she doesn't bake bagels any more, I found her recipe in my files and remembered she was the bagel baker par excellence of the family.

2 packages yeast	4 generous teaspoons salt
1 cup water, warm	¼ cup oil
5 pounds flour	4 eggs, beaten
1 cup sugar	

1. Preheat oven to 350° F.
2. Place yeast in a bowl, add warm water and let sit 5 minutes.
3. Place flour, sugar and salt in a large mixing bowl. Mix, then make a hole in the center. Add yeast mixture, oil and eggs. Add more warm water to make a good dough.
4. Turn onto a floured surface and knead about 10 minutes. Shape dough into a ball and place in a greased bowl, turning dough around so it is all greased. Cover and let rise in a warm place about 1½ hours.
5. Punch down dough and let rise again about 30 minutes. Cut dough into 48 pieces. Roll each piece of dough into a long rod. Wrap around your hand to connect the ends. Seal with water. Place on greased cookie sheets and let rise 15-25 minutes.
6. Heat a pot of water to boiling. Using a slotted spoon, drop each bagel into the boiling water for one and a half minutes then turn and let cook one and a half minutes more. Drain on paper towels, then place on greased cookie sheet. Bake in a 350° F oven for 25 minutes until firm but not quite brown. Switch oven to broil and brown under broiler on both sides.

Preparation and Cooking Time: 3½ hours

My Light Rye Bread

Barbara Gorodetzky
Kansas City, Missouri   Yield: 2 Loaves

*This bread was a redo of two or three rye recipes I came to because
I was probably missing ingredients. I used to make small loaves of
the bread for my kids' friends so each walked away with one small
loaf.*

¾ cup water	1-2 cups rye flour
¼ cup molasses	1 tablespoon caraway seeds
¾ cup warm water	2 tablespoons shortening,
2 packages yeast	melted
1 egg	1 teaspoon salt
1 egg yolk	1 egg white
2-3 cups bread flour	

1. Preheat oven to 400°F.
2. Dissolve ¾ cup water and molasses in one bowl.
3. Dissolve ¾ cup warm water and the yeast in another bowl.
   Let stand 10 minutes.
4. In a large bowl, combine molasses and yeast mixtures with
   egg and yolk, bread flour, rye flour, caraway seeds,
   shortening and salt. Knead. Put dough into a greased
   bowl. Cover and let rise until double in size.
5. Knead dough again. Place into two loaf pans. Let rise
   again.
6. Place pans in 400°F oven and bake for 30 minutes.
7. Brush warm loaves with egg white mixed with water.

Preparation and Cooking Time: 2½ hours

Pareve

Bracha's Saloufa or Mithani

Sybil Kaplan   Yemen/Middle East
Overland Park, Kansas

Bracha was my upstairs neighbor in Jerusalem, and she was
Yemenite. Every Friday afternoon she would bake and cook and then
send samples down for me to taste. She gave me this recipe.

2 pounds sifted flour
3 tablespoons sugar
3-3⅓ cups water
2 tablespoons coarse salt
1¾ ounces cake yeast

1. Place flour in a mixing bowl. Add salt and 2½ tablespoon
   sugar.
2. In second bowl, dissolve yeast in ½ cup lukewarm water.
   Add 1½ teaspoons sugar. Let sit 5 minutes. Add to flour.
3. Add rest of water slowly and knead dough until it is soft
   and flexible like chewing gum. Every 10 minutes, wet
   hands and knead dough. Repeat about 10 times.
4. Sprinkle flour on a board or cookie sheet. Wash hands
   with water. Grab a piece of dough about the size of a
   tennis ball. Place on floured board or sheet. Continue until
   sheet is filled. Place on stove on low heat.
5. Stretch a dough piece to the size of a frying pan. Oil pan
   and cook dough until brown on both sides. Remove to a
   board to cool. Continue with dough balls until all are
   browned.

Preparation and Cooking Time: 2 hours

Spiced Pita Chips

Sybil Kaplan
Overland Park, Kansas

Yield: 48 Chips

6 pieces pita,	**2¼ teaspoons dry basil**
quartered and opened	**½ teaspoon dry dill**
1 stick unsalted margarine	**⅛ teaspoon red pepper**
1 tablespoon dry parsley flakes	**flakes (optional)**
or dry chervil	

1. Preheat oven to 350° F.
2. Melt margarine in a saucepan.
3. Add spices. Place pita pieces on a cookie sheet or sheets. Brush spiced margarine on each piece. Bake in a 350° F oven 25 minutes. Let cool. Store in closed can.

Preparation and Cooking Time: 35 minutes

"and ye shall eat your bread until ye have enough"
(Leviticus 26:5)

Soups

Sour Cherry Soup

Rose Barnes
Scottsdale, Arizona

Yield: 4 Servings

1 can or 1 pound sour cherries, pitted 1 quart water 1 teaspoon salt	2 tablespoons sugar 1 tablespoon flour 1 cup heavy sour cream

1. Place cherries in a pot and add water. If canned cherries are used, bring to boil and boil 10 minutes. If fresh cherries are used, bring to a boil and boil 20 minutes.
2. Add salt and sugar to cherries. Pour a little cherry water into a dish, add flour and make a thickening, then return to cherries. Bring to a boil and cook 5 minuets.
3. Turn off heat and stir in sour cream.

This soup is good warm or cold.

Apples can be substituted for cherries.

Preparation and Cooking Time: 1 hour

Note: © 1994 by Linda F. Radke, Five Star Publications, Chandler, AZ.

Apple and Squash Soup

Barbara Gorodetzky
Kansas City, Missouri   Yield: 6 to 8 Servings

3 tablespoons margarine
1½ pounds butternut squash,
  seeded and chopped into
  8 pieces
1 pound Granny Smith apples,
  peeled and cut into quarters
6 cups water
5 teaspoons chicken
  soup powder
1 bay leaf

½ pound onions,
  thinly sliced
3 slices day-old bread,
  cubed
White pepper to taste
Tarragon to taste
1 cup milk
⅓ cup white wine
  or vermouth
Sour cream
Chives

1. Melt margarine in a soup pot. Add squash, apples, chicken soup, and bay leaf and cook until squash is tender (about 40 minutes).
2. Add onions and bread cubes. Bring to a boil, cover, cook another 10 minutes.
3. Season with pepper and tarragon. Puree in blender and return to pot.
4. Before serving, add milk, wine or vermouth and heat thoroughly.

To serve, top with sour cream and chives.

Preparation and Cooking Time: 1 hour

Cold Red Borscht
Cholodny Krasny Borsh

The Aleph-Bet of Jewish Cooking

Russia
Yield: 4 to 6 Servings

400 grams (14 ounces) beets
Hot water
2 teaspoons salt
4 teaspoons vinegar
600 grams (1¼ pounds)
   potatoes, peeled

1½ teaspoons sugar
Cucumbers, sliced
Hard-boiled eggs,
   chopped
Scallions, chopped
Sour cream

1. Slice beets thin and place in a pot. Pour hot water on top.
   Add salt and vinegar and bring to a boil. Pour off one half
   of the liquid into a bowl to keep. Let it cool.
2. Cook beets in remaining liquid until tender.
3. Cut potatoes into cubes and add to beets. Cook 20
   minutes. Cool.
4. Add reserved liquid and sugar.
5. Pour soup into bowls, garnish with cucumbers, eggs,
   scallions and sour cream.

Preparation and Cooking Time: 45 minutes

Note: Reprinted with permission from Shvut Ami, the
International Center for Soviet Jews, Jerusalem, Israel.

Chanita's Cream of Spinach-Potato Soup

Sybil Kaplan
Overland Park, Kansas

Israel
Yield: 6 Servings

Chanita is Israeli, her husband, Mel, is American and they live in Jerusalem. I met them as part of a potluck soup group which got together regularly when I lived there. The hostess made the soup and others brought the rest of the meal. This was a recipe Chanita made up and gave to me. She said many years before she had a recipe for a spinach milk soup and another for a potato milk soup and she didn't really like them so she combined them and made some changes and this was the result.

3 tablespoons margarine	14 ounces spinach
3¾ ounces Chinese cabbage, chopped	3 tablespoons margarine
6 potatoes, chopped	4½ tablespoons flour
¾ teaspoon salt	3 cups milk
4½ cups milk	3 eggs
	Parmesan cheese

1. Place 3 tablespoons margarine in a saucepan. Add Chinese cabbage and potatoes. Cover and cook over low heat 5 minutes.
2. Add salt, 4½ cups milk and cook 30 minutes.
3. Place spinach in a little water, cover and steam 10 minutes. Drain and chop.
4. In a saucepan, melt 3 tablespoons margarine. Add flour and stir. Pour in milk to make a thick sauce.
5. Add spinach to potato-cabbage mixture. Cook 5-6 minutes. Beat eggs and stir into soup.

To serve, sprinkle cheese on top.

Preparation and Cooking Time: 1 hour

Cream of Veggie Soup

Barbara Gorodetzky
Kansas City, Missouri

Yield: 6 to 8 Servings

2 cups potatoes,
    peeled and chopped
1½ cups winter squash,
    peeled and chopped
1 small eggplant, chopped
¼ cup celery, chopped
1 medium onion, chopped

1 large garlic clove,
    chopped
1 teaspoon dry mustard
Salt and pepper to taste
1 10¾-ounce can
    vegetable soup
1 cup milk

1. In a large soup pot, combine potatoes, squash, eggplant, celery, onion, garlic, mustard, salt, pepper and vegetable soup. Cook until vegetables are tender.
2. Take ¾ of the mixture and blend. Return to pot. Add milk and heat.

Preparation and Cooking Time: 30 to 40 minutes

Mashed Potato Knaidlach (Dumplings)
Torte Kromply-Gombōr

Sylvai Mednick Weiss

Russia
Yield: 4 to 6 Servings

Linda Radke, says this recipe came from her aunt who is married to her Uncle Art, her mother's brother, who was born in Hungary. She wrote the introduction to Linda's book and she is the one who oftentimes grabbed Grandma's handfuls and found the equivalent in measuring spoons or cups.

3 eggs
1 cup hot mashed potatoes
3 tablespoons butter or margarine
3 tablespoons warm clear soup or seltzer water*
1 cup matzah meal

1. In a bowl, beat eggs into hot mashed potatoes. Add butter or margarine, soup or seltzer water and matzah meal to make a smooth mixture.
2. If using cold mashed potatoes, mash them thoroughly, even diluting with some of the warm liquid until smooth. Chill for several hours.
3. Form into balls about half an hour before serving. Heat water with salt in a pot. Drop balls into boiling water and cook 30 minutes. Drain before serving.

The knaidlach may be used in soups, stews or as a side dish.

* Use seltzer water if for a dairy meal.

Preparation and Cooking Time: 45 minutes plus chilling time

Note: From **That Hungarian's In My Kitchen** by Linda F. Radke, Five Star Publications.

Cold Cherry Soup

Marian Kaplan
Leawood, Kansas

Germany
Yield: 8 Servings

This recipe comes from my mother, Marga Kretschmer, born in Berlin, Germany, who now lives in Buffalo, New York. She said this was passed down to her from her mother as a traditional German recipe.

2 pounds of sour or sweet cherries	½ cup sugar
7 cups water	2 tablespoons cornstarch
Small piece lemon peel and juice	4 tablespoons white wine

1. Place cherries (with pits) and 3½ cups water in a saucepan. If using unpitted cherries, place cherries and juice and water in a saucepan. Bring to a boil. Reduce heat and simmer about 10 minutes.
2. If using pitted cherries, drain but save juice, remove pits and return to pan. Measure juice and add enough water to make 7 cups. If using unpitted cherries, measure juice and add enough water to make 7 cups.
3. Add lemon rind and sugar. Pour a little juice in a small dish, add cornstarch, mix, then return to soup to thicken. Add wine if using. Cook until sauce begins to thicken slightly.
Cool and serve cold.

This recipe can also be used for blueberry or other berry soup.

Preparation and Cooking Time: 1 hour

Carrot Soup

Dora Levy
Kansas City, Missouri   Yield: 4 Servings

2 tablespoons olive oil	4 cups carrots, shredded
¼ cup onions, chopped	2 teaspoons soy sauce
4 cups water	Salt and pepper to taste
1 rib celery, chopped	1 cup soy flour

1. Heat oil in soup pot. Sauté onions until clear but not brown.
2. Add water, celery, carrots, soy sauce, salt and pepper. Simmer for 30 minutes. Remove from heat.
3. Stir in soy flour

Preparation and Cooking Time: 45 minutes

French Onion Soup

Sybil Kaplan
Overland Park, Kansas

French Style
Yield: 4 to 6 Servings

I adapted this from a recipe given out by a store.

2 tablespoons margarine	5⅓ cups water
2 teaspoons oil	5 teaspoons pareve beef
4 cups onions, sliced	soup powder
Salt to taste	⅔ cup white wine
¼ teaspoon sugar	1 bay leaf
2 tablespoons flour	Dash sage (optional)

1. Heat margarine and oil in a soup pot. Add onions, cover and cook 15-20 minutes.
2. Stir in salt, sugar, flour and pareve soup powder. Add water, wine, bay leaf and sage if using. Bring to a boil. Reduce heat and simmer 1 hour.

Preparation and Cooking Time: 1½ hours

Low-Calorie Potato Soup

Dora Levy
Kansas City, Missouri

Yield: 6 Servings

1 tablespoon margarine	2 celery ribs with leaves
1 garlic clove, minced	1 tablespoon fresh or
1 cup onions, chopped	½ teaspoon dry dill
4 pareve chicken soup cubes	2-3 sprigs fresh parsley
5 cups hot water	or 1 teaspoon dry
3 medium potatoes,	1 teaspoon salt
peeled and cut in wedges	½ teaspoon pepper
2 medium carrots,	1 tablespoon cornstarch or
peeled and sliced	potato starch
1 zucchini, sliced	3 tablespoons water

1. Melt margarine in a soup pot. Saute onion and garlic until translucent.
2. Dissolve chicken soup cubes in hot water. Add to pot. Add potatoes, carrots, zucchini and celery but save celery leaves. Bring to a boil, reduce heat and simmer 15-20 minutes.
3. Add celery tops, dill, parsley, salt and pepper.
4. Dissolve cornstarch or potato starch in 3 tablespoons water and add to soup. Simmer until slightly thick.

Preparation and Cooking Time: 30 minutes

Helen's Cold Spinach Soup

Sybil Kaplan   Israel
Overland Park, Kansas   Yield: 10 Servings

Helen Goldfoot and her husband, Stanley, from South Africa were among the many interesting people I met while living in Israel. Eating at each other's home was a favorite pastime and I tasted this in her home and asked for the recipe. She told me she'd been making what she called a "garbage" soup with all sorts of green leaves for some time and one day she decided she would make it mainly a spinach soup for piquancy and variety. Following soup, she served Indian curry on rice topped with finely chopped onions, tomatoes, bananas and coconut and Mango chutney.

Oil	1 teaspoon nutmeg
1 large onion, chopped	1 tablespoon soy sauce
2 squash, chopped	2 tablespoons pareve
1 cup cabbage, chopped	chicken soup powder
8 cups water	2-3 cups spinach,
Salt and pepper to taste	cooked and drained
1 large bunch fresh dill	Pecans, chopped

1. Place oil in a soup pot. Fry onion until limp.
2. Add squash, cabbage, water, salt and pepper, dill, nutmeg, soy sauce and chicken soup powder. Bring to a boil. Reduce heat and simmer until vegetables are tender (15-20 minutes).
3. Cool and put through a blender a few seconds. Add spinach and blend. Cool in refrigerator.

Serve with nuts on top and garlic bread.

Preparation and Cooking Time: 1 hour

St. Peter's Fish Soup

Sybil Kaplan   Israel
Overland Park, Kansas   Yield: 6 Servings

*This comes from a brochure, St. Peter's Fish, from the Sea of
Galilee, produced by Carmel Agrexco, Agricultural Export Co. of
Israel. Not until I read the brochure carefully did I discover that the
tilapia I had seen in supermarkets is St. Peter's Fish.*

3 St. Peter's fish (tilapia) about ¾ pound each, cut in halves	1½ tablespoons sherry or brandy
Salt	1-2 egg yolks
1 onion, cut up	Juice of 1 lemon
1 squash, diced	¼ teaspoon lemon peel, grated
1 medium potato, diced *	6 slices bread
6-7 cups water	Garlic
¼ teaspoon white pepper	Oil

1. Dip the fish in salt. Place onion and fish in a soup pot.
   Add squash, potato and water. Bring to a boil. Reduce
   heat and cook 30 minutes.
2. Remove fish from pot, cool, then carve in parallel lines.
   Return to the pot.
3. Add pepper and sherry or brandy.
4. In a bowl, beat egg yolks with lemon juice and lemon peel.
   Pour a little hot soup into the egg yolks and continue
   beating. Pour into the pot.
5. Heat oil in a frying pan. Rub bread with garlic and fry
   until brown on both sides.
6. To serve, place fried bread in soup bowls and pour hot
   soup on top.
   Sour cream or yogurt may be added instead of egg yolks,
   thus making it dairy.

* If you like, add more potatoes.

Preparation and Cooking Time: 45 minutes to 1 hour

Hungarian Fish Soup
Magyar Hal Leves

Susan Weiss

Hungary
Yield: 6 Servings

Linda Radke says this recipe is from her Aunt Susan, who is from Hungary and is married to Linda's mother's oldest brother, Gene.

3 onions, diced	**1 teaspoon salt**
6 slices cod, carp,	**Green pepper, chopped**
or red snapper	**(optional)**
Water	**½ tomato, cut into pieces**
3 teaspoons paprika	**(optional)**

1. In a Dutch oven, put onions and fish. Cover with water. Add paprika, salt and green pepper and tomato if used.
2. Cook about 15 minutes.

Serve with boiled or baked potatoes or with noodles.

Preparation and Cooking Time: 15 minutes

Note: From **That Hungarian's In My Kitchen** by Linda F. Radke, Five Star Publications.

Scandinavian Fish Chowder

Sybil Kaplan
Overland Park, Kansas

Scandinavian Style
Yield: 4 Servings

4 teaspoons butter or
  margarine
4 teaspoons oil
2 medium onions, chopped
1 cup carrots, sliced
2 tablespoons celery, chopped
1⅓ cups hot water
2 teaspoons pareve chicken
  soup powder
½ teaspoon salt
Dash pepper

4 to 6 sprigs parsley,
  chopped
1 bay leaf
½ teaspoon thyme
2 small leeks, chopped
2 garlic cloves, chopped
1⅓ pounds white fish,
  cut in chunks
⅔ cup milk
2 egg yolks
Dill

1. Heat butter or margarine and oil in a soup pot. Brown
   onions. Add carrots, celery, water, chicken soup powder,
   salt, pepper, parsley, bay leaf, thyme, leeks and garlic.
   Bring to a boil. Reduce heat and simmer 25 minutes.
2. Add fish. Simmer 15 minutes.
3. Beat milk in a bowl with egg yolks. Stir into soup. Heat.
   Sprinkle with dill. Serve hot.

Preparation and Cooking Time: 1 hour

Chicken Lemon Soup
Avgolemono

Sybil Kaplan   Greek Style
Overland Park, Kansas   Yield: 4 to 6 Servings

Hotels in Israel often sponsored special food weeks and brought in chefs to create dishes that were kosher. During Greek Week at the Jerusalem Hilton Hotel, I tasted this dish and was given its recipe.

5½ cups water
5½ teaspoons chicken
   soup powder
4 teaspoons cornstarch

3 egg yolks
2 cups rice, cooked
Juice of 1 lemon
Salt to taste

1. Place chicken soup powder and water in a soup pot. Bring to a boil. Reduce heat.
2. Add cornstarch and yolks and blend. Add rice, lemon juice and salt. Simmer until very hot.

Preparation and Cooking Time: 30 minutes to 1 hour

Whoops! The soup is too salty!
Add a sliced, raw potato, bring to a boil and let boil 5 minutes then remove potato.

Lentil Soup
Lentijas

Matilda Rosenberg   Greece
Overland Park, Kansas   Yield: 8 to 10 Servings

*This came from my mother, Alegre Tevet, who came from Drama,
Greece. My mother often has said the secret to cooking well is
taking your time and cooking slow. The slow cooking allows the
flavors to fully develop.*

1 pound stew meat	**Few shakes pepper**
1 onion, diced	**1 cup lentils,**
Few cloves garlic, cut up	**rinsed and sorted**
Water	**½ cup celery, chopped**
1 can beef broth or	**½ cup carrots, chopped**
3-4 cans water	
1 tablespoon Worcestershire sauce	

1. Place stew meat, onion, garlic, and a little water in a soup
   pot. Cook 1 to 1½ hours until meat is done
2. Add beef broth or water, Worcestershire sauce and pepper.
   Add lentils, celery and carrots. Continue cooking for 1
   hour. Add water if soup seems too thick.

This is a wonderful soup, hearty and good enough to serve
for dinner with a salad and fresh bread. This is delicious as
a wintertime soup!

Preparation and Cooking Time: 2½ hours

Polish Lentil Soup

Sonia Golad
Kansas City, Missouri

Poland
Yield: 8 to 10 Servings

My mother, who came from Vilna, Poland, used to make this on Sundays when our store was closed. She would take over the cooking, and we looked forward to her making this soup.

1 pound lentils	1 garlic clove
1 pound stew meat	5 to 6 ribs celery, diced
3 quarts water	2 onions, chopped
2 tablespoons chicken shmaltz (fat)	3 to 4 carrots, chopped

1. Put lentils and meat in a big soup pot with water. Bring to a boil. Reduce heat and simmer 1 hour and 15 minutes.
2. Melt shmaltz in a frying pan. Add garlic, celery and onions. Cook until onion gets golden.
3. Add to soup pot. Add carrots. Bring to a boil, then reduce heat and simmer 30 minutes.

Preparation and Cooking Time: 2 to 2½ hours

"And it came to pass...that Shobi...brought...wheat and barley and meal and parched corn, and beans, and lentils, and parched pulse..."
(II Samuel 17:27-28)

Hot and Sour Soup

Empire Kosher Poultry
Mifflintown, Pennsylvania

Chinese Style
Yield: 6 Servings

This Chinese take-out is very little effort, plus you get only 109 calories per cup. It's complex, soul satisfying and absolutely delicious. It comes from a staff member's mother, one of the best cooks we know. She says: "This soup depends on the shiitake mushrooms and sesame oil for its delicious flavor. No substitutes!" If you like more bite, add hot pepper to taste.

1½ ounces dried shiitake mushrooms	1 tablespoon low-sodium soy sauce
2 cups water	1½ teaspoons fresh ginger, grated
2 boneless, skinless chicken breasts	1 teaspoon dark sesame oil
4½ cups low-sodium undiluted chicken broth	Black pepper to taste
½ cup canned bamboo shoots, cut into strips	½ teaspoon dry mustard
¼ cup rice vinegar	2½ tablespoons corn starch
1 tablespoon sugar	2 tablespoons water
1 tablespoon dry sherry	1 egg, beaten
	2 tablespoons green onion tops, sliced

1. Combine mushrooms and water in a small saucepan and bring to a boil. Remove from heat and let stand 30 minutes. Drain. Cut mushrooms into thin strips. Set aside.
2. Flatten chicken to ¼-inch thickness, cut into thin strips.
3. Combine mushroom strips, chicken strips, broth, bamboo shoots, rice vinegar, sugar, dry sherry, soy sauce, ginger, sesame oil, pepper and dry mustard in a large pot. Bring to a boil, cover, reduce heat and simmer 10 minutes.
4. Combine corn starch with 2 tablespoons water in a bowl. Add to chicken mixture. Cook for 1 minute, stirring constantly.

5. Slowly drizzle egg into the soup. Cook an additional 2
   minutes. Ladle soup into bowls and sprinkle with green
   onions.

Preparation and Cooking Time: 1¼ hours

Chicken-Vegetable Dumplings

Sybil Kaplan
Overland Park, Kansas

Yield: 6 Servings

2 eggs	**2 cups bread crumbs**
½ cup white part of leek, chopped	**1 tablespoon parsley, chopped**
13 ounces raw chicken, cut into small pieces	**1½ teaspoons salt**
½ cup onions, chopped	**1 teaspoon pepper**
½ cup carrots, chopped	**1 teaspoon thyme**
	3 cups chicken soup

1. Blend eggs in blender until thick and double in volume. Add leek and blend, then add chicken, carrots, and onions. Blend until smooth and thick. Place in a bowl.
2. Add bread crumbs, parsley, salt, pepper and thyme and mix. Shape mixture between soup spoons dipped in cold water. Place balls on a cookie sheet.
3. Pour chicken soup into a pot. Heat. Add chicken dumplings and cook until they float to the top (about 5 minutes). Cover and simmer 10 minutes more.

Preparation and Cooking Time: 30 minutes

Pumpkin Soup

Dalia Carmel
New York, New York   Yield: 6 to 10 Servings

After eating pumpkin soup made by my cousin, Eudice, at a party, I got her recipe and then created my own version.

4 tablespoons margarine	¼ teaspoon nutmeg
1 large onion, chopped	¼ teaspoon white pepper
1 medium leek, white only, chopped	½-inch fresh ginger root, cut in two parts
1 26-ounce can pumpkin puree	1 bay leaf
5¾ cups chicken broth	2 cups non-dairy creamer
1 teaspoon salt	4 tablespoons dry sherry
2½ teaspoons curry powder	Parsley, chopped fine

1. Melt margarine in a soup pot. Sauté onions and leek, stirring until soft, about 8 minutes.
2. Stir in pumpkin puree, broth, salt, curry power, nutmeg, pepper, ginger root and bay leaf. Bring to a boil, reduce heat and simmer, covered, for about 15 minutes. Remove bay leaf.
3. Puree in batches in food processor or blender and return to pot. Stir in sherry and non-dairy creamer and stir until heated through. Adjust seasonings. Garnish with parsley.

Serve with guacamole ice cream (see Dessert chapter).

Preparation and Cooking Time: 1 hour

Curried Pumpkin Soup á la Eudice

Dalia Carmel
New York, New York   Yield: 6 to 10 Servings

I ate this at a party at the home of our cousin, Eudice, and I went to heaven! I usually dislike pumpkin, but this soup is something else!

4 tablespoons unsalted margarine	**2½ teaspoons curry**
1 large onion, chopped	**powder**
1 medium leek, white part only,	**¼ teaspoon nutmeg**
chopped	**¼ teaspoon white pepper**
1 pound pumpkin puree,	**¼ teaspoon ginger**
canned or fresh	**1 bay leaf**
4 cups chicken broth	**1 cup non-dairy creamer**
1 teaspoon salt	**Chopped chives (optional)**

1. Melt margarine in a soup pot over moderate heat. Add onion and leek and sauté, stirring often until soft, about 8 minutes.
2. Stir in pumpkin, chicken broth, salt, curry powder, nutmeg, pepper, ginger and bay leaf. Bring to a boil, stirring. Reduce heat and simmer, covered, for 15 minutes. Remove bay leaf.
3. Puree mixture in food processor or blender in two batches. Puree may be refrigerated up to 2 days or frozen. If using soon, return puree to pot, add non-dairy creamer and stir over moderate heat until heated. Adjust seasonings. Garnish with chives if desired.

Preparation and Cooking Time: 30 minutes

Ella Weiser's Brisket Soup

Dalia Carmel   German
New York, New York   Yield: 6 Quarts

3-4 pound first cut of brisket, trimmed of fat
2-3 marrow bones
2 medium turnips, cut into 4 pieces
2 parsnips, peeled and cut in 2 pieces
¼ celery knob, if large, or 1 small, cut into 4 pieces

3 celery ribs
1 onion, peeled, studded with 4 cloves
3 garlic cloves
1 package fresh dill
1 package flat leaf parsley
2 bay leaves
Salt and pepper to taste
Water

1. Place brisket and bones in a large soup pot.
2. Add turnips, parsnips, celery knob, celery, onion and garlic. Place dill, parsley and bay leaves on top. Add salt and pepper. Add water to cover. Bring to a boil. Skim off scum that rises to the surface, but don't stir the soup. Reduce heat, cover and simmer slowly for 3 hours or until meat is tender.
3. Remove meat, bones and bay leaves.
4. Remove vegetables to a bowl then puree in a blender. Store in a container. Chill soup, then defat the next morning. Add vegetable puree to soup to thicken. Reheat before serving.

Serve with slices of radishes on the side and fresh rye bread. Heat meat and either cut up and add to soup or serve separately with horseradish sauce.

Preparation and Cooking Time: 4 hours

Note: This recipe has appeared in **Soup Suppers** by Arthur Schwartz.

A Brisket Story

Winters in Jerusalem could be chilly and bone chilling. The heavy, famous Jerusalem stone structures--so cool in summer-- kept the chill close to the bones while indoors during the rainy periods. There was nothing better than coming home and running up the stairs to be met by wafts of heavenly aromas-- mother's hot beef soup with vegetables.

I never knew what meat was used to make the soup and never bothered to find out--until it was too late. The makings of the soup eluded me and whenever I wanted to duplicate my mother's soup, no cut of beef suggested by butchers or friends' mothers managed to create that same result.

The only clue I had to follow was a childhood memory of my mother's request that I stop at the butcher on the way to elementary school and ask him to prepare a "spitzen brust" to be ready for me to pick up on my way back from school. I presumed that the package, which I picked up, wound up in the pot to make the soup.

Having set up home in New York, I ventured to call some of the butchers in Yorkville, first checking their fluency in German, starting the conversation by inquiring whether they spoke German. I then asked what cut would they sell me if I asked them for "spitzen brust" (meaning the tip of the breast). The replies varied; some suggested either the first or second cut of the brisket. I took the advice and bought the entire brisket, dividing it in two.

One morning I set up a pot of soup with the first cut of the brisket and all the necessary vegetable trimmings, went off for a while and hoped. Upon returning to my apartment, as I walked down the hall I felt that overwhelming sensation of "going home."

The aroma embraced me with childhood memories from school, to the butcher, to our house in Jerusalem and the warmth of home and my mother--all encased in mother's soup.

Dalia Carmel

Note: Dalia Carmel was born in Jerusalem. Her mother was born in Riga, studied medicine in Riga and Germany, then emigrated to Palestine in the early 1930s. Her father was born in Budapest and was a doctor. She moved to New York in 1960 and is married to Herbert Goldstein, works for El Al Israel Airlines and is a collector of cookbooks. (At last count she owned near 4,000!)

Salads
&
Gelatins

Middle Eastern Cream Cheese and Celery Salad

Sybil Kaplan
Overland Park, Kansas

Middle East
Yield: 2 To 3 Servings

¼ cup low-fat cream cheese
2½ teaspoons lemon juice
1½ teaspoons oil

⅓ cup low-fat sour cream
Salt and pepper to taste
2 ribs celery, finely
    chopped

1. Combine all ingredients in a bowl.

This can also be combined in a blender or food processor and blended or processed a few seconds and used as a dip.

Good with pita bread!

Preparation and Cooking Time: 10 minutes

Edna's Oriental Gelatin

Sybil Kaplan
Overland Park, Kansas

Oriental Style
Yield: 4 Servings

Edna and Kobi Greitser came to Chicago from Haifa as schlichim (emissaries) for a couple of years. I ate this in her home and asked for the recipe.

1 package unflavored gelatin
1 cup milk
½ cup water
2 tablespoons sugar
1 tablespoon almond extract

1. Heat milk in a saucepan with water and unflavored gelatin until gelatin dissolves. Add sugar and almond extract.
2. Pour into a greased serving pan or dish. Refrigerate 6 hours

Cut into pieces just before serving.

Good with fruit cocktail or coconut and pineapple.

Preparation and Cooking Time: 6 hours and 15 minutes

Fruit Gelatin Bavarian

Sybil Kaplan
Overland Park, Kansas   Yield: 6 Servings

1 package fruit-flavored gelatin	**1 cup whipping cream,**
1 cup boiling water	**whipped, regular,**
¾ cup cold water	**or pareve**
1 cup sliced fruit	

1. Dissolve gelatin in boiling water. Add cold water and chill 1 hour and 15 minutes.
2. Whip cream and stir into gelatin. Add fruit. Pour into a greased mold.

Chill 4 hours. Unmold just before serving.

Garnish with sliced fresh fruit and whipped cream.

Preparation and Cooking Time: 5½ hours

Pareve

Cranberry Gelatin Mold

Dorothy Kaplan
Kansas City, Missouri   Yield: 12 to 16 Servings

*I found this on a carton and changed it. I use it for crowds,
especially holidays when the whole family gets together.*

Margarine, oil or spray oil
4 slices canned pineapple,
  pear halves, or
  sliced peaches
1 3-ounce package lemon gelatin
1 cup boiling water
1 cup cold water

2½ cups boiling water
2 3-ounce packages
  red gelatin
1 10-ounce frozen,
  cranberry-orange sauce
1 cup crushed pineapple,
  with juice

1. Grease a gelatin mold (10½ inch diameter with hole in center). Layer pineapple or pear halves or peach slices in bottom.
2. In a mixing bowl, dissolve lemon gelatin in 1 cup boiling water. Then add cold water. Pour over fruit. Refrigerate until firm.
3. In a mixing bowl, dissolve red gelatin in boiling water. Add cranberry-orange sauce and pineapple with juice. Let cool in refrigerator but don't let it get firm.
4. Pour cooled red gelatin mixture over lemon gelatin mixture. Refrigerate until firm.

For a variation, one might try this with 10 ounces of whole berry cranberry sauce.

Preparation and Cooking Time: 3 hours

Sandy's Raspberry Bavarian

Sybil Kaplan   Israel
Overland Park, Kansas   Yield: 8 Servings

Sandy and Neil Katz, Americans, were living in Jerusalem when I lived there. One evening I was in their home and this was the dessert Sandy served, so I asked for the recipe.

1 cup boiling water	1 can frozen orange juice concentrate
1 package regular raspberry gelatin	½ cup cold water
1 envelope unflavored gelatin	1 pint vanilla ice cream, cut into chunks

1. Place boiling water and gelatins in blender. Blend on low for 1½ minutes.
2. Add orange juice and cold water and blend on high. Add ice cream and blend on high a few seconds. Pour into a greased mold and refrigerate.

Preparation and Cooking Time: 3 hours

Dairy

Syrian Fattoush

Sybil Kaplan   Syrian Style
Overland Park, Kansas   Yield: 4 Servings

I adapted various recipes until I found it the way I liked it.

½ cup lemon juice
1-2 garlic cloves, crushed
Salt to taste
⅓ cup olive oil
1 cup yogurt
2 cucumbers,
  finely chopped
2 tomatoes, finely
  chopped

4 green onions, minced
½ cup fresh mint,
  chopped
½ cup fresh parsley,
  chopped
½ cup lettuce,
  finely chopped
1 cup pita,
  toasted and bite size

1. Mix lemon juice and garlic in a bowl with salt. Stir in oil and yogurt.
2. In a second bowl, toss together cucumbers, tomatoes, onions, mint, and parsley. Add pita. Pour lemon juice over and toss.

If you prefer, you can use dry parsley and dry mint although the flavor is not as strong. You can also add red pepper.

Preparation and Cooking Time: 10 to 15 minutes

How do you keep a bunch of parsley fresh? Store it in a tightly covered jar in the refrigerator.

Yaffa's Israeli Avocado Salad

Sybil Kaplan   Israel
Overland Park, Kansas   Yield: 2 to 3 Cups

I learned this from an Israeli I met in Chicago.

Flesh of 3 avocados   1½ teaspoons white pepper
6 hard-boiled eggs   2 green onions, chopped
5 to 6 tablespoons mayonnaise   Sliced tomatoes
3 garlic cloves, crushed   Fresh parsley
1½ teaspoons salt

1. Scoop out avocado flesh and process in food processor or blender.
2. Add eggs, mayonnaise, garlic, salt, pepper and green onions. Process or blend a few seconds

   Place on a plate. Garnish with sliced tomatoes and parsley.

Preparation and Cooking Time: 10 to 15 minutes

Pareve

Bean Salad

Dalia Carmel
New York, New York

Yield: 10 Servings

I made this up about 15 years ago.

1 can chick peas
1 can red kidney beans
1 can wax beans
1 can artichoke hearts,
  drained and sliced
1 can white (cannellini) beans
1 large green pepper, cubed
1½ red onions, chopped fine
¾ cup green olives, sliced
Salt and pepper to taste

Dressing
1 teaspoon mint leaves
1 teaspoon basil leaves
1 teaspoon oregano
¼ cup red wine vinegar
½ cup olive oil

1. Rinse and drain chick peas, kidney beans, wax beans, artichoke hearts and cannellini beans and place in a salad bowl.
2. Add green pepper and red onion and olives. Mix with spatula softly so as not to break the beans. Sprinkle with salt and pepper.
3. In a jar or another bowl, combine mint, basil, oregano, vinegar and oil. Mix well and pour over salad. Mix well. Refrigerate for an hour before serving. Let sit to blend tastes.

Preparation and Cooking Time: 1¼ hours

Italian Broccoli Salad
Insalata di Broccoli

Adeline Gniady
Chicago, Illinois

Italy/Sicily
Yield: 4 to 6 Servings

My family is Italian Catholic and comes from Palermo, Sicily. I gave this to Sybil, my upstairs neighbor.

2 pounds broccoli	1 garlic clove, crushed
3 tablespoons olive oil	Salt and pepper to taste
2 teaspoons wine vinegar	Dash mustard powder
2 teaspoons tarragon vinegar	¼ teaspoon dry parsley
2 teaspoons lemon juice	flakes
⅛ teaspoon oregano	½ red pepper, chopped
⅛ teaspoon basil	Black olives (optional)

1. Place water in a saucepan. Add broccoli, bring to a boil. Reduce heat and cook until tender. Drain and cool.
2. Meantime, combine oil, vinegars, lemon juice, oregano, basil, garlic, salt, pepper, mustard powder and parsley flakes in a jar. Shake well. Pour over broccoli in a bowl. Add red pepper and black olives and chill.

Preparation and Cooking Time: 15 to 30 minutes

"dip thy morsel in the vinegar" *(Ruth 2:14)*

Bulgur Salad

Sybil Kaplan
Overland Park, Kansas

Middle East Style
Yield: 4 Servings

1 cup broccoli
7 tablespoons water
½ teaspoon chicken
soup powder
2 tablespoons red wine
vinegar
1 teaspoon Dijon mustard
2 garlic cloves, minced
Salt and pepper to taste
⅔ cup bulgur

3 tablespoons radishes,
chopped (optional)
3 tablespoons celery,
minced (optional)
2 tablespoons green onions,
minced (optional)
Tomatoes, minced
Red pepper, minced
5 teaspoons olive oil
4 teaspoons red wine
vinegar

1. Place broccoli in a saucepan with a small amount of water.
   Bring to a boil. Reduce heat and simmer 5-7 minutes.
   Drain. Leave in a colander.
2. Place 7 tablespoons water, chicken soup powder, wine
   vinegar, Dijon mustard, garlic, salt and pepper in a
   saucepan. Bring to a boil. Add bulgur, stir, reduce heat,
   cover and set aside for 15 minutes.
3. Place bulgur, sauce and broccoli in a salad bowl. Add
   radish, celery, green onions, tomatoes, red pepper, olive oil
   and wine vinegar. Refrigerate until ready to serve.

You can also make this in a food processor but be careful
not to overprocess it too small.

Preparation and Cooking Time: 1½ hours

Note: The true bulgur salad known as tabbouleh comes from
Lebanon and contains finely chopped tomatoes, parsley, mint,
bulgur, olive oil and lemon juice. Bulgur is a type of wheat,
also called bulghur and burghul.

Carrot and Jicama Salad

Dalia Carmel
New York, New York   Yield: 8 Servings

This started out about 10 years ago, as a carrot salad based on a Moroccan-style salad. Later, I decided to add jicama.

1 clove garlic	**Dressing**
1 bunch fresh mint	Juice of 1 lime
1 bunch fresh dill	Juice of 1 lemon
2 pounds carrots	1 tablespoon cider or
1-2 pounds jicama	Balsamic vinegar
⅔ cup raisins	1 teaspoon chili powder
¾ cup almonds. slivered	1 teaspoon cumin
1 medium leek, thinly sliced	Salt and pepper to taste
	½ cup good olive oil

1. Chop garlic, mint and dill in food processor. Transfer to a salad bowl.
2. Grate carrots and jicama on a medium grater. Transfer to the bowl. Sprinkle raisins and almonds on top. Slice the leek over the top.
3. Mix lime juice, lemon juice, cider or Balsamic vinegar, chili powder, cumin, salt, pepper and oil in a processor. Pour over salad and fold to mix ingredients. Adjust seasonings until tastes balance.
   Refrigerate for a few hours before serving.

Preparation and Cooking Time: 15 to 20 minutes

Chinese Vegetable Salad

Sybil Kaplan   Chinese Style
Overland Park, Kansas   Yield: 4 Servings

8 ounces fresh bean sprouts	½ red pepper, chopped
1 can water chestnuts, sliced and drained	¼ teaspoon dry mustard
	2 teaspoons soy sauce
⅔ cup celery, chopped	¼ cup oil
⅓ cup daikon, chopped	2¼ tablespoons white vinegar
1 cucumber, sliced	
1 green pepper, chopped	Salt and pepper to taste

1. Place bean sprouts, water chestnuts, celery, daikon, cucumber and pepper in a salad bowl.
2. In a jar combine dry mustard, soy sauce, oil, vinegar, salt and pepper. Shake. Pour over salad.

Daikon is a white Japanese radish and makes a nice addition to this salad.

Preparation and Cooking Time: 10 to 15 minutes

How do you get cole slaw to taste crunchy? Cut cabbage in half and soak in salted, ice water 1 hour then drain well.

Cucumber Salad

Marian Kaplan   Germany
Leawood, Kansas   Yield: 4 Servings

*This recipe comes from my mother, Marga Kretschmer, born in
Berlin, Germany, who now lives in Buffalo, New York. She said this
was passed down to her from her mother as a traditional German
recipe.*

1 large cucumber, pared and sliced very thin	¾ teaspoon sugar 1 teaspoon vegetable oil
½ teaspoon salt	1 tablespoon parsley,
1 teaspoon lemon juice	chopped

1. Place sliced cucumber in a bowl. Sprinkle with salt. Push
   slices together as much as possible. Weigh down and
   press. Let stand 4 hours minimum.
2. Pour off cucumber juice and add lemon juice, sugar and oil.
   Mix well. Add parsley and refrigerate overnight.

Preparation and Cooking Time: 4¼ hours

"And the daughter of Zion is left
As a booth in a vineyard
As a lodge in a garden of cucumbers"
(Isaiah 1:8)

Pareve

Edna's Eggplant Salad
Salat Chatzilim

Sybil Kaplan   Israel
Overland Park, Kansas   Yield: 8 Servings

Edna and Kobi Greitzer came from Haifa, Israel, and I met them in Chicago when they were shlichim (emissaries) for a few years. She gave me this recipe.

2 to 3 eggplants	2 to 3 garlic cloves,
2 to 3 tablespoons oil	crushed
White pepper	½ cup techina
Black pepper	¼ cup lemon juice
Salt to taste	

1. Place eggplants on a pan under the broiler and broil 20 to 30 minutes until outside is almost black and inside is soft. Rotate often.
2. Remove from oven, remove skin and mash flesh in a bowl with a fork. Add oil, spices, garlic, techina and lemon juice.

   Variation: grill 2 to 3 large green peppers, oiled, with eggplant, peel and add flesh. Add minced onion, oil and lemon juice.

Preparation and Cooking Time: 40 minutes

Note: Techina is a thick paste made of ground sesame seeds and is used in many Middle Eastern dishes.

Eggplant Salad

Janet Siegel
Prairie Village, Kansas

Israel Style
Yield: 8 Servings

I thought this up while living in Israel.

**2 medium eggplants
6 cloves garlic
1 medium onion, chopped
¼ cup lemon juice
½ cup mayonnaise**

1. Preheat oven to 350° F.
2. Place eggplants on a baking pan and bake in a 350° F oven until brown.
3. Cut off ends and scoop out eggplant flesh. Place in a blender. Add garlic, onion, lemon juice and mayonnaise and blend.
4. Place in a bowl and refrigerate.

Preparation and Cooking Time: 40 minutes

If you're out of mayonnaise, place in a food processor:
1 egg, ⅓ cup vegetable oil, 2 tablespoons white wine vinegar. Add: ½ teaspoon salt, ½ teaspoon dry mustard, ¼ teaspoon paprika, ⅔ cup oil. Blend until thick. Store in covered jar in refrigerator.
This makes a nice mustardy mayonnaise.

Green Salad with Avocado Dressing

Sybil Kaplan
Overland Park, Kansas   Yield: 6 Servings

1 medium head Romaine lettuce	Flesh of a ripe avocado
or ¾ large head iceberg lettuce	3 tablespoons lemon juice
4 ounces marinated artichoke	3 tablespoons orange juice
hearts, chopped	3 tablespoons mayonnaise
(save marinade)	2 teaspoons green onions,
½ cucumber, chopped	chopped
8-10 radishes, chopped	

1. Cut up lettuces in a salad bowl. Add artichoke hearts, cucumber and radishes. Set aside.
2. In blender, put avocado and lemon juice, artichoke hearts marinade, orange juice, mayonnaise and green onions. Blend a few seconds. Pour over salad.

Preparation and Cooking Time: 20 to 30 minutes

For Green Herb Dijon, add 2 teaspoons dry dill,
2 teaspoons dry tarragon, and 2 teaspoons dry parsley to
1 cup Dijon mustard.

Jerusalem Artichoke Salad

Sybil Kaplan
Overland Park, Kansas   Yield: 4 Servings

1½-pound head Boston lettuce	⅜ cup oil
1 small red pepper, cut up	2 tablespoons red wine
5 ounces Jerusalem artichokes	vinegar
(also known as sunchokes)	½ teaspoon Dijon mustard
1 teaspoon lemon juice	Salt and pepper to taste

1. Line a salad bowl with Boston lettuce. Add red pepper.
2. Slice Jerusalem artichokes into another bowl. Toss with lemon juice.
3. Combine oil, wine vinegar, mustard, salt and pepper in a jar. Close and shake.
4. Add Jerusalem artichokes to salad bowl. Pour over dressing.

Preparation and Cooking Time: 20 minutes

Note: Jerusalem artichokes are neither from Jerusalem nor an artichoke. They're part of the sunflower family and the name comes from the Italian word for sunflower. They can be eaten raw, in a salad, with a dip, cooked as a side dish and in soup.

How do you make Dijon mustard more flavorful? For Herbed Dijon, add 1 tablespoon mixed herbs and 1 tablespoon dry vermouth to 1 cup Dijon mustard.

Cooked Olive Salad

Dalia Carmel
New York, New York

Moroccan Style
Yield: 6 to 8 Servings

I was given some leftovers from a party held at the Israel Consulate, about five years ago and this olive salad was so fabulous, I asked for the recipe. If you love piquant things, it is easy to prepare, tasty and keeps well up to 10 days in the refrigerator. It is best prepared 24 hours in advance.

1 can pitted olives, drained	**1 tablespoon cumin,**
¼ cup water	**(use less to taste)**
3 tablespoons oil	**½ teaspoon paprika**
3 garlic cloves, smashed	**½ teaspoon hot paprika**
4-ounce can tomato paste	**(optional)**
¼ cup water	

1. Place drained olives in a small pan and cover with water. Bring to a boil, remove from heat and drain. Repeat another time.
2. Place oil in a frying pan. Sauté garlic until golden.
3. Mix tomato paste with water and add to pan. Add cumin, paprika, and hot paprika, if using, and olives. Bring to a boil. Reduce heat, cover and simmer for exactly 20 minutes.

Preparation and Cooking Time: 30 to 40 minutes

Lirit's Italian Rice Salad

Sybil Kaplan   Italy
Overland Park, Kansas   Yield: 4 Servings

*Lirit and Abba Richman lived in Jerusalem when I lived there and
she was originally from Milan and Rome, Italy. She gave me this
recipe which she had learned from her mother, who made it in the
summer. She recalled eating it when she was small and thought her
mother had gotten it from her mother.*

2 tablespoons oil	**3 medium tomatoes,**
1½ tablespoons vinegar	**cut up**
½ teaspoon basil	**1 medium green or**
Salt to taste	**red pepper, cut up**
2 cups rice, cooked	**3 to 4 sprigs fresh parsley**
	minced

1. Beat together in a small bowl oil, vinegar, basil and salt.
2. In serving bowl, combine rice, tomatoes, pepper and
   parsley. Pour dressing on top and toss. Refrigerate until
   ready to serve but bring to room temperature half an hour
   before serving.

Preparation and Cooking Time: 2½ hours

Rice Salad Primavera

Sybil Kaplan   Italian Style
Overland Park, Kansas   Yield: 4 Servings

2 cups leftover cooked rice	¼ cup oil
¼ pound broccoli flowerets	1½ teaspoons lemon juice
12 snow peas	1½ teaspoons tarragon
12 mushrooms	vinegar
12 cherry tomatoes	1 garlic clove, crushed
¼ red pepper	¼ teaspoon dry mustard
¼ green pepper	⅛ teaspoon tarragon
1 green onion	Salt and pepper to taste

1. Place rice in a salad bowl.
2. Place broccoli, snow peas and mushrooms in a saucepan with a little water and cook until limp (about 5 minutes). Drain. Add to salad.
3. Halve or quarter cherry tomatoes, dice peppers and onion and add to salad.
4. In a jar, combine oil, lemon juice, vinegar, garlic, mustard, tarragon, salt and pepper. Shake well. Pour over salad and refrigerate.

Preparation and Cooking Time: 2½ hours

Spinach Salad

Sybil Kaplan
Overland Park, Kansas   Yield: 4 Servings

2 cups fresh spinach, cut up
2 hard-boiled eggs, grated
2 medium kohlrabi, sliced or
  1 can water chestnuts,
  sliced and drained
6-8 cherry tomatoes, halved
½ teaspoon onion, minced
1 garlic clove, crushed
Salt and pepper to taste

Dash dry mustard
Dash celery seeds
1 tablespoon vinegar
1½ teaspoons water
1 tablespoon + 1 teaspoon
  oil
⅛ teaspoon paprika
Cashews or other unsalted
  nuts (optional)

1. Place spinach, hard-boiled eggs, kohlrabi, and cherry
   tomatoes in a salad bowl.
2. In a jar combine minced onion, garlic, salt, pepper, dry
   mustard, celery seeds, vinegar, water, oil and paprika.
   Shake well. Pour over salad. Add nuts if using.

Preparation and Cooking Time: 2 hours

For Citron Dijon, add grated peel of 1 lemon,
1 teaspoon honey and 1 tablespoon lemon juice to
1 cup Dijon mustard.

Pareve

Tomatoes Stuffed with Hearts of Palm

Sybil Kaplan   Israel
Overland Park, Kansas   Yield: 6 to 8 Servings

I found this recipe in a brochure of Israeli recipes from Agrexco.

2 cups hearts of palm, cut into ¼-inch slices	½ teaspoon dry tarragon
2 tablespoons green onions, minced	¼ cup parsley, minced
2 tablespoons tarragon vinegar	Salt and pepper to taste
¼ cup olive oil	6 to 8 large ripe tomatoes
	Lettuce leaves

1. Rinse and drain hearts of palm and cut into ¼-inch slices in a mixing bowl. Add onions, tarragon vinegar, oil, tarragon, parsley, salt and pepper. Toss and chill.
2. Cut out tomato stems. Cut each tomato into 6 wedges but leave base intact. Salt and pepper wedges. Place each tomato on a lettuce leaf. Spoon hearts of palm into centers.

Preparation and Cooking Time: 10 to 15 minutes

Hana's Turkish Salad

Sybil Kaplan   Middle East
Overland Park, Kansas   Yield: 6 to 8 Servings

*Hana is Yemenite and we met in Chicago. I learned this from her
when we led some cooking classes for Israelis.*

Oil
2 large onions, minced
2 medium green peppers,
  minced
4 large tomatoes, minced
2 small green hot peppers,
  minced

2 to 3 cloves garlic, minced
2 tablespoons tomato paste
Salt to taste
1 tablespoon pareve
  chicken soup powder
½ cup water

1. Heat oil in a frying pan. Sauté onion. Add green pepper
   and cook 5 minutes.
2. Add tomatoes, hot peppers and garlic. Cook 5 minutes.
   Add tomato paste, salt, chicken soup powder and water.
   Reduce heat to very low and cook 30 minutes.

Preparation and Cooking Time: 50 minutes

Note: This is a popular, spicy Yemenite salad.

Pareve

Basil Salad Dressing

Sybil Kaplan
Overland Park, Kansas   Yield: 1 Cup

¾ cup olive oil
2 tablespoons red wine
  vinegar
4 teaspoons Dijon mustard
2 to 3 cloves garlic,
  crushed

¼ cup parsley,
  finely chopped
½ cup fresh basil,
  finely chopped

1. Combine all ingredients in a jar. Close and shake well.
   Refrigerate.

Preparation and Cooking Time: 2 hours

Creamy French Nut Dressing

Sybil Kaplan
Overland Park, Kansas

Yield: 1 to 1¼ Cups

I wanted a creamy French dressing so I experimented until I found one I really liked.

¼ cup oil
¼ cup catsup
½ cup red wine vinegar
¼ cup non-dairy creamer
1 tablespoon mustard

Salt and pepper to taste
1 tablespoon parsley, minced
¼ cup nuts, finely minced

1. Combine all ingredients in a jar. Close and shake well. Refrigerate.

Preparation and Cooking Time: 2 hours

Creamy Mustard Dressing

Sybil Kaplan
Overland Park, Kansas   Yield: 1 Cup

I wanted a creamy vinaigrette that was pareve and found one which I changed and adapted. This is the biggest hit among family and friends.

½ cup olive oil
5 tablespoons non-dairy
   creamer
¼ cup red wine vinegar
1 tablespoon Dijon mustard

1 garlic clove, crushed
½ teaspoon dried parsley
1 hard-boiled egg, mashed
   (optional)

1. Combine all ingredients in a jar. Close and shake well. Refrigerate.

Preparation and Cooking Time: 2 hours

For Olive Dijon, add
¼ cup pitted, minced olives to
1 cup Dijon mustard.

Herbed Vinaigrette

Sybil Kaplan
Overland Park, Kansas   Yield: 1¼ Cups

1 cup oil	**½ teaspoon dry chives**
¼ cup red wine vinegar	**1 teaspoon dry tarragon**
1 teaspoon Dijon mustard	**1 tablespoon dry parsley**
1 teaspoon dry chervil	

1. Combine all ingredients in a jar. Close and shake well.
   Refrigerate.

Preparation and Cooking Time: 2 hours

For Celery Dijon, add 1 teaspoon celery seeds and
¼ cup minced celery leaves to
1 cup Dijon mustard.

Ruth's Jerusalem Chinese Salad Dressing

Sybil Kaplan   Oriental Style
Overland Park, Kansas   Yield: ¼ to ½ Cup

I ate this salad at Ruth's apartment in Jerusalem years ago. Ruth had been born in Shanghai. Her family got out of Europe during World War II and although she must have been quite young when they lived in China, as an adult, she enjoyed making Chinese food.

2 tablespoons catsup	**½ teaspoon salt**
2 tablespoons mayonnaise	**4 teaspoons vinegar**
½ teaspoon garlic powder	**2 tablespoons oil**

1. Combine all ingredients in a jar. Cover and shake well. Refrigerate.

   This dressing is good over a salad of spinach, lettuce, bean sprouts, and tomatoes.

Preparation and Cooking Time: 2 hours

Tehina Dressing

Sybil Kaplan   Middle East
Overland Park, Kansas   Yield: ¾ to 1 Cup

1-3 cloves garlic   **½ teaspoon cumin**
Juice of 2½ lemons   **(optional)**
5 ounces techina paste   **Salt to taste**
Cold water

1. Crush garlic. Place in blender with lemon juice, techina, a
   little water, cumin and salt. Blend to make a thick cream.
   Taste and add more lemon juice or white wine vinegar,
   garlic, salt or water.

Preparation and Cooking Time: 2 hours

Note: Techina is a thick paste made of ground sesame seeds
and is used in many Middle Eastern dishes.

Sauces, Jams
&
Miscellaneous

Crushed Olives and Vegetables

Esther Goldman   Italy/Sicily
Overland Park, Kansas   Yield: 1 Quart

This came from Pete Bono. He was my father-in-law's business partner for many years and his family came from Sicily. I ate these olives in his home about 35 years ago, maybe even longer, and asked him for the recipe.

1 quart green Italian olives (with or without pits)	**Celery pieces**
	Onions, thinly sliced
¼ cup olive oil	**Carrots, sliced**
½ cup white vinegar	**Red peppers, sliced in**
½ cup water	**half rings**
1 teaspoon sugar	**Green peppers, sliced in**
½ teaspoon salt	**half rings**
Oregano to taste	**Cauliflower flowerettes**
Garlic to taste	**(optional)**

1. In a large bowl, combine olives, olive oil, vinegar, water, sugar, salt, oregano and garlic. Let stand.
2. Add celery, onions, carrots, red pepper, green pepper and cauliflower if using. Place into jars or a container with a tight cover. Refrigerate.

Preparation and Cooking Time: 2 hours

"When thou beatest thine olive tree, thou shall not go over the boughs again" (Deuteronomy 24:20)

Pareve

Sophie's Kosher Dill Pickles

Esther Goldman
Overland Park, Kansas

Sophie lived across the hall from me when my oldest son was a baby, about 58 years ago. She was like a mother to me because she was such a motherly lady and always full of advice.

Kirby pickling cucumbers	**5 quarts water**
Dry dill stalks	**1 cup kosher salt**
Garlic	
1 heaping teaspoon pickling spices	
(per quart jar)	

1. Pack jars with firm cucumbers. Add dill, garlic and pickling spices.
2. In a pot, combine water and salt, bring to a boil, then pour into jars to the top and cover quickly.

   * For a small batch, reduce your brine: e.g., ½ cup salt for 2½ quarts water; ¼ cup salt for 1¼ cups water.

Preparation and Cooking Time: 24 hours

Citrus Etrog Jam

Sybil Kaplan
Overland Park, Kansas

I created this recipe in Israel while living there in 1970s.

1 large etrog (citron)
1 orange
1 grapefruit
1 lemon
Sugar

1. Wash fruit and cut in halves to remove seeds. Cut in thin slices, cut slices in half. Place in saucepan and cover with water. Soak overnight.
2. Place saucepan on stove and bring to a boil. Drain off water. Bring to a boil again. Drain off water.
3. Measure pulp into a bowl then replace in pan. Add 1 cup sugar for every cup of fruit pulp. Simmer for 30 minutes, stirring frequently.
4. Pour into sterilized jars and seal.

Preparation and Cooking Time: 25 hours

Pareve

Guava Jam

Sybil Kaplan
Overland Park, Kansas

I created this while living in Israel during 1970s.

2 pounds fresh guavas
Sugar
Lemon juice

1. Cut up guavas and place in a saucepan. Cover with water. Bring to a boil, then reduce heat and simmer until soft. Drain off excess water.
2. Puree in a blender and measure into a bowl. Add ½ cup sugar and 1 teaspoon lemon juice for every cup of fruit. Return to saucepan. Cook over low heat 30 minutes, stirring frequently.
3. Pour into sterilized jars and close.

Preparation and Cooking Time: 1 hour

Orange Marmalade

Sybil Kaplan
Overland Park, Kansas

I think I made this up when oranges were so cheap and plentiful in Israel.

4 oranges
2 cups water
1 cup sugar

1. Cut oranges in thin slices. Place in a pot with 2 cups water. Bring to a boil. Reduce heat and let simmer 45 minutes. Drain but save ¾ cup juice.
2. Add sugar to mixture, then puree in blender. Return to pot with juice. Simmer 15 minutes. Pour into jars, close and refrigerate.

Preparation and Cooking Time: 1 hour

"A word fitly spoken is like apples of gold..."
(Proverbs 25:11)

Pareve

Brandied Peach Butter

Sybil Kaplan
Overland Park, Kansas   Yield: 3 to 4 Jelly Jars

I made this up when peaches were so cheap and plentiful.

2 pounds peaches,   Dash cinnamon
  pitted and chopped   Dash ginger
Water   Dash allspice
2 teaspoons lemon juice   1½ tablespoons brandy
1 cup sugar

1. Place peaches in a pot. Cover with water. Bring to a boil,
   reduce heat and simmer 10 to 15 minutes. Drain.
2. Puree in blender and return to pot. Add lemon juice, sugar
   and spices. Cook until as thick as you like it. Add brandy
   and cook a few minutes more. Spoon into jars and close.

Preparation and Cooking Time: 45 minutes

Mint Chutney
Marathi - Pudeena Chutney

Solomon Michael Daniel   India
Bombay, Maharashtra   Yield: 1 Cup

This recipe originated with the Bene-Israel Jews of India.

1 cup loosely filled
  fresh mint leaves
1 garlic clove
1½ inch fresh ginger root
6 green chilies

½ cup loosely filled fresh
  coriander leaves
  (cilantro)
2 teaspoons tamarind paste
¼ teaspoon salt
1 teaspoon sugar

1. Clean and wash all ingredients. Drain water.
2. Grind all ingredients finely into a bowl.

Serve with Bahajias, Samosas (fried, triangular pastries) or with food.

Preparation and Cooking Time: 10 to 15 minutes

Pareve

Eggplant Relish

Sybil Kaplan   Romania
Overland Park, Kansas   Yield: 2 Cups

I got this from my mother, Rae Horowitz; she used to speak of this as a favorite of my father whose family came from Romania.

1 eggplant
¼ cup vinegar
½ teaspoon salt
Dash red pepper
1 garlic clove, chopped fine

1. Preheat oven to 400° F.
2. Place eggplant in a hot oven and bake until soft. Run under cold water and peel off skin.
3. Place flesh in a bowl and mash or chop, then put into a quart jar. Add vinegar, salt, red pepper and garlic. Cover and mix well. Refrigerate.
4. When ready to serve, taste and add more vinegar or salt if necessary.

If this is to be used as an appetizer, use olive oil and chopped onions instead of the vinegar.

Preparation and Cooking Time: 45 minutes

Irit's Pickled Eggplant Slices

Sybil Kaplan   Israel
Overland Park, Kansas   Yield: 8 to 10 Servings

I met Irit when her husband, Gabby, was stationed with the Israel Consul General's office in Chicago. I enjoyed this at her home and she gave me the recipe.

2 medium eggplants	**1 red pepper, minced**
2 teaspoon salt	**½ cup cider vinegar**
Oil	**½ cup water**
4 garlic cloves, chopped	**1 teaspoon salt**
½ bunch fresh parsley,	**½ teaspoon pepper**
chopped	**Dash paprika**

Three days before serving:
1. Slice eggplants into one-inch thick slices. Place in a colander. Sprinkle over salt and let sit 30 minutes. Wash slices and pat dry.
2. Heat small amount of oil in a frying pan. Fry eggplant slices on both sides until brown. Drain on paper towels.
3. In a bowl, place chopped garlic, parsley and red pepper.
4. Place vinegar and water in a saucepan. Add salt, pepper and paprika. Bring to a boil.
5. Layer eggplant slices in a bowl, add garlic-parsley-pepper mixture to each layer. Pour cider mixture over. Cover and refrigerate at least 24 hours. Three days is best!

Preparation and Cooking Time: 3 days

How do you get your garlic stronger? Place it in a press before using.

Pareve

Roast Red Peppers

Sybil Kaplan
Overland Park, Kansas

> **4 red peppers**
> **3 tablespoons oil**
> **2 tablespoons wine vinegar**
> **¼ teaspoon salt**
> **¼ teaspoon oregano**

1. Preheat oven to 450° F. Prick peppers in several places with a fork. Place in a baking pan. Roast 20 minutes.
2. Place in a colander in the sink and rinse with cold water. Open, remove seeds and cut in ½-inch strips. Place in a jar.
3. Add oil, vinegar and spices to jar. Close and shake.

Preparation and Cooking Time: 30 minutes

Eggs, Cheese & Dairy

Blender Cheese Souffle

Sybil Kaplan
Overland Park, Kansas   Yield: 6 Servings

I made this recipe up while living in Israel.

6 eggs
½ cup whipping cream or
  pareve whipping cream
¼ cup Parmesan cheese,
  grated
½ teaspoon mustard

½ teaspoon salt
¼ teaspoon pepper
2 cups yellow cheese,
  grated
1½ cups cream cheese

1. Preheat oven to 375° F.
2. Place eggs, pareve whip or whipping cream, Parmesan cheese, mustard, salt and pepper in blender. Whirl until smooth.
3. Add yellow cheese then cream cheese. Whirl 5 seconds. Pour into a greased souffle dish. Bake in a 375° F oven 45-50 minutes. Serve immediately.

Preparation and Cooking Time: 1 hour

St. Peter's Fish Pizza

Sybil Kaplan   Israel
Overland Park, Kansas   Yield: 4 Servings

*This recipe comes from the brochure, St. Peter's Fish from the Sea of
Galilee, produced by Carmel Agrexco Agricultural Export Co. of
Israel. It explains that tilapia is the name for St. Peter's fish.*

Dough

11 ounces flour	¼-ounce package dry yeast
1 cup milk or lukewarm water	½ teaspoon sugar

Filling

¼ oil	1 teaspoon dry marjoram
4 garlic cloves, mashed	Salt and pepper to taste
1 cup onions, chopped	2 tablespoons sunflower
1 pound 2 ounces	seed kernels, mashed
tilapia fillets, cut into	Margarine
2½-inch pieces	1 cup "Gamba" olive sauce
2 tablespoons parsley, chopped	7 ounces pizza cheese,
	grated

1. Preheat oven to 400° F.
2. Sift flour twice in a bowl (if using unsifted). Mix yeast
   with sugar and a little of the lukewarm milk or water. Add
   2 teaspoons flour to the yeast and set in a warm place to
   ferment.
3. Make a well in the flour and pour in the yeast mixture.
   Cover the bowl and allow the yeast to expand.
4. Add the rest of the liquid and knead the dough into a single
   ball. Set in a warm place to rise. After dough rises, knead
   a few time.
5. Pour oil into a frying pan. Sauté garlic and onion. Add
   fish and fry for 5 minutes. Add parsley, marjoram, salt and
   pepper. Add sunflower seeds.

6. Rub a pizza pan with margarine. Roll out dough on a floured surface into a circle about ½-inch thick. Rub surface of dough with Gamba olive sauce, scatter fish over the dough. Sprinkle with marjoram, then cover with grated cheese. Bake in a 400° F over 25 minutes. Serve hot.

The pizza can be cooled, sealed and frozen. To serve, defrost and heat.

Preparation and Cooking Time: 3 to 4 hours

Spinach Souffle

Dalia Carmel
New York, New York   Yield: 10 to 12 Servings

I ate this at the home of a colleague from El Al and his wife. She gave me her recipe. Then I incorporated some of my changes and some made by the wife of the company doctor. Once I served this for brunch to cousins visiting from Israel. They loved it and took second and third helpings. On the third helping, my cousin asked what was this made of. Knowing how Israelis dislike spinach, I was reluctant to reply, but I told her it was made with spinach. She pushed the plate away (while on the third helping!) and declared, "I do not eat anything made with spinach!"

2 10-ounce packages chopped, frozen spinach, drained and defrosted
½ bunch fresh dill
1 leek, trimmed
6 eggs
½ pound feta cheese
2 4-ounce packages cheddar cheese, shredded
2 pounds cottage cheese
Salt and pepper to taste
Nutmeg to taste
1 bar butter, melted or 6 ounces sour cream
Sunflower seeds (optional)
Pine nuts (optional)

1. Preheat oven to 350° F. Butter one large 12-cup souffle dish or two smaller ones.
2. In food processor, mix spinach, dill, leek, eggs, feta and cheddar cheese.
3. Mix in cottage cheese, salt, pepper, nutmeg, butter or sour cream. Pour into buttered souffle bowl or bowls. Sprinkle sunflower seeds or pine nuts on top if you like. Bake in a 350° F oven for 1 to 1¼ hours or until top is lightly browned.
Serve with large mixed salad.

This can also be cut in half for 4 to 6 servings.

Preparation and Cooking Time: 2 hours

Spinach Vegetable Quiche

Sybil Kaplan
Overland Park, Kansas   Yield: 6 Servings

1 single crust pastry to fit 9-inch pie plate	3 eggs
2 tablespoons margarine	¾ cup milk
½ cup onions, chopped	Salt and pepper to taste
1 garlic clove, minced	½ teaspoon celery salt
1 pound spinach, cooked, drained and chopped	½ teaspoon basil
1½ cups Swiss cheese, shredded	2 tomatoes, sliced thin
	1 tablespoon bread crumbs
	1 tablespoon Parmesan cheese shredded

1. Preheat oven to 425°F.
2. Roll out pastry to 12 inches round to fit a 9-inch pie plate. Fit into plate, turn edges under and flute to make a stand-up edge.
3. Heat margarine in a frying pan. Sauté onion and garlic 5 minutes. Add spinach and cook until excess moisture evaporates. Pour into a bowl.
4. Add cheese, eggs, milk, salt, pepper, celery salt and basil and blend. Pour into the pastry shell. Place tomato slices around edge. Bake in a 425°F oven 15 minutes. Reduce heat to 350°F and bake 10 minutes longer.
5. Combine bread crumbs and Parmesan cheese in a bowl. Sprinkle over tomatoes. Bake 10 minutes or until top is puffy. Let stand 10 minutes before serving.

Preparation and Cooking Time: 1 hour and 15 minutes

Baked Eggs in Tomatoes

Sybil Kaplan   Israel
Overland Park, Kansas   Yield: 6 Servings

I found this in an Agrexco brochure advertising Israeli exported tomatoes.

6 medium ripe tomatoes   **1 heaping tablespoon**
Salt and pepper   **scallions, finely minced**
6 tablespoons heavy cream   **6 large eggs**
1 tablespoon butter, melted

1. Preheat oven to 350° F.
2. Remove top third of tomatoes. Scoop out seeds and pulp. Sprinkle inside with salt and pepper. Turn upside down on paper towels and let drain 10 minutes.
3. Mix heavy cream with cooled, melted butter in a mixing bowl. Add scallions, salt and pepper.
4. Break an egg into each tomato. Spoon 1 tablespoon of the heavy cream mixture over each. Bake in a greased shallow pan in 350° F oven for 15 minutes or until whites are firm.

Preparation and Cooking Time: 45 minutes

Cheesy Egg-Potato Bake

Sybil Kaplan
Overland Park, Kansas   Yield: 6 Servings

*I have no idea where I got this recipe but it has a star by it which
means I've fixed it and it's a great one to repeat.*

6 medium potatoes, sliced	**Salt and pepper to taste**
3 small onions, sliced	**½ teaspoon garlic powder**
¾ cup Swiss cheese, grated	**⅜ cup margarine**
1½ cups milk	**Paprika**
9 eggs	

1. Preheat oven to 350°F.
2. Grease a casserole. Layer potatoes and onions in casserole.
3. In a bowl, combine ½ cup plus 1 tablespoon cheese, milk, eggs, salt, pepper and garlic powder. Mix, then pour over potatoes.
4. Sprinkle 3 tablespoons cheese on top. Dot with margarine pieces. Sprinkle on paprika. Bake in a 350°F oven for 1½ hours.

This is great for a brunch and can be doubled for a larger crowd.

Preparation and Cooking Time: 45 minutes

Doris's Scrambled-ahead Eggs

Sybil Kaplan
Overland Park, Kansas   Yield: 8 To 10 Servings

One of the times I visited in Kansas City from Israel, Doris had some people over for brunch and fixed this. Doris and her husband, Paul, are not only old friends but they would bring groups of tourists to Israel every year when I was living there. This is a wonderful company dish and easy to make. I made it in Israel and I've made it in the States.

1¼ cups mushroom soup	½ teaspoon dill
¼ cup dry sherry	⅛ teaspoon pepper
1½ cups Swiss cheese, shredded	¼ cup margarine
1¼ cups cheddar cheese, shredded	¼ pound mushrooms, sliced
18 eggs	¼ cup green onions, chopped
2 tablespoons milk	Paprika
1 teaspoon parsley flakes	

1. Preheat oven to 300° F.
2. Heat mushroom soup in a saucepan until hot and smooth. Stir in sherry. Set aside.
3. Toss Swiss and cheddar cheese together in a bowl. Set aside.
4. Beat eggs in a bowl with milk. Add parsley, dill and pepper.
5. Melt margarine in a frying pan. Add mushrooms and onions. Cook until onions are limp. Add eggs and stir until set. Spoon half the egg mixture into a greased baking dish. Add half the soup and half the cheese.
6. Add the rest of the eggs, the rest of the soup and the rest of the cheeses. Sprinkle with paprika. Bake in a 300° F oven 35 minutes.

Preparation and Cooking Time: 1 hour

Fresh Tomato Pizza

Sybil Kaplan   Israel
Overland Park, Kansas   Yield: 2 Servings

I found this in an Agrexco recipe for exported tomatoes.

Water
6-8 medium tomatoes
2 pieces pita bread
    sliced horizontally
½ pound mozzarella cheese,
    cut into very thin slices

1 teaspoon basil or
    oregano
¼ cup olive oil

1. Preheat oven to 400° F.
2. Place water in a saucepan and bring to a boil. Drop in
   tomatoes for a few minutes. Remove, peel, remove seeds
   and excess moisture. Cut into thin wedges.
3. Cover pita with tomato wedges. Place sliced mozzarella on
   top. Sprinkle with basil or oregano.
4. Drizzle with olive oil. Bake on a greased cookie sheet in
   400° F oven until top is golden brown and cheese bubbles.

Preparation and Cooking Time: 20 to 30 minutes

Pareve

Egg Foo Yung

Sybil Kaplan   Chinese Style
Overland Park, Kansas   Yield: 4 Servings

1 onion, cut up	Water
2 celery ribs, cut up	1 teaspoon margarine
2 large green peppers, cut up	3 eggs, beaten
2 garlic cloves, crushed	2 cups bean sprouts
1 teaspoon soy sauce	1 teaspoon soy sauce

1. Spray a frying pan with no-stick cooking spray. In the frying pan, add onion, celery, green peppers, garlic and just enough water so vegetables won't stick to the pan. Add 1 teaspoon soy sauce.
2. Make room in the center of the pan to melt the margarine. Pour in the beaten eggs and scramble in center, then mix with vegetables.
3. Add sprouts and 1 teaspoon soy sauce. Simmer until sprouts are done.

Serve with rice.

Preparation and Cooking Time: 10 to 15 minutes

Note: This dish is actually Chinese American in origin.

Hana's Egg Salad
Salat Beitzim

Sybil Kaplan   Israel
Overland Park, Kansas   Yield: 4 Servings

Hana and I became friends when she and her husband, Yehudah, were in Chicago and he was serving as aliyah shaliach (emissary). We had many meals in each other's homes and she gave me this recipe. She now lives in Rishon l'Tzion, Israel.

Oil
1 large onion, chopped
6 hard-boiled eggs
2-3 teaspoons mayonnaise
Salt and pepper to taste

1. Heat oil in a frying pan. Fry onions until light brown.
2. Place fried onions in a bowl. Add eggs and mash.
3. Add mayonnaise, salt and pepper.

Preparation and Cooking Time: 10 to 15 minutes

Shakshouka

Sybil Kaplan
Overland Park, Kansas

Middle East
Yield: 4 Servings

I learned to make this while living in Israel.

2 tablespoons unsalted margarine	**4 eggs**
1 onion, minced	**Salt and pepper to taste**
2 garlic cloves, minced	**1 tablespoons parsley flakes**
3 tomatoes, chopped	

1. Heat margarine in a frying pan. Sauté onion about 3 minutes. Add garlic and cook about 30 seconds. Add tomatoes and cook 4 minutes.
2. Add eggs, salt and pepper. Cook 4-5 minutes. Sprinkle with parsley.

Preparation and Cooking Time: 15 minutes

Note: My research indicates this dish is North African in origin, probably Tunisian, but is popular in many Middle Eastern countries.

Potatoes, Pasta
Rice & Grains

Potatoes Au Gratin

Sybil Kaplan
Overland Park, Kansas   Yield: 4 Servings

I got this from my mother, Rae Horowitz.

4 potatoes, or enough	**Salt and pepper to taste**
to equal 2 cups	**Margarine pieces**
1⅛ pound American	**½ cup milk**
cheese, grated (⅝ cup)	**Paprika**
2 tablespoons onions, grated	

1. Preheat oven to 350° F.
2. Place potatoes in a saucepan, cover with water. Bring to a boil. Reduce heat and cook until partially cooked. Drain, cool, peel and slice.
3. Grease a baking dish. Add one layer of potatoes, grated cheese, grated onion, salt and pepper and dot with margarine. Repeat until all potatoes are used.
4. Add milk and sprinkle with paprika. Bake in a 350° F oven for 30 minutes or until milk is absorbed.

Preparation and Cooking Time: 1 hour

Pasta with Eggs
Tagliatella alle Uova

Adeline Gniady
Chicago, Illinois

Italy/Sicily
Yield: 2 to 3 Servings

*I learned this from my mother who came from Palermo, Sicily. I
became friends with my Jewish neighbor, Sybil, who kept kosher.
I learned about her holidays and cooking and she learned about my
Italian Catholic holidays and cooking. On occasions we exchanged
recipes like this one.*

4 ounces fettucine noodles	Salt and pepper to taste
2 eggs	1 tablespoon parsley
1 to 2 tablespoons olive oil	Parmesan cheese

1. Place water in a saucepan and bring to a boil. Add noodles
   and cook 6 to 8 minutes. Drain but leave a little water to
   cover bottom of pan.
2. Beat eggs in a bowl. Add oil, salt and pepper and parsley.
   Add to noodles in pan. Sprinkle cheese on top and mix.
   Cover and cook over low heat 3 to 5 minutes. Serve
   immediately.

Preparation and Cooking Time: 25 to 30 minutes

Fettucine Verdi

Sybil Kaplan
Overland Park, Kansas

Italian Style
Yield: 4 to 6 Servings

*I once ate something like this in an exclusive restaurant in Chicago.
I called the chef and he gave me the recipe. Then I tried it with my
own adaptations. Eventually this was the result I continued making.*

8 ounces green noodles	**Salt to taste**
Olive oil	**Dash red pepper flakes**
1 to 2 red peppers, minces	**2 anchovies, chopped**
½ cup raw spinach	**A couple shakes**
2 tablespoons pine nuts	**Worcestershire sauce**
2 to 3 tablespoons	
Parmesan cheese	

1. Bring water to a boil in a pot. Add noodles and cook 6 to
   8 minutes. Drain. Set aside.
2. Heat oil in a frying pan. Lightly sauté red peppers. Add
   spinach and lightly cook until wilted. Add pine nuts, pasta,
   Parmesan cheese, salt, red pepper flakes, anchovies and
   Worcestershire sauce. Toss

Preparation and Cooking Time: 25 to 30 minutes

Which sauce do you serve with which pasta?
Heavy pasta - heavy and meat sauce
Thin, small or fragile pasta - simple sauces like
    butter or margarine and cheese
Long and hollow pasta - tomato sauce or a
    simple sauce like oil and garlic
Short pasta - chunky sauces
Plan on 1 cup sauce to 4 ounces pasta

KitchenAid Noodle Kugel

Nellie Foster
Tempe, Arizona

Yield: 10 Servings

Linda Radke, contributed this recipe from her sister-in-law. She reports that when made with raisins, the kugel is less moist and of a firmer consistency. When made with pineapple, the kugel is creamier.

1 stick butter or margarine	½ teaspoon cinnamon
4 eggs	1 cup white raisins or
1½ teaspoons vanilla	1 20-ounce can crushed
½ cup sugar	pineapple with juice
16 ounces light sour cream	1 12-ounce package
16 ounces low-fat	wide noodles
cottage cheese	1 cup graham cracker
	crumbs

1. Preheat oven to 375° F.
2. Place butter or margarine in a 9 x 13-inch baking dish and place in oven to melt.
3. Place eggs in KitchenAid bowl. Attach flat beater and set to stir. Add vanilla, sugar, sour cream, cottage cheese, cinnamon and raisins or pineapple and juice in that order.
4. Heat water in a saucepan. Prepare noodles according to directions. Drain and place in a bowl.
5. Pour butter into cheese and cream mixture. Mix well. Add to noodles and mix well with a wooden spoon. Pour into baking dish in which butter or margarine was melted.
6. Sprinkle with cracker crumbs. Cover with foil and bake in a 375° F oven for 45 minutes. Remove foil and bake an additional 15 minutes. Serve at once or room temperature.

Preparation and Cooking Time: 1 hour, 15 minutes

Corn Meal Mush
Mamaliga

Hilda Meth   Romania
Richmond, Virginia   Yield: 8 Servings

This came from my father who came from Romania. I was born in Soccani. My father was the mamaliga expert in the house, and we all considered it a treat when he made it. Mamaliga is the national Romanian food, and it is similar to corn mush.

5 cups cold water
2 teaspoons salt
1 tablespoon oil
2 cups yellow corn meal

1. Place water in a saucepan with salt and oil. Bring to a boil, then lower heat, pour all the corn meal in and start stirring.
2. Continue stirring until you get the consistency you want.

Soft, hot mamaliga is served as a carbohydrate with meat. It is best when you put some margarine on it.
Leftover mamaliga can be poured into a loaf pan and when it is cold, it solidifies. Then it is usually cut in slices, fried lightly and served for breakfast or lunch with butter or margarine, jam and/or a white salted cheese called Brinza in Romania.

Preparation and Cooking Time: 15 to 20 minutes

Fruited Pecan Wild Rice

The Quaker Oats Company
Chicago, Illinois

Yield: 4 Servings

¼ cup pecans, chopped
1 tablespoon margarine or
butter
1 medium onion, chopped
1 6-ounce package
Near East
Long Grain & Wild Rice
Pilaf mix

2 cups water
½ cup dry fruit bits,
raisins or
dried cranberries
¼ teaspoon cinnamon

1. In medium saucepan, add pecans and cook over medium heat, 5 to 6 minutes or until nuts are light golden brown and fragrant, stirring frequently. Remove from pan; set aside.
2. In same saucepan, melt margarine or butter over medium heat. Add onions and cook 3 minutes, stirring frequently. Add rice pilaf mix and cook 30 seconds, stirring occasionally.
3. Add water, contents of spice sack and cinnamon. Add fruit bits, raisins or dried cranberries. Bring to a boil.
4. Cover, reduce heat to low and simmer 30 minutes or until most of liquid is absorbed. Stir in nuts and serve.

Preparation and Cooking Time: 45 minutes

Apple Walnut Wild Rice

The Quaker Oats Company
Chicago, Illinois

Yield: 4 Servings

*This is a special occasion side dish that makes any day a holiday
with a rich harvest of flavors.*

¼ cup walnuts, chopped
1 tablespoon margarine
  or butter
1 medium onion, chopped
1 6-ounce package Near East
  Long Grain & Wild Rice
  Pilaf mix

1 cup apple juice
1 cup water
¼ teaspoon cinnamon
1 medium red apple,
  cut into ½-inch pieces
  (unpeeled)

1. In medium saucepan, add nuts and heat over medium heat.
   Cook 5 to 6 minutes or until nuts are light golden brown
   and fragrant, stirring frequently. Remove from pan; set
   aside.
2. In same saucepan, melt margarine or butter over medium
   heat. Add onions and cook 3 minutes, stirring frequently.
   Add rice pilaf mix and cook 30 seconds, stirring
   occasionally.
3. Add apple juice, water and contents of spice sack and
   cinnamon. Bring to a boil. Cover, reduce heat to low and
   simmer 30 minutes or until most of liquid is absorbed.
4. Stir in apple and walnuts and serve.

Preparation and Cooking Time: 45 minutes

Three Mushroom Pilaf

The Quaker Oats Company
Chicago, Illinois

French Style
Yield: 4 Servings

1 tablespoon margarine
  or butter
1 cup shiitake mushroom
  caps, sliced
1 cup oyster mushrooms,
  sliced
1 cup crimini (brown)
  mushrooms, sliced
  or 3 cups fresh mushrooms
  sliced

2 cloves garlic, minced
1 teaspoon dried thyme
  leaves
1¼ cups water
¼ cup dry sherry or
  additional water
1 6.09-ounce package
Near East Rice Pilaf mix
⅓ cup green onions,

1. In medium saucepan, melt margarine or butter on medium heat. Add mushrooms, garlic and thyme; cook 3 minutes, stirring frequently.
2. Add water, sherry, rice pilaf mix and contents of spice sack. Bring to a boil.
3. Cover, reduce heat to low and simmer 20 minutes. Stir in green onions. Cover and continue to simmer 5 minutes or until most of the liquid is absorbed.

Preparation and Cooking Time: 30 to 40 minutes

Note: Inspired by the cuisine of the French countryside, this rice pilaf dish features the rich sautéed flavor of three different types of mushrooms.

Mashed Sweet Potatoes

Sybil Kaplan
Overland Park, Kansas

Yield: 4 Servings

½ cup cream or non-dairy
   creamer
4 to 5 tablespoons
   unsalted margarine
Salt and pepper to taste

4 sweet potatoes,
   boiled and skinned
1 tablespoon lemon rind,
   grated (optional)
Juice of ½ lemon

1. In a saucepan, combine cream or non-dairy creamer with
   salt and pepper and margarine. Bring to a boil.
2. Mash potatoes in a bowl. Add liquid and mash more. Add
   lemon rind and lemon juice.

Preparation and Cooking Time: 1 hour

Pine Cone Potatoes

Reva Kaplan
Kansas City, Missouri   Yield: 6 Servings

I got this from my daughter-in-law, Patty, who got it from a rabbi's wife.

6 medium white baking potatoes
Olive oil
Salt or salt substitute
Paprika
Margarine pieces

1. Preheat oven to 450°F.
2. Slice across each potato but not all the way through (slicing horizontally so potato sits).
3. Sprinkle oil on each potato and place in greased baking dish.
4. Sprinkle with salt or salt substitute and paprika. Place margarine pieces on top. Bake in a 450°F oven 1 hour.

Preparation and Cooking Time: 1 hour, 10 minutes

What can you do with a leftover baked potato?
Dip it in water and bake it in a 350°F oven 20 minutes.

Lemon Potatoes

Dalia Carmel
New York, New York

Moroccan Style
Yield: 6 Servings

I took this from a cookbook, tried it and made changes until it comes out this way. This permeates the house with a wonderful aroma!

Oil
2 medium onions, thinly sliced
3 garlic cloves, minced
2 pounds potatoes, peeled
 and sliced into ¼-inch slices
1 tablespoon cumin
1 teaspoon ground coriander

¼ teaspoon cayenne
 pepper
Salt to taste
1½ cups water
5 tablespoons olive oil
Juice of 1½ lemons
Chopped cilantro
 (Italian parsley)

1. Heat oil in a frying pan and sauté onions and garlic until transparent.
2. Add potatoes and make sure they are coated with oil on both sides. Add cumin, coriander, cayenne pepper and salt, water, oil and lemon juice. Bring to a boil. Reduce to medium and cook 25-30 minutes. Stir from time to time so the potatoes will not stick to the pan.

Garnish with cilantro before serving.

Preparation and Cooking Time: 1 hour

Korean Potatoes
Kamcha Namul

Sybil Kaplan
Overland Park, Kansas

Oriental Style
Yield: 2 to 3 Servings

2 tablespoons oil or butter
1 large onion, sliced
2 potatoes, peeled and sliced
½-inch wide by ⅛ thick by
1 to 2 inches long

1 tablespoon sesame seeds,
toasted
3 to 4 tablespoons soy
sauce
1 garlic clove, crushed

1. Heat oil or butter in frying pan. Add onion and potatoes. Cook 2 to 3 minutes.
2. Add sesame seeds, soy sauce and garlic. Cook until potatoes are tender.

This is nice served with stir-fried chicken or beef and vegetables.

Preparation and Cooking Time: 20 to 25 minutes

If the recipe calls for sliced potatoes, place in salted water until ready to use and they won't turn dark.

Sweet Potato Kugel

Dalia Carmel
New York, New York   Yield: 4 Servings

I found this recipe about six years ago, changed and adapted it and this is what comes out.

2 pounds sweet potatoes,
  peeled and quartered
Water
¾ cup apple juice
2 tablespoons lemon juice
2 tablespoons lime juice
1 tablespoon butter
1 1-inch piece of ginger
  finely chopped
¼ teaspoon allspice

½ teaspoon cinnamon
1 teaspoon salt
2 bananas, sliced
1 large apple, peeled,
  cored and cubed
¼ cup dried apricots,
  chopped
2 tablespoons cilantro,
  (optional)
¼ cup nuts, chopped or
¼ cup coconut

1. Preheat oven to 350°F.
2. Place potatoes in a saucepan with water, bring to a boil, reduce heat and simmer until tender. Drain.
3. Puree potatoes in food processor with apple juice, lemon juice and lime juice. Place in a bowl.
4. Heat butter in a frying pan. Sauté ginger, allspice, cinnamon and salt. Add bananas and apple and stir. Cook for 10 minutes, stirring from time to time. Mix with potatoes.
5. Add apricots and cilantro, if using, and fold well together. Grease a square baking pan or pie pan and transfer contents to it. Flatten top and sprinkle on nuts or coconut. Bake in a 350°F oven 45 minutes.

Preparation and Cooking Time: 2 hours

Garlic Noodles

Lil Spungen
Kansas City, Missouri

Yield: 4 to 5 Servings

12 ounces wide noodles
1 stick no-salt pareve margarine
2 cloves garlic, minced
½ pound fresh mushrooms, chopped

1. Cook noodles according to package directions. Drain thoroughly.
2. Melt margarine in a frying pan. Add garlic and mushrooms.
3. Place noodles back in saucepan in which they were cooked. Pour garlic mushrooms on top. Season to taste.

Preparation and Cooking Time: 30 minutes

Rachel's Jerusalem Pudding
Kigel Yerushalmi

Sybil Kaplan   Israel
Overland Park, Kansas   Yield: 4 to 6 Servings

I met Rachel when she and her husband were in Chicago and he was with the Israel Consul General's office. She gave this recipe to me and told me, "They say it's special to Jerusalem because it is sweet and peppered both and is used by religious people with Friday evening dinner or Saturday lunch." Rachel and her family lived in Jerusalem.

>   **8 ounces thin noodles**
>   **1 cup oil**
>   **1 cup sugar**
>   **3 eggs**
>   **Black pepper**

1. Preheat oven to 300°F.
2. Place water in a saucepan and bring to a boil. Add noodles and cook 8-10 minutes. Drain and wash. Place in a bowl.
3. Heat oil in a frying pan. Add sugar and mix. Cook until sugar is golden.
4. Add eggs and pepper to noodles and mix. Add sugared mixture to noodles and stir vigorously. Pour into a greased baking dish. Bake in a 300°F oven for 40 minutes.

Preparation and Cooking Time: 1¼ hours

Note: Some keep this warm overnight so it is eaten on Shabbat lunch.

Leftover Spaghetti Kugel

Sara Sabo   Israel
Herzliva, Israel   Yield: 2 to 4 Servings

*I was born in Tel Aviv in 1923. When I was 4, my parents emigrated
to Beirut, Lebanon. I had my education in an Alliance school and
went to an English college for girls. I met Zeev, my husband, who
was at that time in the British Army. We returned to Palestine. I
have two children and six grandchildren. I am a seventh generation
Israeli and very proud of it. At Chanukah, we celebrated our 51st
wedding anniversary. This recipe was from my Aunt Lea who was a
very good cook.*

2 tablespoons sugar   2 eggs, beaten
Oil   Pepper
1 tablespoon water   Raisins (optional)
Leftover spaghetti   Cinnamon (optional)
Pinch salt

1. In a frying pan, melt sugar in oil to make caramel. Add
   water.
2. Put spaghetti in a bowl. Add salt, eggs, pepper, raisins and
   cinnamon, if used. Add caramel mixture.
3. Heat oil in a frying pan. Add spaghetti mixture. Fry about
   10 minutes until brown on one side. Let cool. Invert on a
   plate. If it looks dry, add a few drops of oil on top.

To bake in oven, use same method, but add a little more
margarine and water and pour into a greased casserole.
Bake in a 350° F oven 20 minutes.

Preparation and Cooking Time: 15 to 30 minutes

Lentils and Rice
Kochari (Midjadara)

Soly Mizrahi   Middle East
Mission, Kansas   Yield: 4 to 5 Servings

*I was born in Cairo, Egypt, and this was served usually once a week.
When we eat this we say, "bil lanam ou sheffa" which means eat in
good health.*

1 cup brown lentils	Salt to taste
¼ cup vegetable oil	¼ cup oil
1 onion, chopped	1 cup long grain rice
2¼ cups water	2 tablespoons margarine
½ teaspoon cumin	2 onions, chopped
Black pepper to taste	Hot pepper sauce (optional)

1. Clean the brown lentils to be sure there are no strange
   particles or small stones. Wash and soak for 10 minutes.
2. In a small frying pan, put ¼ cup oil and fry one chopped
   onion until yellowish brown. Do not burn.
3. Rinse and drain lentils and put in a pot with 2¼ cups
   water. Add sautéed onions, cumin, pepper, salt and ¼ cup
   oil. Cook over medium heat until the lentils are tender (20-
   25 minutes). Cover the pot with the lid slightly but not all
   the way.
4. Add rice on top lentils and cook over medium heat until
   rice is tender and fluffy. Add a little more water if needed.
5. Melt margarine in a frying pan. Sauté remaining 2 onions.

To serve, place lentils and rice in a casserole, put sautéed
onions on top and if using, sprinkle some drops of hot
pepper sauce on top.

Preparation and Cooking Time: 1 to 1½ hours

Pulao (Rice)

Solomon Michael Daniel   India
Bombay, Maharashtra   Yield: 12 Servings

This is traditional of Bene-Israel, Jews of India.

1 kilo (2.2 pounds) Basmati rice	10 onions
3 tablespoons ghee or dalda	5 small sticks cinnamon
50 grams (2 tablespoons) almonds	12 cloves
50 grams (2 tablespoons) pistachios	12 peppercorns
50 grams (2 tablespoons) transparent seedless raisins	Bay leaves
	8 cardamons

1. Wash rice and set aside for water to drain off.
2. Heat ghee in a soup pot. Fry almonds, pistachios and raisins. Set aside in a bowl.
3. Fry onions to golden brown. Set aside in another bowl.
4. To ghee, add cinnamon, cloves, peppercorns, bay leaves and cardamon. Fry 30 seconds. Add rice. Stir continuously until well fried. Add enough water to cover about 2½ inches over the rice. Cook over a medium heat until very little water is left.
5. Sprinkle cardamon seeds powder over rice, cover with lid, turn heat to low. Stir after 5 minutes so rice does not stick to bottom. Add almonds, pistachios and raisins. Cook a few minutes longer. Put fried onions on top of rice.

Serve with chicken or mutton curry.

Preparation and Cooking Time: 45 minutes

Note: Basmati rice is a long-grained rice with fine texture and perfume, nutlike flavor. It is found in Indian markets.
Ghee is butter that has been melted to separate the milk solids from the liquid on the surface. If this rice dish is to be served with a meat course, a pareve margarine or oil should be used instead.
Instead of water, you can use coconut milk.

How do you keep rice white? Add a little lemon juice to the water while it is boiling.

Spinach and Rice
Spinach y arroz

Matilda Rosenberg   Greece
Overland Park, Kansas   Yield: 6 Servings

I got this from my mother, Alegre Tevet, who came from Drama,
Greece.   Vegetables are very important in Sephardic cooking. A
Shabbat dinner is not complete without several vegetables being
served. This dish is wonderful because the fresh lemon brings out
the wonderful flavor of the spinach.

2 bunches fresh spinach	**½ cup rice**
2 tablespoons oil	**½ cup water**
Juice of 1 lemon	**1 can garbanzo beans**
1 teaspoon salt	

1. Wash and clean spinach. Place in a saucepan.
2. Add oil, lemon juice, salt, rice and water. Bring to a boil.
   Reduce heat and cook 20 minutes or until rice is tender. If
   desired, add garbanzo beans or more lemon if you like the
   lemony taste.

This makes a pretty company dish.

Preparation and Cooking Time: 30 minutes

Mushroom Rice

Sybil Kaplan
Overland Park, Kansas

Yield: 4 to 6 Servings

2 cups chicken broth	1½ teaspoons margarine
⅓ cup oil	1 cup mushrooms, sliced
1 teaspoon salt	1½ teaspoons dry parsley
1 cup raw rice	flakes

1. Place chicken broth in a saucepan with oil and salt. Bring to a boil. Add rice and cook until liquid is absorbed. Cover and let sit 10 minutes.
2. In another pan, melt 1½ teaspoons margarine. Heat mushrooms 5 minutes. Stir into rice. Sprinkle with parsley.

Preparation and Cooking Time: 25 to 30 minutes

When preparing rice, add margarine or butter and a little white wine, red wine or sherry. The taste is unusual.

Rice Pilaf

Dalia Carmel
New York, New York   Yield: 8 Servings

3 tablespoons olive oil
1 cinnamon stick
3 whole cloves
¼ cup vermicelli, cut up
  or orzo, or ⅛ cup each
¼ cup pine nuts
1 cup converted rice
  (not instant)

1 chicken soup cube*
1½ cups water
Saffron, creole, achiote or
  coriander seasoning
  packet
Kitchen towel, clean

1. In a heavy pot, heat oil,, cinnamon and cloves. Add vermicelli or orzo or both and pine nuts. Mix together until browned slightly. Add rice and mix well to make sure they all get coated with oil.
2. Reduce heat, add chicken soup cube, water and seasoning packet of your choice. Bring to a boil, reduce heat to the barest minimum, mix contents well, cover and let simmer 17 minutes exactly. Do this exactly 17 minutes!
3. Remove lid quickly, place a clean towel over the pot and immediately cover and let stand for 10 minutes before serving.

* Pareve cube will make this pareve.

Preparation and Cooking Time: 50 minutes

Fish

Baked Haddock

Cindy Megiddo
Forest Hills, New York   Yield: 4 to 6 Servings

My mother, Sara Feinberg, from Providence, Rhode Island, made this delicious dish all through my childhood in the 1940s, when Americans were meat eaters and fish was not so popular. It is deceptive in its simplicity, but it was so popular, this was the one fish recipe all of our non-fish eating guests loved!

3 pounds Haddock fillets	**2 pints sour cream**
(thick pieces)	**Parmesan cheese, grated**
Salt and pepper to taste	**¼ pound butter bits**

1. Preheat oven to 350° F.
2. Grease a baking dish. Place fish in dish. Salt and pepper fish. Cover with sour cream.
3. Sprinkle heavily with grated cheese. Dot with butter. Bake in a 350° F oven 45 minutes to 1 hour, basting very often.

Preparation and Cooking Time: 1 hour

If you're feeling energetic for some do-it-yourself, back-to-scratch cooking, for home-made sour cream, place 3 containers sour cream and a pinch of salt in a clean piece of cloth. Tie it closed. Hang it over your kitchen faucet and let it drip for 24 hours.

Fish in Sour Cream Sauce

Sybil Kaplan
Overland Park, Kansas   Yield: 4 Servings

When I was living in Israel, I met Henrietta, an American from California, and she invited me to participate in a monthly women's cooking group. She had gotten this recipe from a neighbor after eating in her home and thought it was salmon because it was pink. When it was her turn to take the main dish to the cooking group, she brought this because it was good and it was easy.

4 slices frozen fish fillets	**3½ tablespoons catsup**
Margarine bits	**2½ tablespoons lemon**
Tomato slices	**juice**
Mushroom slices	**Dill, chopped**
¾ cup sour cream	

1. Preheat oven to 350° F.
2. Grease a rectangular or square casserole and place fish in it. Dot with margarine pieces. Cover with tomato slices and mushrooms.
3. In a bowl, combine sour cream, catsup, lemon juice and dill. Pour over fish. Bake in a 350° F oven 1 hour.

Preparation and Cooking Time: 1 hour, 15 minutes

The recipe calls for sour cream and you're out.
Blend 1 cup low-cal cottage cheese with
2 tablespoons lemon juice and 3 tablespoons milk.

French Fish with Mushroom Sauce

Sybil Kaplan   French Style
Overland Park, Kansas   Yield: 4 Servings

I adapted this from someone who had adapted it from Juila Child.

½ can cream of mushroom soup	3 tablespoons margarine
⅓ can milk	2½ tablespoons flour
4 fish fillets	½ cup whipping cream or milk
2 tablespoons green onions, chopped	¼ teaspoon lemon juice
1½ tablespoons margarine pieces	Sliced mushrooms
½ cup white wine or vermouth	¼ cup Swiss cheese, grated
	1 tablespoon margarine pieces

1. Preheat oven to 350°F.
2. Place mushroom soup and milk in a saucepan. Blend. Set aside.
3. Arrange fish in a buttered baking dish. Pour mushroom soup on top. Add onions. Dot with margarine. Bake in a 350°F oven 8 to 10 minutes.
4. Melt 3 tablespoon margarine in a saucepan. Blend in flour to make a roux. Add vermouth and ½ cup liquid from fish. Add whipping cream or milk. Bring to a boil. Add lemon juice. Reduce heat and cook until sauce thickens.
5. Drain off rest of liquid from fish and discard. Pour white sauce over fish. Add sliced mushrooms and cheese. Dot with margarine. Bake 20 minutes. Switch to broil and broil to brown top.

Preparation and Cooking Time: 45 minutes to 1 hour

Halibut Caddy Ganty

Sybil Kaplan
Overland Park, Kansas   Yield: 4 Servings

Someone I met in Israel gave this recipe to me and told me she had gotten it from a lodge where she used to go to vacation when she lived in Alaska. She said the person at the lodge received it from a neighbor whose husband had written it down as he had gotten it from a fisherman from Pelican, Alaska, who got it from Caddy Ganty herself!

2 pounds frozen halibut or	2 tablespoons sour cream
haddock, cut in pieces	1 tablespoon mayonnaise
Salt	1 tablespoon onions,
Dry white wine	finely chopped
Bread crumbs	Paprika

1. Preheat oven to 425° F.
2. Place layers of fish in a bowl, salting each layer. Pour over wine to cover. Cover bowl with wax paper. Set aside in cool place for 2 hours.
3. Drain fish and pat fish dry.
4. Place bread crumbs in a shallow dish. Roll fish in bread crumbs. Place in a single layer in a buttered baking dish.
5. In bowl, combine sour cream, mayonnaise and chopped onions. Pour over top of fish. Sprinkle with paprika. Bake in a 425° F oven 15-20 minutes until lightly brown and bubbly.

Preparation and Cooking Time: 2½ hours

Baked Herring
Herring Forshmak or Forshmak Seledochnyi

The Aleph-Bet of Jewish Cooking   Russia

Yield: 4 Servings

4 herring fillets	**1 apple, peeled and cut**
Water	**into cubes**
4 teaspoons unsalted butter	**1 cup sour cream**
2 onions, cut in cubes	**2 teaspoons bread crumbs**
4 pieces white bread	

1. Soak herring in a bowl of water for 10-12 hours, changing water after 4 hours and after 8 hours.
2. Preheat oven to 375° F.
3. Melt butter in a frying pan and fry onions lightly.
4. Chop herring and add fried onions, white bread, apple and sour cream. Mix well and pour into a greased baking dish. Sprinkle bread crumbs on top. Bake in a 375° F oven for 25 minutes. Serve hot.

Preparation and Cooking Time: 10 to 12½ hours

Note: Reprinted with permission from Shvut Ami, the International Center for Soviet Jews, Jerusalem, Israel.

Cooking fish but hate the odor? Add lemon juice or vinegar to the fish.

Another way to eliminate odor when baking or broiling fish--place a piece of aluminum foil in oven sprinkled with cinnamon.

Tuna Crepes

Sybil Kaplan
Overland Park, Kansas

Yield: 10 to 12 Servings

¼ **cup margarine**
¼ **cup onions, chopped**
¼ **cup celery, chopped**
Salt and pepper to taste
¼ **cup flour**

1 cup milk
1½ cups pareve chicken
   soup or bouillon
1 tablespoon sherry
3 cups tuna
8 to 10 cooked crepes
⅓ cup Parmesan cheese

1. Preheat oven to 350° F.
2. Heat margarine in a frying pan. Sauté onion and celery 3 minutes. Add salt and pepper.
3. Stir in flour to make a roux. Add milk and bouillon. Cook over low heat until thick and smooth. Remove from heat.
4. Add sherry. Pour half the sauce into a bowl. Add tuna to that half.
5. Lay out crepes and place 3 tablespoons tuna mixture onto center of each. Fold sides in and roll up. Place crepes in a greased baking dish. Pour remaining sauce on top. Sprinkle with Parmesan cheese. Bake in a 350° F oven for 20 to 35 minutes.

Preparation and Cooking Time: 45 minutes

Indian Banana Peanut Fish

Sybil Kaplan India Style
Overland Park, Kansas Yield: 4 Servings

4 portions fish   **2 tablespoons oil**
Salt and pepper to taste   **2 teaspoons curry powder**
2 teaspoons lemon juice   **¼ cup salted peanuts**
¼ cup oil   **2 small bananas, sliced**

1. Place a piece of foil in a broiling pan. Spray with no-stick cooking spray. Place fish on top. Sprinkle with salt and pepper.
2. Combine lemon juice with ¼ cup oil. Mix, then pour on top of fish. Broil 10 minutes.
3. Heat 2 tablespoons oil in a small pan. Add curry powder, peanuts and banana slices. Sauté until brown. Pour on fish before serving.

Preparation and Cooking Time: 15 to 30 minutes

St. Peter's Fish in Rice

Sybil Kaplan   Israel
Overland Park, Kansas   Yield: 2 to 3 Servings

*Recently while at the fish counter in the grocery store I saw a fish
marked "tilapia." I had never heard of it and no one I asked knew
what it was. While sorting through some cookbooks, I found a
brochure produced by Carmel Agrexco, Agricultural Export Co. of
Israel, St. Peter's Fish from the Sea of Galilee. The recipes were
great and there, on the back, was a translation of St. Peter's Fish--
tilapia.*

1 pound tilapia fish fillets	2 pareve soup cubes
Oil	Water
2¾ cups raw rice	2 teaspoons lemon juice
3 medium onions, thinly sliced	3 medium beets, baked
1 teaspoon cumin	2 tablespoons fresh
½ teaspoon allspice	parsley, chopped
Salt and pepper to taste	Almonds, blanched
½ teaspoon saffron	(optional)
2 teaspoons sumac	
1 cup sunflower seed	
kernels	

1. Slice the fish in the width. Separate the pieces. Heat oil in
   a frying pan and fry the fish until golden on both sides.
   Set aside to cool.
2. Wash the rice and pour over boiling water. Mix. Set aside
   to cool.
3. When rice is cool, wash and drain.
4. Heat oil in frying pan and fry onions until golden. Place
   half the onions in a pot. Add rice and mix. Add cumin,
   allspice, salt, pepper, saffron and sumac and oil from frying
   pan. Stir and add sunflower seed kernels.

5. Dissolve soup cubes in water and add to pot. Add water to about 1 inch above the rice. Stir to loosen up the pot. Bring to a boil, reduce heat and cook covered until the rice is done and water absorbed. Add water only if needed. Remove from heat and keep covered.
6. Sprinkle lemon juice and seasonings over the fish slices and heat in the oven or a frying pan.
7. Pour rice in a serving bowl. Slice beets in half-moon sections and dip in lemon juice. Arrange around the rice. Add onions and a few cubed beets to the fish. Arrange around beets and down center of the rice. Garnish with parsley. Serve hot.

This dish can be prepared ahead of time and reheated in the oven, covered, just before serving. Blanched almonds, lightly browned or fried in oil can also be scattered over the dish.

Preparation and Cooking Time: 1 hour

For a delicate crust on fish, add ½ to 1 teaspoon baking powder to the frying batter. For a special taste, also add 1 tablespoon sherry or brandy when frying fish.

"Crabmeat" Salad

Dorothy Kaplan
Kansas City, Missouri

Yield: 3 to 4 Servings

1 8-ounce package **imitation crabmeat, flaked**	**⅓ cup mayonnaise**
½ cup celery, chopped	**½ teaspoon lemon juice**
2 tablespoons onions, minced	**⅛ teaspoon salt**
	⅛ teaspoon pepper

1. Place imitation crabmeat in a bowl. Add celery, mayonnaise, onion, lemon juice, salt and pepper. Blend. Refrigerate until serving.

Preparation and Cooking Time: 10 to 15 minutes

If a recipe calls for 1 tablespoon fresh herbs, you can substitute ½ teaspoon dried herbs.

Seafood Marinade

Hilda Meth
Richmond, Virginia

3 tablespoons olive oil	**2 to 4 tablespoons**
1 teaspoon fresh ginger,	**margarine**
grated or chopped fine	**¼ cup red dry wine**
1 teaspoon fresh garlic	**1 teaspoon soy sauce**
2 serrano chilies or	
Green onions (for the faint at heart)	

1. Combine all ingredients in a jar.

   All solid ingredients need to be grated or chopped fine.

   This is a wonderful marinade for grilled fish. It will store in the refrigerator for at least two months although I have stored it longer. This version is also for the faint of heart!

Preparation and Cooking Time: 10 minutes

If a recipe calls for 1 garlic clove, you can substitute ⅛ teaspoon garlic powder or ½ teaspoon minced garlic.

"Whatever in the water has fins and scales, whether in the seas or in the rivers--that you may eat."
(Leviticus 11:9)

Poultry

Baja California Chicken

Sonia Golad
Kansas City, Missouri   Yield: 8 Servings

This recipe I found when I was visiting my daughter in California. A distant cousin, who, like me, came from Vilna, Poland, passed away and while we were looking at her albums and her books, I found this recipe with a picture of my grandfather and grandmother. I didn't have any pictures of my mother's parents so I took it and enlarged it. Her children didn't even know who was in this picture.

8 chicken breasts, boned	**¼ cup olive oil**
Salt and pepper to taste	**¼ cup tarragon vinegar**
2 garlic cloves, crushed	**¾ cup dry sherry**

1. Preheat oven to 350°F.
2. Sprinkle chicken with salt and pepper
3. Combine garlic, oil and vinegar in a frying pan and heat. Add chicken and sauté until golden brown, turning often.
4. Place chicken in a baking dish. Pour sherry over. Bake in a 350°F oven 10 minutes or until chicken is done.

Preparation and Cooking Time: 20 to 30 minutes

Chicken and Dumplings
Csirke As Gombōc

Ruth Gluck   Hungary
Phoenix, Arizona   Yield: 6 to 8 Servings

Linda Radke's Aunt Ruth, sister of her mother, says this recipe comes from her mother, Emma Weiss, who was born in Hungary.

1 medium onion, sliced fine	½ cup water
Shortening	2 cups flour
4 pounds chicken, cut up	3 eggs
4 cups water	Salt and pepper to taste
Salt and pepper to taste	Paprika to taste
Paprika to taste	Boiling water
3 tablespoons flour	1 teaspoon salt

1. In a pot, sauté onion in shortening. Add chicken and 4 cups water. Add salt, pepper and paprika and cook slowly over medium heat until chicken is tender, about 30-40 minutes.
2. Meantime, in a bowl, make a paste of the 3 tablespoons flour and ½ cup water. Pour over chicken and let come to a boil for 1 minute. Remove from heat.
3. For the dumplings: in a bowl, mix 2 cups flour and eggs. Add salt, pepper and paprika and enough water to make a soft batter. Beat well. Heat soup pot of water with 1 teaspoon salt.
4. Dip a teaspoon into the boiling water to prevent sticking of batter. Drop the batter, ½ teaspoon at a time into boiling water. Cook until tender. Remove to a colander and rinse with warm water. Place dumplings on top of the chicken.

Preparation and Cooking Time: 1 to 1½ hours

Note: From **That Hungarian's In My Kitchen** by Linda F. Radke, Five Star Publications.

Chicken Marbella

Sonia Golad
Kansas City, Missouri   Yield: 10 to 12 Servings

I made this up about 10 years ago and called it "marbella" like marbles because of the red and green and brown colors.

4 chicken, quartered	1 cup prunes, pitted
(2 pounds each)	½ cup red wine vinegar
1 head of garlic cloves, pressed	½ cup Spanish green olives
¼ cup dry oregano	½ cup capers with juice
Salt and pepper to taste	6 bay leaves
½ cup olive oil	1 cup white wine

Night before serving:
1. In a large bowl, combine chicken pieces with garlic, oregano, salt and pepper, oil, prunes, vinegar, olives, capers and bay leaves. Cover and let marinate in refrigerator overnight, turning chicken a few times.
Next day:
2. Preheat oven to 350° F.
3. Arrange chicken in a baking pan. Spoon marinade over. Pour white wine around. Bake in a 350° F oven 1 hour, basting often.

Serve with rice.

Preparation and Cooking Time: 13½ hours

Chicken and Linguine

Empire Kosher Poultry   Italian Style
Mifflintown, Pennsylvania   Yield: 4 Servings

The flavor of this comes from the oil and margarine plus the herbs and garlic.

4 tablespoons margarine
2 tablespoons olive oil
6 to 8 cloves fresh garlic, minced
¼ cup onions, finely chopped
½ cup good chicken broth
½ cup white wine
1 cup mixed fresh herbs (parsley, tarragon, basil thyme, one or more)

2 tablespoons fresh lemon juice
½ pound boneless, skinless chicken cutlets or chicken thighs
Linguine or fettucini
Parsley, chopped

1. Melt margarine with oil in a saucepan. Add garlic and onion and sauté lightly. Be careful not to burn the garlic.
2. Add chicken broth, white wine, herbs and lemon juice. Cook over low heat for about 10 minutes.
3. Cut chicken into thin strips or dice and add to sauce. Poach until cooked, about 10 minutes, stirring to make sure chicken is evenly cooked. If sauce seems thin, add a little cornstarch mixed with 1 tablespoon of cold water to thicken.
4. Cook linguine or fettucine according to directions. Drain. Mix sauce into pasta. Serve with parsley on top.

Preparation and Cooking Time: 30 to 40 minutes

"Schnitzel" - Italian Style

Sybil Kaplan
Overland Park, Kansas

Italian Style
Yield: 4 Servings

4 pieces boneless chicken	**Bay leaf**
Flour	**Dash of thyme**
Salt and pepper to taste	**1 teaspoon dry parsley**
3 tablespoons oil	**4 ounces mushrooms**
1 onion, chopped	**flakes**
2 tomatoes, quartered	**⅔ cup olives, sliced**
⅓ cup white wine	

1. Dredge chicken in flour seasoned with salt and pepper.
2. Heat oil in a frying pan. Brown chicken. Add onion, tomatoes, wine, bay leaf, thyme, parsley and mushrooms. Bring to a boil. Reduce heat, cover and simmer until chicken is done. Add olives and stir.

Preparation and Cooking Time: 30 to 40 minutes

Note: Schnitzel is the German word for cutlet and refers to a piece of meat dipped in egg, breaded and fried.

"A land of wheat and barley, and vines and fig trees and pomegranates; a land of olive trees and honey"
(Deuteronomy 8:8)

Lemon Chicken

Dalia Carmel
New York, New York   Yield: 8 Servings

I love short recipes that work out and are hardly anything to do and you get a fabulous dish. This is a good example!

8 chicken thighs or thighs and legs	1½ whole lemons, sliced, with seeds removed
Salt and pepper to taste	Paprika to taste
3 tablespoons margarine	½ cup shallots, chopped
1 tablespoon olive oil	½ cup white wine, dry sherry or vermouth

1. Salt and pepper the chicken parts. Heat margarine and oil in a frying pan.
2. Brown the chicken on both sides. Place a slice of lemon on each piece of chicken, sprinkle with paprika then the shallots. Cover the pan well and simmer 10 to 15 minutes.
3. Add the wine and continue simmering 50 minutes.

Serve with rice.

Preparation and Cooking Time: 1 hour, 15 minutes

"Also fowl were prepared for me..."
(Nehemiah 5:17)

Moroccan Chicken Stew with Couscous

Sybil Kaplan
Overland Park, Kansas

Middle East
Yield: 4 to 6 Servings

This recipe originated in Israel with modifications over the years.

Oil
2 to 2½ pounds chicken parts
1 onion, minced
¾ teaspoon turmeric
½ teaspoon cumin
⅜ teaspoon allspice
¼ teaspoon cayenne
1 garlic clove, crushed
1½ bay leaves

1¼ cups chicken soup
1½ carrots, chopped
1 turnip, sliced
½ pound cabbage, cut up
⅜ pound eggplant, cut up
1½ zucchini, cut
1 cup can chick peas
½ cup raisins
Couscous

1. In a soup pot, heat oil. Brown chicken. Add onion and sauté 5 minutes.
2. Add turmeric, cumin, allspice, cayenne, garlic, bay leaves and cook 5 minutes.
3. Add chicken soup, carrots, turnip, cabbage, eggplant and zucchini. Bring to boil. Reduce heat, cover and simmer 40 minutes. Add chick peas and raisins.
4. Cook couscous according to directions. To serve, place couscous in a soup bowl, spoon chicken and vegetables on top.

Preparation and Cooking Time: 1 to 1½ hours

Note: Couscous is semolina steamed in a colander-type pan above the pot (called a couscoussiere) in which stew is cooking. The steam coming from the bottom cooks the couscous on top. It is primarily a staple food in Morocco, Tunisia and Algeria. It is also made sweet like a cereal or a dessert and as a basis for salads.

Leftover Chicken Chinese Casserole

Sybil Kaplan   Chinese Style
Overland Park, Kansas   Yield: 4 Servings

I adapted this recipe from one a friend gave me using tuna.

½ cup Chinese noodles
1¼ cups water combined with
5 teaspoons pareve cream of
  mushroom soup mix
1 cup chicken, cooked and
  slivered
½ cup celery, chopped
¼ cup water chestnuts, sliced or
  bamboo shoots

¼ cup onions, chopped
¼ cup green pepper,
  chopped
1 teaspoon soy sauce
1 teaspoon sherry
¼ cup Chinese noodles

1. Preheat oven to 350° F.
2. Place ½ cup Chinese noodles in a mixing bowl. Add
   mushroom soup, chicken, celery, water chestnuts, onions
   and green pepper and blend. Add soy sauce and sherry.
3. Pour into a greased casserole. Top with ¼ cup noodles.
   Bake in a 350° F oven for 30 minutes.

Preparation and Cooking Time: 40 minutes

How do you cut vegetables for Chinese cooking? The
general rule of thumb is cut hard vegetables diagonally and
tender vegetables vertical.
Celery - cut in wedges
Carrots - cut in wedges
Peppers - cut in ½ to ¾-inch strips, matchstick length or
strips then diagonal to make triangles
Onion - in eighths
Scallions - crossways
Turnip - matchstick size

Indian Chicken

Sybil Kaplan
Overland Park, Kansas

India Style
Yield: 4 to 6 Servings

3 pounds chicken, cut into
serving pieces
2 tablespoons oil
1 onion, chopped
1 green pepper, diced
1 teaspoon curry powder
2 tomatoes, quartered

1 teaspoon coriander
1 teaspoon cumin
1 teaspoon turmeric
¼ teaspoon garlic powder
Salt and pepper to taste
½ cup water
¼ teaspoon cinnamon

1. Heat oil in a pan. Brown chicken. Add onion, green
   pepper, curry powder, tomatoes, coriander, cumin, turmeric,
   garlic powder, salt and pepper, water and cinnamon.
2. Bring to a boil. Reduce heat, cover and cook 25 to 30
   minutes or until chicken is done.
   Serve with rice, chutney, raisins, peanuts and coconut.

Preparation and Cooking Time: 1 hour

Greek Chicken Avgolemono with Orzo Pilaf

Sybil Kaplan Greek Style
Overland Park, Kansas Yield: 4 Servings

¼ **cup margarine**
½ **cup orzo**
2 **cups water**
½ **cup rice**
1½ **teaspoons chicken-flavored**
  bouillon
1 **tablespoon margarine**
1 **garlic clove, sliced**
4 **chicken breasts or thighs**

¼ **cup water**
1 **medium squash, sliced**
2 **egg yolks**
1½ **teaspoons cornstarch**
½ **teaspoon chicken**
  bouillon
2½ **tablespoons lemon**
  juice

1. Melt ¼ cup margarine in a saucepan. Add orzo. Cook 10 minutes.
2. Add water, rice and 1½ teaspoons chicken bouillon. Bring to a boil. Reduce heat and simmer 30 minutes. Set aside.
3. Heat 1 tablespoon margarine in a frying pan. Brown garlic then discard. Add chicken and brown. Add ¼ cup water and bring to a boil. Reduce heat, cover and simmer 10 minutes.
4. Add squash and cook 10 minutes more or until chicken and squash are tender.
5. Beat egg yolks in a saucepan with a wooden spoon. Add cornstarch and chicken bouillon. Stir over medium heat 10 minutes. Add lemon juice.
   Place chicken on a platter, spoon sauce on top. Serve with pilaf.

Preparation and Cooking Time: 1½ to 2 hours

Korean Chicken with Vegetables
Joon-kol

Sybil Kaplan

Overland Park, Kansas

Oriental Style

Yield: 4 Servings

4 chicken breasts or thighs
¼ cup soy sauce
1 tablespoon brown sugar
1 clove garlic, pressed
Dash pepper
¼ cup almonds, chopped
½ cup chicken broth
Oil
1 medium onion,
  thinly sliced

4 medium carrots,
  thinly sliced
1 bunch green onions,
  minced
2 cups bean sprouts
1 pound spinach, chopped

1. Slice chicken. In a bowl, combine soy sauce, brown sugar, garlic and pepper. Marinate chicken 30 minutes. Sprinkle with almonds. Add marinade to chicken broth.
2. Add 1 tablespoon oil to a frying pan or wok. Cook chicken 1 minute. Add onion. Cook 1 minute. Add carrots, green onions and broth. Cover and cook 5 to 7 minutes.
3. Add bean sprouts and spinach. Cover and cook 1 minute. Stir. Serve over rice.

Preparation and Cooking Time: 45 minutes

Thai Style Fried Chicken

Empire Kosher Poultry
Mifflintown, Pennsylvania

Oriental Style
Yield: 4 Servings

This oven-baked chicken gets rid of many fat calories, but gives the same illusion of indulgence! The coconut lends a little extra flavor, texture and sweetness that make this recipe a favorite of all ages. Why Thai? Because Thai cooking uses a lot of coconut and coconut juices. Add lime for tartness.

2 tablespoons margarine
2 eggs or egg substitute
1 can flaked coconut
¾ cup cracker or
   pretzel crumbs,
   finely crushed

2 teaspoons fresh
   lemon peel, grated
1 teaspoon ginger,
   freshly grated or
½ teaspoon dried
1 cut-up 3-to 5-pound
   chicken

1. Preheat oven to 375° F.
2. Melt margarine in a baking dish which is large enough to accommodate the chicken pieces. You can also spray with no-stick cooking spray instead of margarine.
3. Beat the eggs with a little water in a shallow bowl.
4. Mix coconut, crumbs, lemon and ginger in a second bowl. Dip chicken pieces in egg, then in crumb mix. If you wish, you can double bread for more coating. Return the chicken into the egg after the first crumb bath, then back into the crumbs.
5. Place chicken in the baking dish and bake in a 375° F. oven for 1 hour. Turn over chicken every 15 minutes.

Preparation and Cooking Time: 1¼ hours

Chicken á la Sabra

Sybil Kaplan   Israel
Overland Park, Kansas   Yield: 8 Servings

This recipe came from the Tel Aviv Sheraton. The Israeli hotels often invited journalists to food tastings and handed out recipes. This probably came to me this way.

2 broiling chickens	2 large onions, sliced
Oil	Salt and pepper to taste
Seasoned flour	1 teaspoon thyme
2 cups orange juice	2 tablespoons brown sugar
1 cup dry white wine	1 teaspoon orange peel
1 can mushrooms with juice	

1. Preheat oven to 350° F.
2. Heat oil in a large frying pan or two.
3. In a second pan, place 2 tablespoons seasoned flour, orange juice, wine, juice of the mushrooms, onions, salt and pepper, thyme, brown sugar and orange peel. Bring to a boil. Reduce heat and simmer 3 minutes.
4. Place chickens in a roasting pan. Pour sauce on top. Bake in a 350° F oven 1 hour, basting every 20 minutes. Scatter mushrooms over chicken. Continue baking 30 minutes.

Preparation and Cooking Time: 1 hour, 45 minutes

Baked Honey Chicken

Sybil Kaplan
Overland Park, Kansas   Yield: 4 Servings

I got this recipe from my mother, Rae Horowitz.

1-3 pounds chicken, cut up	2 tablespoons soy sauce
3 tablespoons onions, chopped	1 teaspoon ginger
2 tablespoons honey	1 teaspoon garlic, minced

1. Preheat oven to 425° F.
2. Arrange chicken in a greased 9 x 13 inch baking dish.
3. In a bowl, combine onion, honey, soy sauce, ginger and garlic. Spoon over chicken. Marinate for 1 hour.
4. Bake chicken in 425° F oven 30 minutes, turn pieces over and continue baking 10 to 15 minutes more or until chicken is tender.

Preparation and Cooking Time: 1 hour, 45 minutes

Chicken Croquettes

Sybil Kaplan
Overland Park, Kansas   Yield: 4 Servings

¼ cup salted margarine	1 tablespoon onions, grated
⅓ cup flour	1 tablespoon lemon juice
1 cup non-dairy creamer	1 egg, beaten
2 cups cooked chicken, diced	⅓ cup bread crumbs
1 teaspoon dry tarragon	Oil
1 tablespoon dry parsley flakes	

1. Melt margarine in a saucepan. Add flour to make a roux. Add non-dairy creamer and cook about 3 minutes until thick. Set aside to cool.
2. In a bowl, mix together chicken, tarragon, parsley, onion and lemon juice. Add cream sauce. Blend and chill.
3. Remove from refrigerator and shape into croquettes. Dip first in beaten egg, then in bread crumbs. Heat oil in a frying pan. Fry croquettes until brown on both sides. Drain on paper toweling

Preparation and Cooking Time: 1 to 1½ hours

What makes breading or flour stick to chicken better?
Chill the chicken pieces 1 or more hours then bread.

Marinated "Schnitzel"

Sybil Kaplan   Israeli Style
Overland Park, Kansas   Yield: 4 Servings

8 pieces boneless chicken	1 garlic clove, minced
⅔ cup white wine vinegar	⅓ teaspoon thyme
⅓ cup oil	⅓ teaspoon chili powder
⅓ cup catsup	Dash cayenne
⅔ medium onion, minced	Salt to taste

1. Place chicken in a shallow baking dish.
2. In a bowl, combine vinegar, oil, catsup, onion, garlic, thyme, chili powder, cayenne and salt. Blend, then pour over chicken. Let sit several hours.
3. Spray a broiling pan rack with no-stick vegetable spray. Place chicken on top and broil on both sides, basting with leftover marinade, until cooked to taste.

Preparation and Cooking Time: 2 to 2½ hours

Note: Schnitzel is an Israeli favorite--boneless chicken or turkey.

How do you turn a chicken or chicken part without piercing the flesh and losing the juice?
Turn it with wooden spoons.

Chicken in Wine

Sybil Kaplan
Overland Park, Kansas

Yield: 4 Servings

1 pound chicken, cut into parts
2 tablespoons oil
1½ tomatoes, chopped
1½ cloves garlic, minced
¼ cup cognac
1¼ cups dry white wine
1 celery rib with leaves,
   chopped

8 green olives, pitted
Salt and pepper to taste
2 bay leaves
⅛ teaspoon thyme
Dash ginger
1 orange, sliced and
   unpeeled

1. Heat oil in a frying pan. Brown chicken. Add tomatoes and garlic and cook a few minutes.
2. Add cognac, white wine, celery, olives, salt and pepper, bay leaves, thyme and ginger. Reduce heat and cook 20-30 minutes.
3. Add sliced orange and cook over low heat a few minutes.

Good served with mushroom rice.

Preparation and Cooking Time: 40 minutes

Baked Chicken

Sybil Kaplan
Overland Park, Kansas

Yield: 5 to 6 Servings

My mother, Rae Horowitz, gave this to me.

1 5-pound chicken	**Your favorite stuffing**
¼ teaspoon ginger	**½ teaspoon ginger**
1 onion, sliced	**¾ cup boiling water**
½ cup celery, chopped	**6 potatoes, cut up**

1. Preheat oven to 400° F.
2. Clean out chicken and pat dry. Sprinkle cavity with ¼ teaspoon ginger.
3. Stuff with favorite stuffing. Add ½ teaspoon ginger to stuffing. Place chicken in roasting pan. Roast in 400° F oven for 10 minutes. Add onion-celery mixture.
4. Turn chicken over. Bake 20 minutes more. Reduce heat to 350° F. Add boiling water and potatoes. Bake 1½ hours more.

Preparation and Cooking Time: 2¼ hours

How do you get a crisp, brown crust on a roast or broiled chicken?
Rub mayonnaise over the skin.

Quick Chicken Aloha

Dorothy Kaplan
Kansas City, Missouri   Yield: 6 Servings

I'm not sure where I got this recipe, but I've been making it about 20 years. I always keep an extra can of pineapple slices on the shelf to use when I want to make a chicken dish in a hurry.

6 boned chicken breasts or other chicken pieces you like	1 teaspoon rosemary
2 teaspoons Dijon mustard	1 20-ounce can pineapple slices
2 teaspoons Worcestershire sauce	Juice from pineapple
2 teaspoons cornstarch	1 lemon, thinly sliced
⅛ teaspoon garlic powder	

1. Preheat oven to 400° F.
2. Grease an ovenproof baking dish. Place chicken in dish and broil until brown.
3. Drain pineapple and put aside. Place juice in a mixing bowl. Add mustard, Worcestershire sauce, cornstarch, garlic powder and rosemary. Pour over chicken.
4. Bake in a 400° F oven 30 minutes. Add lemon and pineapple slices around side of chicken. Spoon sauce on top. Bake 5 minutes more.

Preparation and Cooking Time: 1 hour

Chicken with Mushrooms and Wine

Janet Siegel
Prairie Village, Kansas

Yield: 4 Servings

I thought up this recipe myself.

2 eggs or 1 portion "egg beaters"
¼ cup water
Flavored bread crumbs
4 double chicken breasts,
  skinless and boneless

1 8-ounce package
  mushrooms
2 8-ounce cans tomato
  sauce
2 shakes nutmeg
½ cup red wine

1. Beat eggs or "egg beaters" and water in a shallow dish. Place bread crumbs in a second shallow dish.
2. Dip chicken cutlets first in egg, then in bread crumbs. Spray a pan with no-stick vegetable spray. Fry 10 minutes on each side.
3. Clean frying pan with a paper towel. Slice mushrooms into pan and cook for 2 minutes.
4. Add tomato sauce and nutmeg and cook another 2 minutes. Add wine and cook another 2 minutes. Pour sauce over cutlets and serve.

This dish can be made beforehand and then put in a preheated 325° F oven to heat until hot.

This dish can also be made ahead and put in a container for the freezer and frozen for future use.

Note: This dish can also be made without the sauce, just breading and frying cutlets. In this case, it gets an Israeli name--"Chicken Schnitzel."

Preparation and Cooking Time: 35 to 45 minutes

Stuffing for Fowl

Bertha Kaplan, mother of Helen Hiller
Chicago, Illinois   Yield: 6 to 8 Servings

My mother told me that she copied the recipe for the stuffing from the first box of cornflakes she had which was a sample at the door, 75 years ago.

¼ **cup chicken fat**	¼ **cup flour**
1 medium onion, sliced	**1 teaspoon salt**
¼ **cup celery, diced**	**Dash cinnamon**
2 tablespoons green pepper, diced	**Dash pepper**
2 cups cornflakes	

1. Heat chicken fat in a frying pan. Sauté onion, celery and green pepper until soft and transparent.
2. Pour vegetables into a mixing bowl. Add cornflakes, flour, salt, cinnamon and pepper. Mix well. Taste for added seasonings.

This recipe is sufficient for a 4-to 5-pound veal breast or a 5-to 6-pound chicken.
For a 10 to 12 pound turkey, double the recipe. Do not overstuff the fowl. If you have leftover stuffing, make into balls and bake alongside the meat or fowl.

Preparation and Cooking Time: 15 minutes

Malka's Chinese Chicken "Spare Ribs"

Sybil Kaplan
Overland Park, Kansas

Oriental Style
Yield: 4 Servings

Malka Nisan is a great cook who came on aliyah from Canada with her husband, Mordechai. They live in Jerusalem and this is one of many recipes she gave me when I lived in Jerusalem.

2 pounds chicken wings
7 tablespoons brown sugar
7 tablespoons soy sauce
7 tablespoons water
1 to 2 garlic cloves, crushed

1. Preheat oven to 350°F.
2. In a bowl, combine sugar, soy sauce, water and garlic.
3. Place chicken wings in a greased casserole. Pour sauce on top. Bake in a 350°F oven for 1½ hours, basting occasionally.

Preparation and Cooking Time: 1 hour, 45 minutes

Frank's Peruvian Style Chicken Salad

Sybil Kaplan
Overland Park, Kansas

South American
Yield: 4 Servings

When I lived in Israel, Frank Nothman was public relations director for the Jerusalem Hilton. He was from Peru. He gave this recipe to me.

2 pounds chicken
Juice of 5 lemons
9 ounces mushrooms, halved
2 ribs celery, cut-up

Salt and pepper to taste
2 cups pareve whipping cream
3 teaspoons sugar

Day before serving:
1. Place chicken in a pot. Add a little water and cook until done. Cool. Cut in bite-size pieces. Place in a bowl.
2. Add lemon juice. Marinate 24 hours.
   Next day:
3. Add mushrooms and celery to chicken. Season with salt and pepper. Add whipping cream and sugar and toss.

Preparation and Cooking Time: 25 hours

Chicken Stuffed with Potato
Kuritsa Farshirovannaya Kartoshkoy

The Aleph-Bet of Jewish Cooking

Russia
Yield: 6 to 8 Servings

2 cups boiled potatoes,
  mashed
2 teaspoons chicken fat,
  melted
½ cup chopped onions,
  fried
1 teaspoon salt

¼ teaspoon pepper
1 2-2½ kilos
(4¼-5 pounds)
  whole chicken
½ teaspoon ground garlic
2 teaspoons salt
¾ teaspoon pepper

1. Preheat oven to 375° F.
2. Prepare boiled potatoes. Drain and mash.
3. Fry onion and set aside.
4. Mix potatoes with melted chicken fat, fried onion,
   1 teaspoon salt and ¼ teaspoon pepper.
5. Stuff potato mixture inside chicken and sew closed or
   secure. Rub garlic, remaining salt and pepper into chicken
   skin.
6. Place in a greased baking dish. Bake in a 375° F oven for
   45 minutes until brown.

Preparation and Cooking Time: 1¼ hours

Note: Reprinted with permission from Shvut Ami, The
International Center for Soviet Jews, Jerusalem, Israel.

My Favorite Turkey

Ruth deSola Mendes
Pound Ridge, New York   Yield: Depends on size

*This is my favorite way of doing turkey; it's failproof for a juicy and
tender bird. It was the recommended method used by The White
Turkey Inn in Danbury, Connecticut, a Connecticut landmark
renowned for its flock of turkeys which roamed the grounds.*

Turkey
Garlic powder
Pepper
Apples, cored and peeled or stuffing

1. Preheat oven to 250° F.
2. Rub turkey with garlic powder and pepper to taste. A
   kosher turkey will not require additional salt.
3. Fill cavity with cored, peeled apples or stuffing.
4. Place turkey on a rack about 1 inch high in a shallow pan,
   breast down. Cover with a moistened cloth. If the bird is
   fat, leave alone; if the bird is lean, rub with melted
   margarine to ensure even browning. Turning the bird
   breast down is a self-basting method and permits the fat
   from the back to melt and continuously baste the less moist
   breast underneath.
   For a 12-to 14-pound bird, cook 3½ to 4 hours at 250° F.;
   for a 14-to 18-pound bird, cook 4 to 4½ hours; for a 20-
   pound bird, cook 4 to 5 hours.

Preparation and Cooking Time: Depends on size

Turkish-style Chicken Kebab

Sybil Kaplan
Overland Park, Kansas

Middle East
Yields: 4 Servings

1½ pounds chicken pieces	1 garlic clove, minced
¼ cup oil	¼ teaspoon cinnamon
¾ cup wine vinegar	3 onions, quartered
¼ cup dry red wine	1 eggplant, cut in cubes
1 medium onion, chopped	4 bay leaves
1 teaspoon pepper	¼ cup oil

1. In a bowl, combine ¼ cup oil, wine vinegar, red wine, 1 chopped onion, pepper, garlic and cinnamon. Add meat and marinate at least 3 hours.
2. Thread on skewers quartered onions, meat, eggplant and bay leaves. Brush with oil. Broil until done.

This can also be made with lamb.

Preparation and Cooking Time: 3¼ to 3½ hours

Note: The word *kebab* is Turkish for roasted meat and the style of taking cubes of meat, marinating them and cooking them on a skewer. It comes from the Turkish soldiers who cooked pieces of meat over the open fires on their swords.

Shish kebab is also the term used from the Turkish word, *sis*, meaning skewer. *Kebab* is another word used for the same skewered and grilled, marinated cubes of meat.
Shashlik or *shishlik* is a Russian word for the same idea.
Kofta is minced meat which is put on skewers like a sausage and grilled.

Middle Eastern Turkey Steaks

Empire Kosher Poultry
Mifflintown, Pennsylvania

Middle East
Yields: 4 Servings

This recipe comes from our favorite kosher chicken restaurant as a special favor. This is a very simple recipe for turkey thighs and is one instance where you don't have to use slow, moist heat. You actually sear in the flavor and tenderness very quickly. The texture and flavor are much like beef without the fat and calories. With turkey tenders or chicken cutlets, the flavor won't be as pronounced.

1 pound turkey thighs,
   cut into large cubes,
   butterflied and pounded
   until ¼ inch thick*
2 tablespoons cumin

1 tablespoon paprika
½ teaspoon coarsely
   ground black pepper
2 tablespoons full-flavored
   olive oil

1. If using turkey tenders, cut each fillet into three pieces crosswise, then butterfly each piece and pound until ¼-inch thick (between pieces of waxed paper, with a mallet, your fist or a rolling pin). If using chicken cutlets, pound each piece separately.
2. Rub with cumin, pepper and paprika. Sprinkle with oil. Cover and marinate overnight in the refrigerator. Next day:
3. Preheat grill. Grill for 2 minutes, turn and grill another 2 minutes. Don't overcook!

Serve with rice pilaf and a fresh onion and tomato salad.

* This can also be made with turkey tenders or boneless, skinless chicken breasts.

Preparation and Cooking Time: 24¼ hours

Barbeque Turkey Wings

Sybil Kaplan
Overland Park, Kansas

Yields: 4 Servings

4 turkey wings	**½ cup water**
12 ounces chili sauce	**1 teaspoon garlic powder**
2 onions, chopped	**1 teaspoon Worcestershire**
½ cup brown sugar	**sauce**

1. Preheat oven to 350° F.
2. Place turkey wings in a greased baking dish.
3. In a bowl, combine chili sauce, onions, brown sugar, water, garlic powder and Worcestershire sauce. Pour over wings. Bake in a 350-375° F oven 1 hour.

Preparation and Cooking Time: 1¼ hours

If a recipe calls for 1 teaspoon poultry seasoning, you can substitute ½ teaspoon sage, ½ teaspoon thyme and ½ teaspoon rosemary (optional).

"Bring me game and make savory food for me..."
(Genesis 27:6)

Amish Turkey

Empire Kosher Poultry
Mifflintown, Pennsylvania   Yields: 4 to 6 Servings

The Empire Kosher plant is located in central Pennsylvania, in the midst of a large Amish population. Many first-time visitors to the area at times may get the Amish farmer and the Orthodox rabbi confused, at least from a distance! The Amish conduct their lives in strict keeping with their religious faith, with daily routines that closely follow that of their ancestors in 18th century Europe. This recipe for Amish Turkey is invariably served at their weddings, customarily held in the fall, where the bride's family may cook for several hundred people.

The original recipe calls for a dozen eggs. We omitted the eggs and used about half the margarine that the recipe specifies. It's a very simple dish to prepare, and permits you to carve a holiday turkey one day and serve a family turkey that doesn't resemble a tired left-over the third day. When roasting the turkey, save the juice and brown bits from the bottom of the pan if you don't make gravy.

> **2 cups or more white or dark turkey, cooked and cut into chunks**
> **4 to 6 cups prepared bread stuffing or equivalent in bread cubes with your favorite herb mix**
> **½ cup parsley, chopped**
> **1 cup onions, chopped**
> **1 cup celery, chopped**
> **Pepper to taste**
> **2 cups turkey broth from the pan or chicken stock**
> **½ stick margarine, cut into chunks**

1. Preheat oven to 325° F.
2. Mix stuffing, parsley, cooked turkey and broth in a roasting pan.
3. Top with onions, celery and margarine. Bake in a 325° F oven 1 to 1½ hour, covered. Add more broth if necessary. The top should be crisp, the interior soft and fragrant.

Preparation and Cooking Time: 1½ to 1¾ hours

Meat

Barbecued Ribs of Beef

Sybil Kaplan   Israel
Overland Park, Kansas   Yields: 4 to 6 Servings

I received this recipe from an Israeli wine company while living in Israel.

3 pounds short ribs of beef	1 tablespoon sugar
Oil	1 tablespoon Worcestershire sauce
2 teaspoons salt	½ cup catsup
1 teaspoon pepper	¾ cup dry red wine
1 teaspoon paprika	½ cup onions, minced
1 teaspoon dry mustard	1 garlic clove, minced

1. Preheat oven to 350° F.
2. Heat oil in an ovenproof casserole or pot. Brown ribs. Pour off fat.
3. In a bowl, combine salt, pepper, paprika, dry mustard, sugar, Worcestershire sauce, catsup, wine, onions and garlic. Pour over ribs in a baking pan, sprayed with no-stick vegetable spray. Place in 350° F oven. Bake, basting often, 1 hour, or until as done as you like them.

Preparation and Cooking Time: 1½ to 1¾ hours

Rachel's Tunisian Couscous

Sybil Kaplan
Overland Park, Kansas

Middle East
Yields: 4 Servings

Rachel was my neighbor in Jerusalem and she let me watch her make this dish and introduced me to couscous.

1½ pounds couscous
1 teaspoon salt
3 tablespoons oil
1 cup cold water
1 tomato, cut up
2 zucchini squash,
 cut up
2 carrots, sliced
1 turnip, sliced
Piece cabbage, sliced
Piece pumpkin
(use sweet potato or
rutabaga, peeled and
sliced as substitute

1 teaspoon coriander
1 teaspoon dill
1 teaspoon parsley
1 pound stew meat or
 chicken
Salt and pepper to taste
1 teaspoon beef or chicken
 soup powder
1 to 2 cups water

1. Spread couscous in a pan. Stir in salt and oil, then water. Pour into a sieve. Push through while rubbing. As an option, use packaged couscous and follow directions on package. Set aside.
2. In soup pot, place tomato, squash, carrots, turnip, cabbage, pumpkin or sweet potato or rutabaga if using, coriander, dill, parsley, stew meat or chicken, salt and pepper and soup powder. Add 1 to 2 cups water. Bring to a boil. Reduce heat and cover. Cook until done.
 When regular couscous is used, it is placed in couscoussiere atop soup pot and left to cook by the steam from the soup.

To serve, place couscous in individual soup bowls, top with meat or chicken and vegetables.

This dish is eaten by Tunisians every Friday night.

Preparation and Cooking Time: 1 to 1½ hours

Carbonades Flamandes

Sybil Kaplan   Belgium
Overland Park, Kansas   Yields: 4 Servings

*An American friend who got it from a Flemish chef, gave this recipe
to me.*

3½ ounces unsalted margarine	2 tablespoons flour
2 pounds stew meat or	2 cups light beer
shoulder meat,	1 cup malt beer
cut in cubes	1 bay leaf
1 medium onion, chopped	Salt and pepper to taste
4 garlic cloves, chopped	
1 can tomato paste	

1. Melt margarine in a soup pot. Add meat and onion. Cook
   a few minutes. Add garlic and tomato paste. Cook 3
   minutes.
2. Stir in flour. Cook another few minutes.
3. Add beers, bay leaf, salt and pepper. Bring to a boil.
   Skim off top. Reduce heat and simmer 1½ hours.

Preparation and Cooking Time: 2¼ hours

Note: Carbonade a la flamande is a Belgian beef stew from
Flanders.

Emma's Hungarian Goulash
Magyar Gulyäs

Ethel Quarnstrom/Emma Weiss   Hungary
                                                Yields: 8 Servings

Linda Radke explains that this recipe was from her Hungarian-born Aunt Ethel, who was like a second mother to her. Emma was Linda's grandmother, her mother's mother.

4 tablespoons white vegetable shortening	1 teaspoon paprika
2 large onions, diced	1 teaspoon black pepper
2½ pounds beef, diced	2 teaspoons salt
Boiling water	1 teaspoon garlic salt
1 tablespoon parsley, chopped	6 large red potatoes, diced
6 medium carrots, sliced round	2 teaspoons flour

1. In a large pot, sauté onion in 2 tablespoons of the shortening. Add beef. Brown for 20 minutes.
2. Add enough boiling water to cover the meat 1 inch. Add parsley, sliced carrots and spices. Cook about 2 hours, then add potatoes. Continue cooking half an hour or until potatoes and meat are done.
3. In a frying pan, melt remaining 2 tablespoons shortening. Add flour to make a sauce. Add sauce to the goulash. Mix well and serve.

Preparation and Cooking Time: 3 to 3½ hours

Note: From **That Hungarian's In My Kitchen** by Linda F. Radke, Five Star Publications.

Sate

Hilda Meth   Oriental Style
Richmond, Virginia   Yields: 3 to 4 Servings

*I picked up this recipe in the Orient and adapted it to American
ingredients and my taste. It is of Thai origin. Sate is a form of
skewered and marinated food which is grilled using small bamboo
skewers. It works well with lamb and chicken. I don't like it with
beef but someone else might. If you make multiple batches, it will
keep in the refrigerator up to six months.*

1 cup soy sauce	1 clove garlic, minced
1 teaspoon dark molasses	Juice from 1 lemon or
2 teaspoons red hot pepper	3 tablespoons lemon juice
¾ cup hot water	1 to 2 pounds beef,
½ cup chunky peanut butter*	cut in chunks

1. Place soy sauce, molasses, red hot pepper, hot water,
   peanut butter, garlic and lemon juice in a sauce pan.
   Simmer until they are smoothly combined.
2. Marinate the meat of your choice in this for about two
   hours before cooking.**
3. Skewer meat on bamboo skewers, grill and serve over rice
   with dipping sauce.

   * If you use smooth peanut butter, use ⅓ cup and add ¼
   cup chopped peanuts.

   ** Reserve marinade sauce. This can be refrigerated for a
   future use.

Preparation and Cooking Time: 2¼ to 2½ hours

Note: Sate is originally Indonesian and is a favorite snack
food, appetizer or main entree.

Dipping Sauce for Sate

Hilda Meth   Oriental Style
Richmond, Virginia   Yields: 3 to 4 Servings

½ small can of tomato sauce
¼ cup water
3 tablespoons lemon juice
1 teaspoon Tabasco sauce

1. Combine ingredients in a sauce pan. Bring to a boil.
   Remove from heat and cool.

   This is a very versatile sauce and can be used successfully
   as a dip for a meat fondue.

Preparation and Cooking Time: 10 to 15 minutes

For Oriental cooking

If you don't have	Use
water chestnuts	celery, onion or kohlrabi
bamboo shoots	turnip, zucchini, cauliflower stalk, celery or onion
Chinese cabbage	lettuce, cabbage or celery heart
bean sprouts	shredded turnip, shredded cabbage, shredded zucchini, shredded celery heart

London Broil with Sauce

Lil Spungen
Kansas City, Missouri   Yields: 6 Servings

This recipe was given to me by a very dear friend in St. Louis.

Marinade:
¼ pound no-salt pareve
  margarine
2 cloves garlic, crushed
2 teaspoons seasoned salt
½ teaspoon chili powder
¼ teaspoon dry mustard
1½ tablespoons
  Worcestershire sauce
2 tablespoons vinegar
Dash Paprika
3 to 4 pound London broil

Sauce:
1 small clove garlic,
  crushed
1 teaspoon dill
1 medium onion, sliced
¼ cup no-salt pareve
  margarine
½ pound fresh
  mushrooms, sliced
2 tablespoons chili sauce
¼ teaspoon thyme
⅛ teaspoon Tabasco sauce
1 teaspoon Worcestershire
  sauce
½ cup dry red wine
1 teaspoon pareve beef
  powder

1. Preheat oven to 400° F.
2. Place marinade margarine, crushed garlic, seasoned salt, chili powder, dry mustard, Worcestershire sauce, vinegar and paprika in a sauce pan. Heat. Let cool.
3. Pour into a large plastic bag. Slip in London broil. Marinate as long as desired (the longer the better).
4. Barbeque meat on a spit or broil until brown. Place in baking pan in 400° F preheated oven and cook 15 to 20 minutes or until tender.

5. While meat is cooking, sauté garlic, dill, mushrooms and onion in margarine 5 minutes. Blend in 1 teaspoon flour until smooth.
6. Add chili sauce, thyme, Tabasco sauce, Worcestershire sauce, wine and beef powder. Simmer 10 minutes. This yields 1 cup sauce.

Preparation and Cooking Time: 2 to 3 hours

What if you're out of chili powder?

Combine:

1 teaspoon turmeric, 2 teaspoon garlic powder,
1 teaspoon cumin, 2 teaspoons oregano,
¼ teaspoon cayenne pepper, and
3 tablespoons paprika.

Rouladen, Potato Dumplings and Sauerkraut
Schlessische Rouladen

Margarete Jacoby   Poland
Kansas City, Missouri   Yields: 4 Servings

I was born and raised in Schlessia (on the Polish border with Germany). As a child, I used to watch my mother in the kitchen. Unfortunately, I don't remember too much about her cooking, but this was one of my favorite dishes, and the only beef I would eat as a child. Of course I had no measurements so I had to come up with them myself until I perfected them to my liking.

4 4x6-inch, ½-inch-thick	**Margarine**
slices shoulder beef	**Flour**
4 ½-inch thick slices salami	**Salt and pepper to taste**
1 small pickle	**5 medium potatoes**
¾ cup onions, diced	**1 egg**
Dijon mustard	**Dash nutmeg**
Oil	**½ cup flour**

1. Cut salami in julienne slices. Cut pickle in julienne slices.
2. Pound each slice of meat well with a cleaver. Spread with mustard, sprinkle with diced onions, top with salami and pickle, salt and pepper.
3. Roll up meat pieces and fasten each with toothpick.
4. Heat oil in a frying pan. Brown meat rolls. Add 1 cup hot water, reduce heat and simmer 1½ hours. Add more water if needed.
5. Remove meat rolls to a plate. Melt margarine in pan. Add flour to the drippings. Add water and stir until you have a gravy.

Preparation and Cooking Time: 2 hours

Potato Dumplings

Margarete Jacoby   Poland
Kansas City, Missouri   Yields: 4 Servings

5 medium potatoes, peeled   **½ cup flour**
Salt and pepper to taste   **Water**
1 egg   **1 teaspoon salt**
Dash nutmeg

1. Place potatoes in a saucepan with water. Bring to a boil. Cook until done. Drain. Put through ricer. Cool and dry on paper towels.
2. Place riced potatoes in a mixing bowl. Add salt, pepper, egg, nutmeg and work in flour with your hands until mixture is smooth and holds together. (Adjust flour as needed so add a little at a time.)
3. Shape into egg-size balls.
4. Heat a pot with water to which 1 teaspoon salt has been added. Bring to a boil. Drop potato balls into water. Boil gently, uncovered, 2 to 3 minutes.
5. When dumplings rise to the top, remove with a slotted spoon and transfer to paper towels to drain.

Preparation and Cooking Time: 35 to 45 minutes

Sauerkraut

Margarete Jacoby   Poland
Kansas City, Missouri   Yields: 4 Servings

1 pound sauerkraut
¼ cup onions, minced
2 garlic cloves, minced
3 to 4 tablespoons oil
Pepper

1. Wash and drain sauerkraut. Place in a saucepan, cover
   with water and cook 30 minutes. Drain.
2. Add onions, garlic, oil and pepper. Mix well.

Preparation and Cooking Time: 40 minutes

Rachel's Hungarian Roast Beef

Sybil Kaplan   Hungary
Overland Park, Kansas   Yields: 6 to 8 Servings

I met Rachel when her husband was with the Israel Consul General's office in Chicago in the 1980s. She gave me this recipe and said she learned it from the Hungarian-born grandmother of her husband who came to Palestine in the 1930s.

3-to 4-pound boneless shoulder roast	4 to 5 tablespoons oil
Paprika	2 medium onions, sliced
Black pepper	3 to 4 garlic cloves, minced
Garlic salt	5 cups water
Salt	½ cup dry red wine

1. Sprinkle paprika, pepper, garlic salt, and salt on the meat and rub in well.
2. Heat oil in a low stewing pot. Add onions and sauté until golden.
3. Add meat and brown on both sides. Add garlic and enough water to cover meat. Cover pot and cook over medium heat 1½ hours.
4. Add wine and continue to cook over low heat until sauce is thick and brown. Let cool.
5. Remove meat to a platter and slice. Place sauce in a saucepan. Heat sauce just before serving and pour over meat.
   Serve with potatoes, boiled rice or cooked vegetable.

Preparation and Cooking Time: 2 to 3 hours

Italian Steak, Olives and Potatoes

Dalia Carmel   Italian Style
New York, New York   Yields: 6 Servings

I am a collector of cookbooks, so I adapted this from a recipe I received from a woman who wrote several cookbooks about old Italian neighborhoods that no longer exist in Wisconsin. D.C.

2 cups flavored
  bread crumbs
2 teaspoons Italian
  seasoning
1 tablespoon parsley,
  chopped
Salt and pepper
Olive oil
1 medium onion, sliced

3 pounds round steak
  or London broil,
  cut into serving pieces
2 cups tomatoes, chopped
  or 1 can tomatoes,
  crushed
4 to 5 potatoes, peeled
  and quartered
1 can black olives, drained
  and pitted

1. Preheat oven to 325° F.
2. Mix bread crumbs with Italian seasonings, parsley, salt and pepper in one dish. Pour olive oil in a second shallow dish.
3. Add olive oil to a frying pan. Sauté onion until soft. Add chopped tomatoes and season with salt and pepper. Cook briefly.
4. Dip each piece of meat in oil then in breadcrumbs mixture. Arrange around pan.
5. Pour onion/tomato mixture over steak and potatoes. Top with olives. Bake, uncovered, in 325° F oven 1½ hours.

Preparation and Cooking Time: 2 hours

Rolled Cabbage

Janet Siegel England
Prairie Village, Kansas Yields: 6 to 8 Servings

I got this recipe from my grandmother via my mother from England.

1 whole cabbage, medium size	2 8-ounce cans tomato sauce
2 pounds chopped beef or turkey	2 tablespoons lemon juice
4 tablespoons oil	¼ cup brown sugar
1 onion, chopped	2 6-ounce cans tomato paste

1. Preheat oven to 375° F.
2. Place whole cabbage in a pot with cold water. Bring to a boil and cook 20 minutes. Drain and cool in pot.
3. Peel off leaves of cabbage and cut out thick ends.
4. Take chopped meat and place in each cabbage leaf. Fold each envelope style.
5. Place oil and onion in a pot and cook for 3 minutes. Place rolled cabbage pieces in pot then add tomato sauce and paste over the rolls. Add lemon juice and brown sugar. Add more brown sugar if you like.
6. Simmer for 1½ hours. Taste and adjust seasoning. If pot can be used in oven, place in oven, otherwise transfer to an oven casserole. Cook in 375° F oven 45 minutes.

This dish can be made beforehand and reheated before serving.

Preparation and Cooking Time: 3 hours

Hungarian Stuffed Cabbage
Magyar Tõltõtt Kãposzta-Tõltõtt Paprika

Ethel Quarnstrom/Emma Weiss   Hungary
                                                      Yields: 12 Servings

*Linda Radke, explains that this recipe came from her Aunt Ethel,
who was born in Hungary and was like a second mother to her.
Emma was Linda's grandmother, her mother's mother.*

Water	2½ to 3 pounds ground
2 medium-size	beef
cabbages	1½ cups long grain rice
Vegetable shortening	Salt and pepper to taste
2 pounds onions,	1 46-ounce can tomato
chopped	juice

1. Preheat oven to 350° F.
2. Trim and core cabbages. In a large pot, bring water to
   boil. Add cabbage heads. Lower heat and simmer 15
   minutes on each side until cabbage is softened.
3. Remove from pot to a colander. Carefully detach leaves.
4. In a frying pan, sauté onions in vegetable shortening. Place
   beef in a large mixing bowl. Add sautéed onions, rice and
   seasonings.
5. Lay each cabbage leaf on a flat surface. Place 1 to 2
   tablespoons sautéed beef mixture on each leaf. Roll leaves
   loosely. Place in large roaster. Cover with chopped
   leftover cabbage and onion. Pour tomato juice on top.
   Cover and cook slowly at 350° F 1 to 1¼ hours.

Preparation and Cooking Time: 2 hours

Note: From **That Hungarian's In My Kitchen** by Linda F.
Radke, Five Star Publications.

Stuffed Tomatoes
Farshirovaniya Pomidori

Svetlana Sorkin   Russia
Overland Park, Kansas   Yields: 6 to 8 Servings

I learned this from my Bubby who came from the Ukraine.

Oil   ½ pound ground beef
1 box mushrooms, minced   Salt and pepper to taste
1 onion, minced   1 tablespoon catsup
1 carrot, grated   20 to 30 Roma tomatoes
1 cup raw rice
3 tablespoons fresh
   parsley, minced

1. Preheat oven to 500° F.
2. Heat oil in a frying pan. Fry mushrooms approximately 10 minutes until cooked. Remove from pan to a bowl.
3. Fry carrot until cooked. Add to mushrooms.
4. Fry onion until golden in color. Remove and add to vegetables.
5. Wash rice and put in a saucepan. Cover with water and cook over low heat until all the water is absorbed. Add to vegetables.
6. Brown meat in pan. Add to vegetables and rice. Add salt, pepper, catsup and parsley and blend. Add more catsup if needed.
6. Cut off top of each tomato, scoop out insides and be careful to leave a bottom so each can stand up.
7. Stuff each tomato. Add a little water to a baking dish and stand up tomatoes in dish.
8. Reduce oven to 325° F to 350° F and place baking dish in oven. Bake approximately 10 minutes.

Preparation and Cooking Time: 30 minutes

Note: This is meant as a side dish.

Kubbeh, Kibbeh or Kibbee

Sybil Kaplan   Middle East
Overland Park, Kansas   Yields: 3 to 4 Servings

Cones	Filling
½ pound burghul	¼ cup margarine
Boiling water	1 to 2 onions, chopped
½ pound ground beef	¼ pound ground meat
1 onion, grated	⅛ cup pine nuts, or
½ teaspoon mint	sesame seed kernels
Salt and pepper to taste	Pinch cumin
¼ teaspoon cumin	Pinch cinnamon
½ teaspoon cinnamon	Oil
½ cup cold water	

1. Place burghul in a bowl. Pour boiling water on top. Let sit 30 minutes.
2. Add ½ pound meat, grated onion, mint, salt, pepper, cumin and cinnamon. Grind ingredients. Add water to make a smooth dough. Refrigerate.
3. Meantime, sauté 1 to 2 chopped onions in margarine. Add ¼ pound meat and brown. Add pine nuts or sesame seed kernels, cumin and cinnamon.
4. Remove shell mixture from refrigerator. Take a lump of mixture, form a cone, place 1 tablespoon filling inside and close. Make in torpedo shape. Continue until all burghul shell mixture and fillings are used.
5. Heat oil in a pan. Drop in cones and deep fry.

Preparation and Cooking Time: 1 to 1½ hours

Note: Burghul is a form of wheat, also called bulghur and bulgar.

Stuffed Grape Leaves

Sybil Kaplan   Middle East
Overland Park, Kansas   Yields: 20 Leaves

Someone in Israel gave this recipe to me.

Filling

Oil	½ teaspoon mint
1 onion, chopped	½ teaspoon cinnamon
⅜ cup rice	20 grape leaves
¾ pound ground meat	2 tablespoons lemon juice
Salt and pepper to taste	2 garlic cloves, slivered
1 small tomato, chopped	Water
1 tablespoon parsley, chopped	

1. Heat oil in a frying pan. Fry onion until golden. Add rice and continue to fry about 10 minutes. Remove to a bowl.
2. Add meat, salt, pepper, tomato, parsley, mint and cinnamon.
3. Place water in a pot. Heat to boiling. Plunge in leaves for a few minutes to soften. Remove to a board or table.
4. Place 1 heaping teaspoon filling in the center of each leaf near stem end. Roll up like a cigar, folding together sides toward middle. Place leaves on bottom of pot. Pack tightly.
5. Add lemon juice and water to cover and garlic. Place a plate over the leaves to prevent them from coming undone. Cover pot and cook 1 to 2 hours at low heat.

Preparation and Cooking Time: 2½ hours

Note: Grape leaves are really the large green leaves of the grapevine and are used in Greek and Middle Eastern recipes. Simmering in water for 10 minutes makes them pliable enough to use in this recipe.

Rachel's Tunisian Boulette

Sybil Kaplan
Overland Park, Kansas

Middle East
Yield: 16 Meatballs

Living in Israel was a great adventure for me. In one particular apartment building my neighbors were from Tunisia, Syria, the U.S. and several other backgrounds. I watched my neighbor, Rachel, make this dish and jotted it down as she explained it.

2 to 3 potatoes, peeled	2 slices bread
Salt	Salt and pepper to taste
2 large onions, grated	Cinnamon
1 pound ground meat	1 egg, beaten
½ cup parsley, minced	Oil
¼ cup mint, minced	2 tablespoons tomato paste
¼ cup dill, minced	1 tablespoon chicken soup
Little coriander	powder
(Italian parsley)	

1. Cut potatoes into slices 3 inches long and 2½ inches wide. Place in colander. Sprinkle salt on top.
2. Place onions with meat, parsley, mint, dill and coriander in one bowl.
3. Place bread in another bowl with water and break up pieces. Add salt, pepper, and cinnamon and meat. Make meat mixture into meatballs. Wrap a potato slice around each meatball. Place egg in a bowl and beat. Dip potato-covered meatballs in egg.
4. Heat oil in a pan. Fry each potato-covered meatball until brown. Place in a soup pot. Add a little water but not enough to cover the meatballs. Add tomato paste and soup powder and cover pot. Cook on low heat 20 to 30 minutes or until water cooks down to half.

Preparation and Cooking Time: 1 hour

Irit's Stuffed Cauliflower

Sybil Kaplan   Israel
Overland Park, Kansas   Yield: 4 Servings

Irit's husband was part of the Consular Corps from Israel in Chicago, and she gave me this recipe.

1 to 2 pound cauliflower, washed and quartered	Flour
	Oil or margarine
1 teaspoon salt	1 to 2 onions, sliced
1 pound ground beef	2 tablespoons catsup
Salt and pepper to taste	3 tablespoons water
1 medium onion, minced	
1 to 2 eggs	

1. Place quartered cauliflower in a bowl with water and 1 teaspoon salt. Leave 15 minutes then drain. Make sure it is clean.
2. In a bowl, mix meat, salt, pepper and minced onion. Stuff inside flowerets.
3. Beat eggs in a shallow bowl; place flour in a second bowl. Dip cauliflower first in eggs then in flour.
4. Heat oil in a frying pan. Fry cauliflower until brown. Place in a soup pot.
5. Add oil or margarine to the frying pan and brown the sliced onion. Add catsup and water and mix to a paste. Pour over cauliflower. Add enough water to cover half the cauliflower in depth. Bring to a boil. Reduce heat and cook until tender.

Serve as an appetizer with olives and parsley garnishes or as a main entree with rice, eggplant soufflé, salad and wine.

Preparation and Cooking Time: 30 to 45 minutes

Greek Macaroni-Meat Pie
Pastitso

Sybil Kaplan   Greek Style
Overland Park, Kansas   Yield: 4 Servings

I created this from a combination of many recipes so it would be kosher.

2 to 2½ cups elbow or shell macaroni	1 tablespoon parsley, chopped
2 tablespoons margarine	¼ teaspoon sugar
⅛ teaspoon nutmeg	Salt and pepper to taste
Salt and pepper to taste	2½ tablespoons margarine
2 eggs	¼ cup flour
1 tablespoon margarine	1½ cups non-dairy creamer
½ onion, chopped	
1 garlic clove, crushed	⅛ teaspoon nutmeg
¾ pound ground meat	Salt and pepper to taste
1½ tablespoons tomato paste	1 egg
¼ cup wine	1 tablespoon margarine pieces
¼ cup beef bouillon	Paprika

1. Preheat oven to 350°F.
2. Place water in a saucepan. Add macaroni to boiling water with salt. Cook until tender, drain and set aside in a bowl.
3. Add 2 tablespoons margarine, nutmeg, salt and pepper on macaroni and toss. Let cool.
4. When cool, add 2 eggs, toss and set aside.
5. Heat margarine in a frying pan. Sauté onion and garlic until onion is soft. Add meat and brown. Add tomato paste, wine, bouillon, parsley, sugar, salt and pepper. Cover and simmer 20 minutes.
6. Melt 2½ tablespoons margarine in a saucepan. Stir in flour to make a roux. Cook 2 minutes. Add non-dairy creamer and bring to a boil. Cook 1 minute. Add nutmeg, salt and pepper. Set aside to cool. Add egg.

7. Add ¼ of the sauce to the meat mixture and stir. Grease a casserole. Spoon half the macaroni, all the meat sauce, rest of the macaroni and top with cream sauce. Scatter margarine pieces on top. Sprinkle with paprika. Bake in a 350° F oven for 50 minutes.

Preparation and Cooking Time: 1½ hours

"Thus shall they prepare the lamb, the grain offering and the oil..." (Ezekiel 46:15)

Irit's Moussaka

Sybil Kaplan   Israel
Overland Park, Kansas   Yield: 6 To 8 Servings

*I met Irit and her husband, Gabby, in Chicago when he was part of
the Israel Consul General's office. One of their families came from
Turkey and Irit gave me this recipe.*

2 medium eggplants	Topping
Salt	2 tablespoons margarine
⅓ cup olive oil	2 tablespoons flour
1 medium onion, chopped	1 cup water
1 to 2 pounds ground beef	2 eggs
2 garlic cloves, minced	½ teaspoon salt
½ teaspoon oregano	Dash nutmeg
½ teaspoon thyme	
Dash cinnamon	
Dash pepper	
1 cup tomato paste	

1. Slice eggplants lengthwise ½-inch thick. Salt slices. Let
   sit in colander 20 to 30 minutes. Wash in water and dry.
2. Heat oil in a frying pan. Sauté eggplant a few minutes.
   Remove to a plate. Blot on paper towels.
3. Sauté onion. Add beef and brown about 10 minutes. Add
   garlic, oregano, thyme, cinnamon, pepper and tomato paste.
   Stir. Reduce heat, cover and cook 30 minutes. If sauce is
   cooking out, add hot water.
4. Melt margarine in a saucepan. Stir in flour. Add water to
   make a sauce. Beat eggs in a dish and add to sauce. Add
   salt and pepper.
   Grease a baking dish. Place ⅓ eggplant slices, ½ meat
   sauce, second third eggplant, rest of meat sauce, last of
   eggplant and white sauce on top. Bake in a preheated
   350°F oven for 40 minutes.

Preparation and Cooking Time: 2 to 2¼ hours

Note: Moussaka is originally from Greece but is popular throughout the Mediterranean.

Letcho with Meat

Dalia Carmel   Hungary
New York, New York   Yield: 4 to 6 Servings

*My mother was born in Riga and emigrated to Palestine in the
1930s. This was the way she used to make this Hungarian dish.*

3 tablespoons margarine	Salt and pepper to taste
1 tablespoon olive oil	1 teaspoon caraway seed
3 large onions, chopped	(optional)
4 large peppers, chopped	4 to 8 frankfurters or
1 heaping tablespoon	Hungarian thin salami,
sweet paprika	sliced
5 large tomatoes, chopped	2 eggs

1. Heat margarine and oil in a large pan. Sauté onions until
   limp. Add peppers and sauté, mixing a lot, until limp and
   onions are slightly brown.
2. Add paprika and mix well for a few minutes. Add
   tomatoes and bring mixture to a boil. Reduce heat. Add
   salt, pepper and caraway seeds. Cover and simmer.
3. Boil frankfurters in a pot. If using salami, add here. Cool
   under water and slice ½-inch thick. Add to vegetables.
   Bring to a simmer and mix well. When done and tomatoes
   have exuded their liquid and franks are hot, beat the two
   eggs together in a bowl and add into the hot mixture,
   mixing all the time so the eggs do not curdle.

This can be served as an appetizer or main dish.

If preparing ahead of time, prepare up to addition of eggs.

Preparation and Cooking Time: 30 minutes

Mutton Vindaloo

Solomon Michael Daniel   India
Bombay, Maharashtra   Yield: 4 Servings

This recipe came from the Bene-Israel Jews.

2 pounds mutton *   1 teaspoon cumin seeds
¾ cup vinegar   10 peppercorns
½ cup oil   10 red chilies
12 garlic cloves   Salt to taste
2-inch ginger piece
10 cloves
5 cinnamon sticks
3 teaspoons coriander seeds

1. Wash and drain meat thoroughly.
2. Grind all spices in vinegar.
3. Heat oil in a pot. Add spices and fry for a few minutes
   until oil separates out. Add mutton, salt and remaining
   vinegar and cook in its own water on a low heat until meat
   is ready and oil separates out. This will remain in good
   condition for a long time. Serve with bread or chapati.

   * Mutton is lamb more than a year old, has a stronger
   flavor and is less tender.

Preparation and Cooking Time: 1 to 2 hours

Mutton Alveress
Marathi - Mutton Alveress

Solomon Michael Daniel
Bombay, Maharashtra

India
Yield: 4 Servings

This recipe is followed by all Bene-Israelis of India from generation to generation.

Black peppercorns
Cloves
Cardamon
Cinnamon or 2 teaspoons
  Garam Masala powder
1 kilo (2.2 pounds) mutton
Salt
6 green chilies
6 red chilies
3-inch piece ginger

12 flakes garlic
1 teaspoon Khus Khus
1 coconut, prepared
10 onions
8 potatoes
Salt to taste
¾ teaspoon turmeric
  powder
2 teaspoons ground
  coriander
6 tablespoons oil

1. Pound pepper, cloves, cardamon and cinnamon together to make Garam Masala.
2. Clean, wash and salt mutton. Set aside. Wash again and drain.
3. Grind chilies, ginger, garlic, Khus Khus and coconut to a fine paste.
4. Peel onions and potatoes. Cut into thick rounds. Soak potatoes in water for a little while to remove starch.
5. Apply salt, turmeric, coriander, Garam Masala and ground spices to mutton, then onions, then potatoes.
6. Heat oil in a deep and broad vessel like a casserole with a tight-fitting lid.
7. Arrange onions, meat and potatoes in layers until the top layer is potatoes. Put on lid, cook on top of stove over medium heat. Do not stir.
8. When meat is cooked, serve from bottom layer first.

Preparation and Cooking Time: 1 to 2 hours

Note: Mutton is lamb that is a year old or older. Garam
Masala is a blend of ground spices. It is available in Indian
markets. Khus Khus are poppy seeds.
Coconut has to be cracked open, coconut removed from shell,
and grated.

How do you make your own curry powder?

Blend ½ teaspoon poppy seeds, ½ teaspoon mustard seeds,
½ teaspoon ginger, ½ teaspoon black pepper,
½ teaspoon chili powder, 1 teaspoon cumin, and
2 teaspoons turmeric.

Store in airtight jar.

Middle East Lamb Riblets, with Eggplant

Sybil Kaplan
Overland Park, Kansas

Middle East
Yield: 4 Servings

¾ **pound lamb riblets**
⅓ **cup tomato juice**
1 **tablespoon**
  Worcestershire sauce
½ **teaspoon dry mustard**
1½ **teaspoons brown sugar**
1½ **tablespoons vinegar**
1½ **tablespoons onion, chopped**

1 **eggplant, chopped**
1 **8-ounce can tomato paste**
½ **teaspoon beef soup**
  powder
⅓ **cup red wine**
2 **garlic cloves, crushed**

Night before:
1. Place lamb in a glass baking dish.
2. In a bowl, combine tomato juice, Worcestershire sauce, dry mustard, brown sugar, vinegar and onion. Pour over lamb and refrigerate overnight.
Next day:
3. Preheat oven to 350°F.
4. Arrange eggplant around dish with lamb in center. Pour marinade on top.
5. In a bowl, combine tomato paste, beef soup powder, wine and garlic. Pour on top. Bake in a 350°F oven for 1 hour.

Serve with rice.

Preparation and Cooking Time: 13¼ hours

Greek Veal Stiffado

Sybil Kaplan   Greece
Overland Park, Kansas   Yield: 4 Servings

*When I lived in Jerusalem, it was common practice for the various
hotels to sponsor ethnic food weeks. On one occasion, the Jerusalem
Hilton had a Greek week and the Athens Hilton chef came and
cooked kosher Greek dishes. This was a recipe they gave out to
members of the press invited to sample the special fare.*

3 pounds veal cubes	1 cup white wine
1 cup olive oil	Salt and white pepper
1 cup onions, chopped	to taste
2 cups canned stewed	4 garlic cloves, crushed
tomatoes	1 teaspoon rosemary
Pearl onions	

1. Preheat oven to 300° F.
2. Place veal in a greased roasting pan. Roast until half
   cooked in a 300° F oven about 20 minutes.
3. In a saucepan, heat oil. Sauté onions. Add tomatoes, pearl
   onions, white wine, salt, pepper, garlic and rosemary.
   Reduce heat and simmer 1 hour.
4. Add sauce to veal and continue cooking 15 to 20 minutes.

Serve with roast potatoes.

Preparation and Cooking Time: 2 hours

Stuffed Breast of Veal
Chazirello (Pancetta di Vitella Ripiena) Piglet

Edda Servi Machlin   Italy
Croton-on-Hudson, New York   Yield: 6 Servings

Some time ago I received a telephone call from the widow of the historian Cecil Roth who asked me whether I knew why the Jews of Pitigliano called this delicious kosher dish, chazirello, piglet. She and her late husband had found the recipe in ancient Italian-Judaeo dialect (which used Hebrew lettering) during one research trip they took many years ago to Pitigliano. I didn't know for certain, but I could imagine the reason. In the early autumn, in the main piazza in Pitigliano, a big open-air fair took place....In the middle of the square loomed a pushcart that sold hot slices of porchetta, a stuffed roasted piglet which sent forth delicious aromas. The Jews, who refrained from eating pork to obey their dietary laws, were envious of their fellow Pitiglianesi and invented this dish which, of course, doesn't use any pork.

Edda Servi Machlin was born in Pitigliano, Italy, the descendant of Italian-Jewish families who had lived in Italy for almost 2,000 years.

4 pounds breast of veal
2 cloves garlic, crushed
Salt
Freshly ground pepper
1 teaspoon fennel seeds
½ boneless, skinless
   chicken breast
¾ pound cubed,
   lean beef

2 thick slices stale bread
   cooked into a pap*
1 egg, slightly beaten
¼ cup raw, unsalted
   pistachio nuts or
   walnut meats
Dash or two nutmeg
1 teaspoon fresh or
½ teaspoon dry
   rosemary

1. Preheat oven to 350° F.
2. Open the pocket of the breast of veal completely as you open a book or have your butcher do it. Painstakingly remove and discard as much fat as possible. Rub with garlic on both sides, then sprinkle with salt and pepper to taste.
3. Spread open the breast, rib side down, over a working surface and sprinkle with fennel.
4. Grind together chicken breast and beef. Combine meats with pap, egg, nuts, nutmeg and salt and pepper to taste. Mix well.
5. Spread this mixture over the rib half of the open breast then close the other half over it. Sew the sides closed, using thread and needle or fasten with a string.
6. Sprinkle all over with rosemary. Place in a baking pan, rib side down. Bake in a 350° F oven for 2½ hours or until quite brown and crisp. Remove from oven, cover with clean kitchen towel, and let stand 10 minutes before serving.

* To make the bread pap that is generally used to soften ground-meat patties and loaves, place the stale bread in a saucepan with cold water to cover and let it soak until swollen and soft. Pour out any excess of water and cook the bread, stirring until quite dry.

Preparation and Cooking Time: 3 hours

From: The **Classic Cuisine of the Italian Jews II**, Giro Press, P.O. Box 203, Croton-on-Hudson, New York 10520

South American Liver in Wine Sauce

Hilda Meth
Richmond, Virginia

South American Style
Yield: 3 to 4 Servings

2 tablespoons margarine
1 pound liver,
  cut in pieces
¼ cup dry sherry or
  Madeira wine

2 tablespoons parsley,
  chopped
1 tablespoon lemon juice
1 teaspoon salt

1. Melt margarine in a frying pan. Add liver, cook and stir 4 to 5 minutes.
2. Add wine, parsley, lemon juice and salt. Cook until done.

Serve on rice.

Preparation and Cooking Time: 15 minutes

Baked Franks

Dorothy Kaplan
Kansas City, Missouri   Yield: 4 To 6 Servings

8 to 10 frankfurters	¼ teaspoon salt
¼ cup onion, chopped	3 tablespoons vinegar
Oil	6 tablespoons catsup
2 teaspoons sugar	2 teaspoons
¾ teaspoon dry mustard	Worcestershire sauce
1 teaspoon paprika	½ cup water

1. Preheat oven to 350° F.
2. Split franks in half lengthwise. Place cut side down in a 6x10-inch greased baking dish.
3. In a frying pan, heat oil and sauté onion until golden. Add sugar, dry mustard, paprika, salt, vinegar, catsup, Worcestershire sauce and water to pan and stir well. Bring to a boil, reduce heat and simmer 15 minutes. Pour over franks. Bake in a 350° F oven for 15 minutes. Baste frequently.

Preparation and Cooking Time: 45 minutes

Vegetables

Israeli Vegetable Souffle

Sybil Kaplan   Israel
Overland Park, Kansas   Yield: 4 Servings

*I started making this dish in Israel and although it is a guess, I think
I received the recipe from an Israeli friend, Yehudit, a noted artist. I
ate many meals in her home, particularly on Friday evenings and
Shabbat, and she always fixed special dishes. Since the main meal
was mid-day, even Friday evening was often dairy and I seem to
recall this was one of the recipes she made and gave to me.*

Cauliflower, squash, corn	**Salt and pepper to taste**
or mushrooms for 4	**2 eggs**
2 tablespoons margarine	**Yellow cheese slices**
2 tablespoons flour	**Parmesan cheese**
1½ cups milk	**Paprika**
½ cup vegetable water	

1. Preheat oven to 350°F.
2. Cook vegetable in water to soften. Drain but save the
   water.
3. Melt margarine in a saucepan. Add flour to make a roux.
   Add milk, vegetable water, salt and pepper and cook until
   thick.
4. Separate eggs. Add yolks to cream sauce. Whip whites
   until stiff, then gently fold into sauce.
5. Place vegetables in greased casserole. Lay yellow cheese
   on top. Pour the white sauce over. Sprinkle with
   Parmesan cheese and paprika. Bake in a 350°F oven for
   25 to 30 minutes. Serve immediately.

Preparation and Cooking Time: 1 hour

Irit's Okra au Gratin

Sybil Kaplan
Overland Park, Kansas

Israel
Yield: 4 To 6 Servings

Members of the Israel Consul General's office in Chicago were always holding wonderful small dinner parties where the dishes of the wives were always special. Because I was a lecturer associated with their speaker's bureau, I often was invited to these dinners and Irit and I became friends. She gave me this recipe.

Oil
1 onion, sliced
2 pounds okra, washed,
  peeled and dried
Water
1 garlic clove, crushed

Salt and pepper to taste
1 tablespoon tomato paste
  (optional)
Parmesan cheese
2 slices Swiss cheese

1. Preheat oven to 350°F.
2. Place oil in a saucepan. Sauté onion until brown. Add okra, water, garlic, salt and pepper. Simmer until okra is tender. Add tomato paste.
3. Grease a baking dish. Place okra and onions in dish. Sprinkle Parmesan cheese on top. Bake in a 350°F oven for 10 to 15 minutes. Switch to broil, add Swiss cheese on top and brown before serving.

Preparation and Cooking Time: 30 to 40 minutes

Dairy Moussaka

Sybil Kaplan
Overland Park, Kansas

Greece
Yield: 6 to 8 Servings

One week, the Jerusalem Hilton hotel declared a Greek food festival and offered all kinds of wonderful Greek foods cooked by the Athens Hilton chef. This was one of the recipes offered to the press and I received it.

Oil	½ cup flour
1 pound eggplant, peeled and sliced	2 cups milk
1 pound squash, sliced	Tomatoes, sliced
3 tablespoons butter	1 cup yellow cheese, grated

1. Preheat oven to 350°F.
2. Place oil in a frying pan. Fry eggplant and squash until just beginning to get tender (5 minutes).
3. Melt butter in a saucepan. Add flour and stir. Add milk and mix well to make a thickening sauce.
4. Grease a casserole. Put layers of eggplant, tomato slices, squash and sauce. Repeat, ending with sauce on top. Sprinkle on yellow cheese. Bake in a 350°F oven for 20 to 30 minutes.

Preparation and Cooking Time: 45 minutes

Baked Tomatoes Italian

Shara Zimmerman
Overland Park, Kansas

Italian Style
Yield: 4 Servings

Sybil says she thinks her daughter, Shara, got some of the family cooking creativity and made this up.

4 tomatoes, cut in half
Salt and pepper to taste
2 tablespoons bread crumbs
2 tablespoons olive oil

1 garlic clove, crushed
Pale yellow Romano-type
cheese, grated
Basil

1. Cut tomatoes in half. Place in greased baking dish. Sprinkle each with salt and pepper.
2. Mix together bread crumbs, oil and garlic. Sprinkle over tomatoes. Sprinkle on cheese and basil. Broil until brown.

Preparation and Cooking Time: 15 minutes

How do you make your own Italian seasoning?

Combine: 2 tablespoons rosemary, 2 tablespoons thyme, 3 tablespoons basil, 3 tablespoons marjoram, and 2 tablespoons oregano.

Store in a jar.

Ella's Creamed Spinach

Dalia Carmel
New York, New York

Israeli
Yield: 6 Servings

This is my mother's recipe. She always kept a portion for me when I came home on the weekend. My mother was born in Riga, studied medicine in Riga and Germany and emigrated to Palestine in the early 1930s. I was born in Jerusalem.

2 cups water
Salt
4 10-ounce packages frozen
  chopped spinach
3 to 4 tablespoons margarine
  or butter
2 tablespoons flour

½ cup slivered almonds
  (optional)
1 to 2 cloves of garlic
¼ to ½ teaspoon nutmeg
Pepper
Half-and-half
1 tablespoon butter or
  margarine, cut into bits

1. Bring water and salt to a boil in a saucepan. Add spinach. Bring to a boil again, reduce heat and simmer 10 minutes. Drain and squeeze as much water out as possible but retain some of the water on the side.
2. Heat the butter or margarine in a sauce pan. Add the flour to make a roux. Mix until golden. If you use slivered almonds, add and sauté until light brown.
3. Puree spinach in food processor with garlic, adding some of the spinach cooking water, nutmeg, pepper and additional salt if necessary.
4. Transfer spinach to pan and stir vigorously, incorporating the roux and almonds. To get a creamy consistency, add half-and-half, stirring a little at a time until you get the creaminess desired.
5. Before serving, add butter or margarine bits, reheat and serve.

Preparation and Cooking Time: 35 to 45 minutes

Turkish-Style Eggplant and Vegetables

Dora Levy   Middle East
Kansas City, Missouri   Yield: 4 to 6 Servings

*My husband Sam's parents came from Istanbul, Turkey. I know
eggplant is very popular in Turkey, though I don't have any recipes
from his family, so when I found this I started making it.*

Olive oil
1 onion, chopped
1 green pepper, chopped
1 rib celery, chopped
2 garlic cloves, crushed
1 eggplant,
  peeled and cubed
Salt and pepper to taste

1 8-ounce can tomato
  sauce or
1 8-ounce can tomato paste
or 1 16-ounce can whole
  tomatoes
½ teaspoon oregano
  (optional)

1. Heat olive oil in a frying pan. Sauté onion, green pepper,
   celery and garlic a few minutes. Add eggplant, salt and
   pepper and continue sautéing until vegetables start to get
   soft.
2. Add tomato sauce or paste or tomatoes and oregano if
   using. Cover and simmer for 20 minutes.

This is a nice side dish for a meat meal.
For a dairy meal, place vegetables in a greased casserole
after adding tomato product, add Parmesan cheese or
mozzarella cheese on top and bake in a 350°F oven 20 to
30 minutes.

Preparation and Cooking Time: 30 minutes to 1 hour

Squash-Potato Pancakes

Marilyn Landes   Israel
Jerusalem, Israel   Yield: 4 Servings

*Marilyn has lived in Israel since 1949, having come from Revere,
Massachusetts, originally. She teaches at the David Yellin Teachers
College, is active in organizations, does folk dancing, has authored
several books and commutes to Tel Aviv area often to see her
grandchildren. She was a neighbor and friend of your editor and she
gave this recipe to me more than 20 years ago.*

1 pound squash, peeled and grated coarsely	Dash pepper
2 very large potatoes, peeled and grated coarsely	¼ cup cornmeal or flour *
	½ onion, grated
	Carrot, grated (optional)
1 egg	Oil
Dash salt	

1. Mix together in a bowl, squash, potatoes, egg, salt, pepper,
   cornmeal, onion and carrot if used. Blend well.
2. Heat oil in a frying pan. Spoon pancakes in oil and fry
   until brown on both sides. Drain on paper toweling.

   * On Pesach, matzah meal or potato flour can be used.

   This can also be put into a greased casserole and baked as
   a kugel in a 350° F oven for 30 minutes.

Preparation and Cooking Time: 30 minutes to 1 hour

Vegetarian Falafel Loaf

The Quaker Oats Company
Chicago, Illinois

Middle East Style
Yield: 4 Servings

This meatless and mildly spicy dish combines the wholesome goodness of wheat germ, garbanzo beans, and fava beans with spices, onion, garlic and parsley for an authentic Middle East dish. Preparing this dish in a loaf pan is an interesting alternative to the traditional party method.

2 6-ounce packages Near East falafel vegetable burger mix 1 8-ounce can no-salt or regular tomato sauce ½ cup water	2 eggs, lightly beaten ½ cup carrots, shredded ½ cup celery, finely chopped ½ cup onions, finely chopped

1. Preheat oven to 350° F. Lightly butter a 9x5-inch loaf pan.
2. Combine in a bowl falafel, tomato sauce, water and eggs. Stir in carrots, celery and onions and mix well.
3. Lightly pat mixture into pan, making surface smooth and even. Bake in a 350° F oven for 55 to 60 minutes. Let stand 5 minutes before removing from pan and slicing.

Preparation and Cooking Time: 1 hour, 10 minutes

Middle East Beets

Sybil Kaplan
Overland Park, Kansas

Middle East
Yield: 4 Servings

2 cups sliced beets	½ teaspoon horseradish
1½ teaspoons oil	Salt to taste
1 tablespoon lemon juice	2 tablespoons beet juice
1 teaspoon mayonnaise	

1. Place beets in a bowl or jar.
2. Add oil, lemon juice, mayonnaise, horseradish, salt and beet juice. Shake well. Refrigerate 1 hour.

Preparation and Cooking Time: 1 hour, 10 minutes

What's a unique way to serve beets?

Buy them fresh and bake them like potatoes, served with margarine or butter.

Pareve

Egyptian Broad Beans
Ful

Sybil Kaplan
Overland Park, Kansas

Middle East Style
Yield: 6 Servings

Like many of the big hotels in Israel, the Tel Aviv Sheraton often invited members of the press to special meals where their chefs were trying out new dishes. This is one created by one of their chefs who passed out this recipe to me.

2 pounds fava or
   broad beans
Water
Oil
1 tomato, sliced
1 onion, sliced

7 ounces tomato paste
1 8-ounce can tomato
   sauce
1 green pepper, sliced
1 red pepper, sliced

Day before serving:
1. Place beans in a soup pot. Cover with water and soak overnight.
Next day:
2. Put beans on to cook, bring to a boil and cook for 3 hours or until soft. Drain.
3. Place oil in a frying pan. Fry tomato and onion until limp. Add tomato paste, tomato sauce, green pepper and red pepper. Cook until peppers are soft.
4. In another pan, add some oil and fry beans for a few minutes. Pour sauce on top.

Preparation and Cooking Time: 27 hours

Baked Eggplant

Dora Levy
Kansas City, Missouri   Yield: 4 Servings

I took this recipe out of a newspaper more than 20 years ago and changed it.

1 medium eggplant, peeled and sliced	¼ cup vinegar
Salt and pepper to taste	¼ cup olive oil
Onion, sliced	½ cup water
Tomatoes, sliced	1 can tomato sauce
Green pepper, sliced	1 tablespoon sugar

1. Preheat oven to 325° F.
2. Grease a rectangular baking dish. Layer eggplant in the bottom. Sprinkle with salt and pepper.
3. Layer all of the onion on top of the eggplant slices, then add the tomatoes on top of the onion slices. Layer the green pepper slices on top of the tomatoes.
4. Mix in a bowl the vinegar, oil, water, tomato sauce and sugar. Pour on top of the vegetables in the baking dish. Bake in a 325° F oven for 20 to 30 minutes.

Preparation and Cooking Time: 40 minutes

If a recipe calls for 2 cups tomato sauce, you can substitute 5½ ounces tomato paste plus water to equal 2 cups.

Pareve

Okra and Tomatoes

Sybil Kaplan
Overland Park, Kansas   Yield: 6 Servings

I picked this recipe up in Israel. It's very popular in the Middle East.

1 pound okra, cut in half	4 tomatoes, diced
Water	Salt and pepper to taste
1 tablespoon margarine	½ teaspoon dry oregano
¼ cup onions, chopped	

1. Remove stems from okra, cut in half and place in a saucepan. Add 1 cup water, cover and cook 5 to 10 minutes, drain.
2. Melt margarine in another saucepan. Sauté onion, tomatoes, salt, pepper and oregano 10 minutes. Add okra. Cook another few minutes. Serve hot.

Preparation and Cooking Time: 25 minutes

Turnip/Parsnip Puree or Vegetable Pâte

Dalia Carmel
New York, New York   Yield: 1 Quart

1 pound turnips,*	3 tablespoons margarine
peeled and cut up	1 tablespoon olive oil
1 pound parsnips,	12 garlic cloves
peeled and cut up	Salt and pepper to taste
Water	Nutmeg (optional)
1 teaspoon salt	

1. Place turnips and parsnips in a saucepan. Add water and salt and parboil for 7 minutes. Drain.
2. In a heavy pan, melt margarine and oil. Add turnips and parsnips and garlic and cook on medium to low heat, covered, until vegetables are cooked through (about 15 minutes).
3. Place in food processor. Add salt, pepper and nutmeg, if using, and puree.

* You can also use only turnips or only parsnips.

This can be served as is, as a side vegetable or combined with the additional purees for a Vegetable Pâte.

Preparation and Cooking Time: 30 minutes

Parsnip/Carrot Puree or Vegetable Pâte

Dalia Carmel
New York, New York   Yield: 1 Quart

1 pound parsnips, peeled and cut into chunks	3 tablespoons margarine
1 pound carrots, peeled and cut into chunks	1 tablespoon olive oil
Water	12 garlic cloves
1 teaspoon salt	Salt and pepper to taste
	A few drops hot sauce
	Pinch nutmeg

1. Place parsnips and carrots in a saucepan. Add water and salt and parboil for 7 minutes. Drain.
2. In a heavy pan, melt margarine and oil. Add parsnips and carrots and garlic and cook on medium to low heat, covered, until vegetables are cooked through (about 15 minutes).
3. Place in food processor. Add salt, pepper, hot sauce and nutmeg and puree.

This can be served as is, as a side dish vegetable or combined with the additional purees for a Vegetable Pâte.

Preparation and Cooking Time: 30 minutes

Pea Puree or
Vegetable Pâte

Dalia Carmel
New York, New York   Yield: 1 Quart

1 24-ounce package	Nutmeg to taste
frozen green peas	3 tablespoons cream
Water	(for dairy meal) or
4 tablespoons margarine	3 tablespoons chicken soup
3 tablespoons flour	or non-dairy creamer
½ cup almonds, slivered	(for meat meal)*
Salt and pepper to taste	

1. Cook peas in a saucepan with water according to the package instructions. Drain well.
2. Puree peas in food processor.
3. In saucepan, melt margarine. Add flour and nuts and blend well. Brown a little over medium heat. Add peas, salt, pepper, nutmeg, cream or chicken soup or non-dairy creamer. Mix well.

* Since the other purees to be used in the vegetable pâte are pareve, you can use a pareve chicken soup or non-dairy creamer to keep it pareve.

This can be served as is, as a side vegetable or combined with the additional purees for a Vegetable Pâte.

Preparation and Cooking Time: 30 minutes

Vegetable Pâte

Dalia Carmel
New York, New York   Yield: 10 to 12 Servings

1 quart turnip/parsnip puree
1 quart parsnip/carrot puree
1 quart pea puree

1. Take a large glass loaf pan. Divide its space into three.
2. Layer the turnip/parsnip layer first, then a pea layer and finally the parsnip/carrot layer.

   Serve with a large ice-cream scoop. This will not unmold as none of the purees are mixed with gelatin or eggs to hold the form.

   You can also serve the purees on a plate with a small scoop or egg-shaped scoop and thus have three varied color balls on the plate.

Preparation and Cooking Time: 30 minutes

Tarragon mustard is good with fish or vegetables.
Combine in a processor or blender 1 cup dry mustard, ½ cup sugar, ⅜ cup tarragon vinegar and 1 tablespoon dry tarragon with ½ teaspoon salt. Gradually add ¼ cup olive oil. Blend or process until like mayonnaise.
Store in jar with lid.

Greek Stuffed Green Peppers

Soly Mizrahi   Greece
Mission, Kansas   Yield: 6 Servings

*I was born in Cairo, Egypt, but my mother came from Larissa,
Greece. I learned this from her and added my imagination.*

3 green peppers	**¼ teaspoon cumin**
¼ cup oil	**Dash black pepper**
1 onion, chopped	**Salt to taste**
1 cup instant rice	**1 15-ounce can crushed**
½ teaspoon oregano	**tomatoes**
½ teaspoon garlic, minced	**1 egg, beaten**
½ teaspoon dry dill	**¼ cup oil**
½ teaspoon dry parsley	**½ cup water**

1. Preheat oven to 350°F.
2. Wash and cut green peppers in half lengthwise. Remove
   crowns and seeds and throw away.
3. Pour ¼ cup oil in a frying pan and sauté onion until
   yellowish brown. Turn off heat. Add rice, oregano, garlic,
   dill, parsley, cumin, pepper, salt, ½ cup crushed tomatoes
   and beaten egg. Mix together and cook for 1 minute.
4. Stuff the green pepper halves ¾ full with the mixture,
   leaving room for the rice to swell.
6. Spray the bottom and sides of a glass baking dish with non-
   stick cooking spray. Arrange the stuffed peppers in the
   dish, placing them close together.
7. In a bowl, combine rest of crushed tomatoes, ¼ cup oil and
   water. Mix together.
8. Pour tomato mixture on top of peppers. Cover with foil.
   Bake in a 350°F oven for 1 hour and 20 minutes. After 1
   hour, check to see if there is any liquid left: if not, add a
   little water.

Preparation and Cooking Time: 1½ hours

Pareve

Ruth's Iraqi Stuffed Pumpkin

Sybil Kaplan
Overland Park, Kansas

Israel
Yield: 4 To 6 Servings

I know Ruth from Jerusalem, her family came from Iraq. She was a most inventive and creative cook who invited me often to share meals with her. I cannot remember an occasion when I did not walk away with a recipe such as this, something she had created that day. She told me the day she created this she had bought a whole pumpkin. Since it was small, she wanted to use it whole and not cut it. Cooking it this way, it kept its shape and color. When I asked for the recipe and we wanted to give it a name, we called it Iraqi Stuffed Pumpkin because Ruth's family came from Iraq--not the recipe!.

1 pound raw pumpkin
Margarine pieces
½ cup raw rice
Cinnamon
Ginger
½ teaspoon salt

1 cup water
¼ cup raisins
2 tablespoons nuts,
  chopped
Brown sugar

1. Preheat oven to 350°F.
2. Place pumpkin piece in a greased baking dish. Dot with margarine, sprinkle cinnamon on top. Bake in a 350°F oven for 30 minutes.
3. Place rice in a slightly oiled saucepan. Add cinnamon and ginger on top. Add the water and salt. Bring to a boil. Reduce heat, cover and simmer 15 minutes. Add inside pumpkin. Bake 1 hour.
4. Add raisins and nuts. Sprinkle brown sugar on top. Bake a few minutes more.

Preparation and Cooking Time: 2 hours

Squash Kugel

Sybil Kaplan
Overland Park, Kansas   Yield: 3 To 4 Servings

I made up this recipe in Israel when squash was plentiful, and I wanted a different side dish.

1½ **pounds squash,** **grated**	½ **cup flour**
1 **small onion, grated**	2 **eggs**
Salt	2 **tablespoons oil**
1 **small potato,** **peeled and grated**	1¼ **teaspoons** **baking powder**
	½ **teaspoon salt**

1. Preheat oven to 350°F.
2. Place squash and onion in a colander. Toss and sprinkle with salt. Let sit 1 hour. Rinse, drain and put in a bowl.
3. Add grated potato, flour, eggs, oil, baking powder and salt to squash and onion mixture. Mix well. Pour into a greased casserole. Bake in a 350°F oven 1 hour and 20 minutes. Cut into squares.

Preparation and Cooking Time: 1½ hours

Pareve

Ruth's Stuffed Squash

Sybil Kaplan   Israel
Overland Park, Kansas   Yield: 4 to 6 Servings

Ruth (mentioned earlier) and her family live in a Jerusalem suburb.
Friday evening dinner in their eclectically designed home was always
a chance for lots of different foods to be prepared. This is one she
created and she gave the recipe to me.

1 pound green squash	1 tomato, cut up
Oil	½ cup water
1 onion, chopped	4 ounces tomato paste
½ cup raw rice	1½ cups water
Turmeric or dill	½ teaspoon soy sauce
Pepper	to taste
Paprika	Salt and pepper to taste

1. Preheat oven to 275° F.
2. Lightly peel squash. Cut in half through middle, scoop out insides using a grapefruit spoon but don't break the skin. Place insides in bottom of greased casserole.
3. Heat oil in a frying pan. Fry outside of squash a few minutes. Remove. Add onion, rice, turmeric or dill, pepper, paprika and tomato. Cook until rice becomes light brown. Add ½ cup water. Simmer until water is cooked out.
4. Stuff this rice mixture into each squash. Place on top insides in casserole.
5. Mix tomato paste with 1½ cups water, soy sauce, salt and pepper. Pour over squash. Place in 275° F oven and cook about 1 hour, adding water if necessary until rice is soft.

Preparation and Cooking Time: 1½ hours

Tomatoes Printannieres

Sybil Kaplan
Overland Park, Kansas

Israel
Yield: 6 Servings

This recipe was given to me by the Tel Aviv Sheraton on an occasion when members of the press corps were invited, as we often were, to try out new dishes created by their chefs.

6 tomatoes, ripe,
   firm, same size
2 tablespoons mushrooms,
   minced
2 tablespoons parboiled
   peas

1 garlic clove, minced
Salt and pepper to taste
Margarine pieces

1. Preheat oven to 425°F.
2. Slice off the top of each tomato. Scoop out the pulp.
3. Combine mushrooms, peas, garlic, salt and pepper. Stuff inside each tomato. Top with margarine piece. Bake in a 425° F oven 6 to 8 minutes.

Preparation and Cooking Time: 15 minutes

Pareve

Irit's Cooked Turnips

Sybil Kaplan
Overland Park, Kansas   Yield: 4 Servings

*Irit and her family lived in Chicago for several years, where we met,
when her husband was part of the Israel Consulate General's office.
She was a great cook and I ate in her home often and she gave me
this recipe.*

Oil	**1 cup water**
1 large onion, sliced	**Salt and pepper to taste**
1 pound turnips,	**3 tablespoons flour**
peeled and sliced	**½ teaspoon rum**

1. Place oil in a saucepan. Sauté onions until light brown.
2. Add turnips, water, salt, pepper and flour. Reduce heat and
   cook over low heat until tender (15 to 20 minutes) and
   sauce is thick. Stir in rum.

Preparation and Cooking Time: 30 minutes

Hungarian Lecho

Sybil Kaplan   Hungarian Style
Overland Park, Kansas   Yield: 2 to 3 Servings

I picked up this recipe in Israel when I worked at a company that served this often in the cafeteria.

1 tablespoon oil	1½ cups tomatoes,
1 tablespoon margarine	chopped
¾ cup onions, chopped	1 teaspoon paprika
2½ cups green peppers,	Salt to taste
chopped	2 teaspoons chicken soup
	powder*

1. Heat oil and margarine in a soup pot. Fry onions until almost golden.
2. Add green peppers and tomatoes. Fry a few minutes.
3. Add paprika, salt and soup powder. Add a little water if needed. Bring to a boil. Reduce heat and simmer 20 minutes.

* To make pareve, use pareve chicken soup powder.

Preparation and Cooking Time: 50 to 60 minutes

Balkan Ghivetch

Sybil Kaplan   Balkan Style
Overland Park, Kansas   Yield: 6 Servings

I picked up this recipe in Israel.

½ cup beef broth or   Pepper to taste
  ½ cup water with   2 cups cauliflower
½ teaspoon beef soup   flowerets
  powder added*   1 eggplant, cut in
2 tablespoons oil   ½-inch pieces
1½ teaspoons tarragon   1 cup carrots, chopped
1½ teaspoons savory   1 onion, sliced
2 small garlic cloves,   2 small turnips, sliced
  minced   2 green pepper, sliced
2 bay leaves   2 tomatoes, cut up

1. Preheat oven to 350° F.
2. Place beef broth or water and beef soup powder in a soup
   pot. Add oil, tarragon, savory, garlic, bay leaves and
   pepper. Cook 5 minutes.
3. Place cauliflower, eggplant, carrots, onion, turnips, green
   pepper and tomatoes in a bowl and toss. Place in greased
   casserole. Pour soup mixture on top. Bake covered in
   350° F oven for 35 minutes.

   * To make this pareve, use pareve beef soup powder.

Preparation and Cooking Time: 45 minutes

Red Cabbage with Apples

Sybil Kaplan   Germany
Overland Park, Kansas   Yield: 4 to 6 Servings

This recipe comes from my mother, Marga Kretschmer, born in Berlin, Germany, who now lives in Buffalo, New York. She said this was passed down to her from her mother as a traditional German recipe.

Red cabbage	**½ cup sugar**
2 cups water	**2 tablespoons chicken fat**
Salt	**or gravy**
6 small cooking apples	
peeled	

1. Quarter cabbage, cut out most of the white and shred. Rinse.
2. Put in a saucepan with water and salt sprinkled over. Add apples, sugar, chicken fat or gravy. Cover and bring to a boil. Reduce heat and simmer until cabbage is soft and all apples blended. Add water if necessary.

This is better when reheated before serving.

Preparation and Cooking Time: 30 minutes

Shmaltz too high in cholesterol?

Sauté 1 large, minced onion in 2 cups vegetable oil with 2 grated carrots about 15 minutes until vegetables are soft. Strain, remove vegetables and pour oil in dish to cool. You can also add 1 teaspoon chicken soup powder to mixture while it sautés.

Cakes

Walnut Chocolate Chip Cake

Debra Levine   Russia
Phoenix, Arizona   Yield: 12 Servings

3 cups all-purpose flour	1¼ cups sour cream
3 teaspoons baking powder	½ cup sugar
1 teaspoon baking soda	1 teaspoon cinnamon
¼ pound + 1 tablespoon butter	1 teaspoon cocoa
1 cup sugar	½ cup walnuts, chopped
3 eggs	1 cup chocolate chips

1. Preheat oven to 350° F.
2. In a mixing bowl, sift together flour, baking powder and baking soda. Set this mixture aside.
3. In a second mixing bowl, cream together butter and sugar. Add eggs, one at a time, mixing well.
4. Add sour cream to creamed mixture. Add all to the dry ingredients.
5. Grease a tube pan. Pour in half the batter. Combine ½ cup sugar, cinnamon, cocoa, nuts and chocolate chips in a bowl.
6. Sprinkle half the sugar-cocoa-nut-chip mixture over batter. Pour on the rest of batter and remainder of topping. Place in a 350° F oven and bake approximately 1 hour or until a toothpick inserted comes out clean.

Preparation and Cooking Time: 1¼ hours

Note: From **Not just Desserts**.

Golden Butter Puffs or
Pull-a-Part Cake
Arangaluska

Ruth Gluck   Hungary
Phoenix, Arizona   Yield: 10 To 12 Servings

Linda Radke, says she received this recipe from Ruth, her mother's
sister, born in Hungary.

1 package yeast	1 cup warm milk
¼ cup warm water	½ pound butter, melted
1 teaspoon sugar	1 teaspoon lemon rind,
4 cups flour	grated
¼ cup sugar	1 cup sugar
¼ teaspoon salt	2 cups walnut meats,
4 eggs, beaten	ground

1. Preheat oven to 350°F.
2. Dissolve yeast in lukewarm water in a bowl with 1
   teaspoon sugar. Set aside for a few minutes.
3. In a large bowl, mix flour with ¼ cup sugar and salt. Add
   beaten eggs, milk, 4 tablespoons melted butter and yeast
   mixture. Mix and blend well.
4. Cover with a cloth and let stand in a warm place for about
   ½ hour until it rises to about double in bulk.
5. Mix lemon rind, sugar and walnuts in a bowl. Set aside.

6. Roll out dough on a floured surface to ⅛-inch thickness. Cut out rounds with a small cookie cutter. Butter a tube pan well. Sprinkle bottom with some of the lemon rind mixture. Arrange one layer of dough rounds, sprinkle with melted butter and nut mixture. Repeat the process until the pan is about three fourths full. Set aside and let rise in a warm place until dough rises to almost top of the pan. Bake in a 350° F oven for 35 to 40 minutes.

Preparation and Cooking Time: 2 hours

Note: From **That Hungarian's In My Kitchen** by Linda F. Radke, Five Star Publications.

"She took the dough and kneaded it into cakes...and baked the cakes" *(II Samuel 13:8)*

Dvora's Coconut Crumb Cake

Sybil Kaplan
Overland Park, Kansas   Yield: 12 Servings

Dvora and her family and I met more than 25 years ago as we all stood in line to board the boat to take us to Israel. We became friends on the boat and maintained the friendship during my years in Jerusalem and theirs, first on a kibbutz, then up north. They originally came from California with three teenagers. All of their children subsequently settled in Israel. Dvora gave me this recipe.

250 grams (9 ounces) margarine	**2 cups stale cake crumbs**
½ cup sugar	**1 cup coconut**
½ cup brown sugar	**1 cup peanuts, chopped**
4 eggs	**3 teaspoons baking powder**
2 teaspoons vanilla	**1 cup milk**

1. Preheat oven to 350°F.
2. In a mixing bowl, blend margarine, sugars, eggs and vanilla.
3. In a second bowl, combine cake crumbs, coconut, nuts, and baking powder. Add to creamed mixture alternately with milk.
4. Pour batter into a greased rectangular cake pan. Bake in a 350°F oven for 35 minutes.

Preparation and Cooking Time: 45 minutes

Safra's English Cake

Sybil Kaplan   Israel
Overland Park, Kansas   Yield: 12 Servings

*Safra and Amnon became friends of mine when they lived in Chicago
and he was head of the Israel Government Tourist office there. She
gave me this recipe, but I have no idea of its origin.*

1½ cups sugar	1½ cups flour
200 grams (7 ounces)	1 teaspoon baking powder
unsalted margarine	1 teaspoon instant coffee
4 eggs	1 teaspoon cocoa
6 ounces plain yogurt	2 teaspoons boiling water
1 teaspoon lemon juice	Raisins (optional)
1 teaspoon vanilla	Nuts, chopped (optional)

1. Preheat oven to 350°F.
2. In a mixing bowl, cream sugar with margarine and eggs.
   Add yogurt.
3. Add lemon juice and vanilla. Add flour and baking
   powder. Blend well. Pour three-quarters of the batter into
   a greased cake pan.
4. In a bowl, combine coffee, cocoa and water. Mix with
   remaining one-quarter batter. Add raisins and nuts if using.
   Pour on top. Bake in a 350°F oven for 35 minutes.

Preparation and Cooking Time: 45 minutes

Fluden

The Aleph-Bet of Jewish Cooking   Russia
                                              Yield: 12 Servings

Dough	Filling
⅔ cup water or milk	150 grams (5 ounces) jam
3 teaspoons sugar	4 teaspoons walnuts,
1½ teaspoons salt	chopped
40 grams (1½ ounces) yeast	4 teaspoons sugar
2 cups flour	Cinnamon
2 teaspoons butter, melted	1 egg, beaten

1. Preheat oven to 350°F.
2. Pour milk or water into a saucepan. Add sugar and salt and heat, stirring all the while.
3. Stir in yeast and flour. Remove from heat. Knead dough. Place in a bowl and let rise 20 to 30 minutes.
4. Add melted butter and knead again, adding more flour if too moist. Let stand in a warm place 40 to 50 minutes.
5. In a bowl, combine jam, walnuts, sugar and cinnamon.
6. Divide dough into two parts. Roll out each on a floured surface about 1 cm. (½-inch) thick. Place one layer of dough in a greased baking pan. Spread a layer of filling, cover with second layer of dough and pinch ends to seal. Place in a warm place to rise for 20 minutes.
7. Brush beaten egg on top. Bake in a 350°F oven until brown.

Preparation and Cooking Time: 2¼ hours

Note: Reprinted with permission from Shvut Ami, the International Center for Soviet Jews, Jerusalem, Israel.

Sweet Rice Cakes

Una Chang Strauss   China
Kansas City, Missouri   Yield: 6 Servings

*This recipe is traditionally eaten during the Chinese New Year,
usually some time in February of each year. I am Chinese, born in
Taiwan and emigrated to the United States in 1980; however, I still
love good Chinese food!*

3 cups half-and-half or
  2% milk
	1 teaspoon almond or
	  vanilla extract

1 tablespoon baking powder	1 pound "sweet rice flour"
1 stick margarine	Sesame seeds (optional)
3 eggs, well beaten	1 can red bean paste
2¼ cups sugar	

1. Preheat oven to 350° F.
2. In a mixing bowl, combine half-and-half or milk, baking
    powder, margarine, eggs, sugar, extract and flour. Mix
    well.
3. Batter can be baked in two ways.
    a. Spread batter in a greased baking pan. Sprinkle sesame
    seeds on top
    b. Divide the batter into two portions. Spread half into the
    greased baking pan. Spread 1 can red bean paste on top.
    Spread rest of batter on top. Sprinkle with sesame seeds on
    top batter.
4. Bake in a 350° F oven 1 hour.

Preparation and Cooking Time: 1¼ hours

Sherry Cake

Sybil Kaplan
Overland Park, Kansas   Yield: 8 Servings

I found this recipe in my files with my mother's name, Rae Horowitz, on it.

6 tablespoons margarine, unsalted	½ teaspoon salt
1 cup sugar	⅓ cup sherry
2 eggs	¼ cup milk
1 teaspoon cardamon	1 teaspoon lemon juice
1½ cups flour	⅓ cup sugar
1½ teaspoons baking powder	3 tablespoons sherry

1. Preheat oven to 300°F.
2. In a mixing bowl, cream margarine and sugar until fluffy.
   Add eggs and cardamon.
3. Combine flour, baking powder and salt in a second bowl.
4. Combine ⅓ cup sherry, milk and lemon juice in a third
   bowl. Add flour mixture alternately with creamed mixture.
   Pour batter into a greased casserole. Bake in a 300°F oven
   for 55 to 70 minutes.
5. While baking, combine ⅓ cup sugar and 3 tablespoons
   sherry. Remove cake from oven. Pour over hot cake.
   Cool before cutting.

Preparation and Cooking Time: 1 hour, 25 minutes

Margarete's Own Birthday Torte

Margarete Jacoby
Kansas City, Missouri   Yield: 12 Servings

*I started making this 50 years ago and it became our traditional
birth torte for the whole family.*

Cake
1 package yellow cake mix
3 large eggs
½ cup oil
1⅓ cups water

Filling
1 package vanilla pudding
2 cups milk
1 tablespoon shortening
2 teaspoons rum extract
½ pound unsalted butter
1 package frozen
   strawberries

Topping
¾ cup almond slivers, slightly toasted

1. Preheat oven to 350° F.
2. Combine ingredients for layer cake as directed on cake mix
   package using eggs, oil and water. Bake in a 9-inch
   springform pan. Cool.
3. With a long cake knife, cut cake into four layers.
4. In a bowl, combine pudding, milk and shortening. (If using
   regular pudding, let cook before continuing.)
5. Whip butter until light and creamy in a bowl. Add pudding
   by tablespoons, mixing after each addition. Add rum
   extract and mix well. This is the butter cream.
6. Place first layer of cake on a plate. Cover with one third of
   the butter cream. Add second layer. Place strawberries on
   top. Cover with third layer. Add second third of the butter
   cream. Cover with fourth layer. Spread last one third of
   butter cream on top. Sprinkle with toasted almonds.*

* To toast almonds, spread on a cookie sheet, toast in
350° F oven 5 to 7 minutes.

Preparation and Cooking Time: 45 minutes to 1 hour

KitchenAid Never-Fail Cupcakes

Nellie Foster
Tempe, Arizona

Yield: 16 Cupcakes

Linda Radke says this recipe comes from her sister-in-law, Nellie Foster.

1 egg	1 teaspoon baking soda
½ cup cocoa	1 cup sugar
½ cup shortening	1 teaspoon vanilla
1½ cups flour	½ cup hot water
½ cup sour milk	

1. Preheat oven to 350°F.
2. Place egg, cocoa, shortening, flour, sour milk, baking soda, sugar, vanilla and hot water in KitchenAid bowl in that order. Attach bowl and flat beater. Set mixer to Stir position for 30 seconds or until all ingredients are just combined.
3. Stop and scrape bowl. Turn to speed 2 and mix for an additional 2 minutes.
4. Line cupcake pan with cupcake papers. Fill with a scant ¼ cup batter. Bake in a 350°F oven for 20 minutes.

Preparation and Cooking Time: 30 minutes

KitchenAid Buttercream Frosting

Nellie Foster
Tempe, Arizona

½ **cup shortening or butter, softened**
¼ **cup milk or water**
1 **pound or 4 cups powdered sugar, sifted**
½ **teaspoon flavoring**

1. Place shortening or butter and water or milk into KitchenAid bowl. Attach bowl and flat beater. Set mixer to Stir position and slowly add powdered sugar and flavoring.
2. Increase speed to setting 4 and mix until smooth. Additional liquid or powdered sugar may need to be added to adjust consistency.

Preparation and Cooking Time: 10 minutes

What do you do when you're out of confectioners' sugar?

Place in a blender: 1 teaspoon cornstarch or flour and 1 cup granulated sugar and whirl until powdered.

Sugar-Free Chocolate Cupcakes

Sybil Kaplan
Overland Park, Kansas

Yield: 8-inch Square Cake
or 8 Cupcakes

3 tablespoons unsweetened cocoa	½ teaspoon baking soda
½ cup hot water	¼ teaspoon salt
Liquid sweetener to equal 1 cup	½ cup milk or
2 tablespoons oil	non-dairy creamer
2 eggs	1 teaspoon vanilla
1½ cups flour	½ cup nuts, chopped
2 teaspoons baking powder	(optional)

1. Preheat oven to 375°F.
2. In a bowl, combine cocoa with hot water.
3. In another mixing bowl, combine liquid sweetener with oil and eggs. Add flour, baking powder, baking soda and salt and blend. Add nuts if using.
4. Pour in cocoa, milk and vanilla and blend. Spoon into greased cupcake cups. Bake in a 375°F oven for 18 to 20 minutes.

This recipe can also be used for an 8-inch square cake, but bake in a 350°F oven for 30 to 35 minutes.

Preparation and Cooking Time: 35 to 45 minutes

Pumpkin Spice Cake

Sybil Kaplan
Overland Park, Kansas   Yield: 12 Servings

*I don't know where I got this recipe, but I've made it over the past 20
or more years.*

2 cups flour	1⅓ cups brown sugar
2 teaspoons baking powder	¼ cup milk or
¼ teaspoon baking soda	non-dairy creamer
½ teaspoon salt	2 eggs
½ teaspoon cinnamon	½ cup unsalted margarine
½ teaspoon cloves	softened
½ teaspoon ginger	¾ cup pumpkin

1. Preheat oven to 350°F.
2. In a mixing bowl, combine flour, baking powder, baking
   soda, salt, cinnamon, cloves and ginger.
3. Add brown sugar, milk or non-dairy creamer, eggs and
   margarine and blend. Blend in pumpkin. Pour into a
   greased cake pan and bake in a 350°F oven for 50 to 55
   minutes.

Preparation and Cooking Time: 1 hour, 10 minutes

Pumpkin Nut Bread

Sybil Kaplan
Overland Park, Kansas   Yield: 1 Loaf

2 cups flour	1 cup sugar
2 teaspoons baking powder	½ cup milk or
½ teaspoon baking soda	non-dairy creamer
1 teaspoon salt	2 eggs
1 teaspoon cinnamon	¼ cup soft butter or
½ teaspoon nutmeg	unsalted margarine
1 cup canned pumpkin	1 cup nuts, chopped

1. Preheat oven to 350°F.
2. In a mixing bowl, combine flour, baking powder, baking soda, salt, cinnamon and nutmeg.
3. In a second bowl, combine pumpkin, sugar, milk and eggs and blend.
4. Add creamed mixture to dry mixture and add butter or margarine. Stir in nuts. Spread batter in a greased loaf pan. Bake in a 350°F oven for 45 to 55 minutes.

Preparation and Cooking Time: 1¼ hours

Henrietta's Choco-Date Cake

Sybil Kaplan
Overland Park, Kansas   Yield: 8 Servings

Henrietta and I met in Jerusalem when I lived there. She was an
American and she gave me this recipe.

1 cup dates, chopped
1 cup boiling water
½ cup unsalted margarine
1 cup sugar
1 teaspoon vanilla
1 egg
2 tablespoons cocoa

1⅔ cups flour
1 teaspoon baking soda
½ cup semi-sweet
   chocolate, broken
   into pieces*
½ cup nuts, chopped

1. Preheat oven to 350° F.
2. Place dates and hot water in a cup. Set aside.
3. Combine in a mixing bowl margarine, sugar, vanilla and egg and beat.
4. Combine cocoa, flour, and baking soda in another bowl. Add to creamed mixture alternately with date-water. Pour into a greased cake pan. Sprinkle chocolate pieces and nuts on top. Bake in a 350° F oven for 35 to 40 minutes.

* If these contain milk, recipe is dairy.

Preparation and Cooking Time: 50 to 60 minutes

If a recipe calls for 1 teaspoon vanilla extract, you can substitute 1 teaspoon coffee, orange or almond flavored liqueur.

Brandy Banana Bread Cake

Sybil Kaplan
Overland Park, Kansas

Yield: 12 Servings

I don't know where I found this, but I was looking for a pareve banana cake at the time and this one came from El Salvador. I adapted and adopted and experimented and this was the conclusion.

1 cup sugar	2 cups whole wheat or
½ cup margarine, unsalted	white flour
2 eggs	1 teaspoon baking powder
3 bananas, mashed	¼ teaspoon salt
2 tablespoons brandy	Almonds

1. Preheat oven to 350°F.
2. In a mixing bowl, cream sugar and margarine. Blend in eggs and bananas.
3. Add brandy, flour, baking powder and salt. Pour into a greased loaf pan. Sprinkle almonds on top. Bake in a 350°F oven for 1 hour

For a different taste, use Sabra liqueur instead of brandy and sprinkle chopped nuts and coconut on top.

Preparation and Cooking Time: 1¼ hours

Elaine's Carrot Pie-Cake
Gezer Pashtida

Sybil Kaplan   Israel
Overland Park, Kansas   Yield: 8 to 10 Servings

Elaine and Eddy were Canadians who lived in Netanya. On one occasion of our being together, she gave me this recipe but I don't know its origin.

½ cup unsalted margarine,   ½ cup bread crumbs
  melted   3 tablespoons lemon juice
1 large tart apple, grated   1 teaspoon cinnamon
1 cup carrots, grated   3 eggs, separated
½ cup raisins   ¾ cup nuts, chopped
½ cup sugar

1. Preheat oven to 350° F.
2. Combine melted margarine with grated apple and carrots in a mixing bowl.
3. Add raisins, sugar, bread crumbs, lemon juice, cinnamon, egg yolks and all but 1 tablespoon chopped nuts. Mix.
4. Beat egg whites in a separate bowl until stiff. Fold into main mixture. Pour batter into a greased round or 8-inch square baking pan. Sprinkle remaining 1 tablespoon nuts on top. Bake in a 350° F oven for 40 minutes.

Preparation and Cooking Time: 1 hour

Date-Nut Carob Torte

Sybil Kaplan
Overland Park, Kansas   Yield: 6 Servings

I made this recipe up while living in Israel because we had lots of dates and I liked using carob powder.

1 cup nuts, ground
1 cup dates, chopped
¼ cup carob powder
4 eggs, separated
¼ teaspoon cream of tartar

1. Preheat oven to 375°F.
2. In a mixing bowl, toss dates and nuts with carob powder. Mix in egg yolks and blend.
3. Beat egg whites with cream of tartar until they form peaks. Gently fold into other mixture. Pour into a greased cake pan. Bake in a 375°F oven for 15 to 25 minutes. Remove from oven and cool 10 minutes.

Preparation and Cooking Time: 45 minutes

Date Loaf Cake

Sybil Kaplan
Overland Park, Kansas

Yield: 1 Loaf

This recipe came from my mother, Rae Horowitz.

1 tablespoon instant coffee	¾ cup sugar
1 cup boiling water	½ teaspoon salt
1¼ cups dates, chopped	1 apple, grated
2¼ cups flour	2 tablespoons unsalted
2 teaspoons baking powder	margarine
½ teaspoon baking soda	1 egg
	½ cup nuts, chopped

1. Preheat oven to 350° F.
2. In a mixing bowl, combine coffee, water and dates.
3. In a second bowl, combine flour, baking powder, baking soda, sugar and salt. Combine date mixture with dry mixture. Add apple, margarine, egg and nuts. Pour into a greased loaf pan. Bake in a 350° F oven for 1 hour.

Preparation and Cooking Time: 1¼ hours

"The rightous shall flourish like a date-palm..."
(Psalms 92:13)

Barbara's Cinnamon Mocha Cake

Sybil Kaplan
Overland Park, Kansas

Yield: 12 Servings

Barbara and I met when I was on a speaking tour in Canada where she lived and she was in a group of people planning aliyah (immigration to Israel). We became friends when she and her family moved to Jerusalem, and she gave me this recipe. She told me she adapted this recipe from a well-known American cookbook because it was easy, reliable and her children liked it. It was a solid cake and one of the three chocolate cakes she made in rotation. Because it is made in a bundt pan, it always looks fancy.

2½ cups flour	1¾ cups sugar
1 teaspoon baking powder	1 cup unsalted margarine
½ teaspoon baking soda	3 eggs
1 teaspoon salt	2 teaspoons vanilla
1 tablespoon instant coffee	¼ cup cocoa*
2 teaspoons cinnamon	1 cup water

1. Preheat oven to 350°F.
2. Sift flour, baking powder, baking soda, salt, coffee and cinnamon in a mixing bowl.
3. Cream sugar and margarine. Add eggs and vanilla. Add cocoa. Beat in flour mixture alternately with water. Pour into a greased bundt pan. Bake in a 350°F oven for 60 to 65 minutes. Cool 15 minutes before turning out onto a plate.

* Carob powder can be substituted for cocoa.

Preparation and Cooking Time: 1½ hours

Jelly Roll

Sybil Kaplan
Overland Park, Kansas

Yield: 8 to 10 Servings

*While looking through my recipe files, I found a handwritten recipe
of my grandmother, Sade Lyon, but like many that were saved, there
was no title. When I started to compare the ingredients and a few of
the directions with the jelly roll recipe of my mother, Rae Horowitz, I
discovered they were the same!*

1 cup flour	1 teaspoon vanilla
1 teaspoon baking powder	3 tablespoons water
¼ teaspoon salt	Jelly or custard
3 eggs	Powdered sugar
1 cup sugar	

1. Preheat oven to 375°F.
2. Combine flour, baking powder and salt in a mixing bowl.
3. In a second bowl, beat eggs then add sugar, vanilla and
   water. Carefully fold in flour mixture.
4. Cover a cookie sheet with wax paper and grease it. Pour
   mixture onto sheet and bake in a 375°F oven for 12
   minutes.
5. Invert at once on a tea towel that has been spread with
   powdered sugar. Spread with jelly or custard and roll up to
   cool.

Preparation and Cooking Time: 30 minutes

Pareve

Ruchi's Orange Chiffon Cake

Sybil Kaplan
Overland Park, Kansas

Yield: 12 Servings

Ruchi and I became friends when she and her husband came from a kibbutz in Israel to Chicago to be schlichim (emissaries) for a youth movement. She gave me this recipe.

2½ cups flour
1½ cups sugar
4 teaspoons baking powder
½ teaspoon salt (optional)
½ cup oil
6 eggs, separated
¾ cup orange juice
2 teaspoons vanilla
2 tablespoons orange peel, grated
½ teaspoon cream of tartar

Icing
1 egg yolk
1 tablespoon unsalted margarine, melted
1 to 2 tablespoons orange juice
1 tablespoon orange peel, grated
1 cup confectioners' sugar

1. Preheat oven to 325° F.
2. Sift into a mixing bowl flour, sugar, baking powder and salt.
3. Make a well in the center. Add oil, egg yolks, orange juice, vanilla and orange peel.
4. In another bowl, beat egg whites and cream of tartar until stiff. Fold into main mixture. Pour into a greased tube pan. Bake in a 325° F oven for 55 minutes.
5. Meantime, combine egg yolk, melted margarine, orange juice, orange peel and confectioners' sugar. Spread on warm cake.

Preparation and Cooking Time: 1¼ hours

My Sabra Orange Cake

Sybil Kaplan   Israeli Style
Overland Park, Kansas   Yield: 12 Servings

I made this up while living in Israel.

⅔ cup margarine, unsalted
1 cup sugar
4 eggs
2 cups flour
6 tablespoons orange juice
½ teaspoon orange peel, grated
2 tablespoons Sabra liqueur
2 tablespoons nuts, chopped
2 tablespoons semi-sweet
  chocolate, grated

Glaze
¼ cup orange juice
2½ tablespoons
  Sabra liqueur
1 tablespoon orange peel,
  grated

1. Preheat oven to 350°F.
2. Cream margarine and sugar in a mixing bowl. Add eggs and beat.
3. Blend in flour, orange juice, orange peel and liqueur. Pour batter into a greased cake pan.
4. In a small bowl, combine nuts and chocolate. Sprinkle on top. Bake in a 350°F oven for 30 minutes.
5. Meanwhile, combine orange juice, liqueur and orange peel for glaze. When cake is baked, punch holes in the top with a toothpick and pour glaze on top.

Preparation and Cooking Time: 40 minutes

Tomato Soup Cake

Sybil Kaplan
Overland Park, Kansas

Yield: 10 to 12 Servings

When I was in seventh grade, we had a student teacher from Hawaii. When she completed her teaching, we had a party and she brought this cake. I got the recipe from her then and have been making it ever since, surprising people by not telling them the secret ingredient until after they taste it!.

1 cup sugar	2 teaspoons baking powder
½ cup margarine, melted	1 teaspoon cinnamon
2 cups flour	1 teaspoon baking soda
1 teaspoon salt	1 can tomato soup
1 teaspoon cloves	½ cup nuts, chopped
1 teaspoon nutmeg	

1. Preheat oven to 350°F.
2. In a mixing bowl, cream sugar and margarine.
3. In a second bowl, combine flour, salt, cloves, nutmeg, baking powder and cinnamon. Add baking soda to tomato soup and stir.
4. Blend creamed mixture with dry mixture. Add tomato soup and blend. Add nuts. Pour into a greased cake pan and bake in a 350°F oven for 45 minutes.

Preparation and Cooking Time: 1 hour

"Helly's" Boston Bread

Sybil Kaplan   South Africa
Overland Park, Kansas   Yield: 1 Loaf

*Helen came from South Africa and we met in Jerusalem. Every time
I ate in her home I came back with another of her special recipes,
and this is one of them. At the time, she told me that although we
may think this bread is from New England, it was a very well known
South African recipe which she remembered as a regular feature at
her mother's tea table.*

1 cup dates, chopped	1 teaspoon baking powder
1 teaspoon baking soda	½ teaspoon cloves
¾ cup boiling water	½ teaspoon cinnamon
2 tablespoons butter,	Pinch salt
softened	½ cup pecans, chopped
¾ cup brown sugar	½ cup raisins
1 egg	Lemon Juice
1 teaspoon vanilla	
1¾ cups flour	

1. Preheat oven to 350°F.
2. Place dates and baking soda in a dish with boiling water.
    Set aside.
3. In a mixing bowl, cream butter and sugar. Beat in egg and
    vanilla extract.
4. Add flour, baking powder, cloves, cinnamon and salt. Add
    date mixture and blend.
5. Stir in pecans and raisins. Pour batter into a greased loaf
    pan. Sprinkle top with lemon juice. Bake in a 350°F oven
    for 1 hour.

Preparation and Cooking Time: 1¼ hours

Pareve

Zucchini Bread

Sybil Kaplan
Overland Park, Kansas

Yield: 1 Loaf

I got this recipe from my mother, Rae Horowitz.

3 eggs	3 cups flour
2 cups sugar	¼ teaspoon baking powder
1 cup oil	1 teaspoon baking soda
1 teaspoon vanilla	1 teaspoon cinnamon
2 cups zucchini, peeled and grated	½ cup nuts, chopped

1. Preheat oven to 325°F.
2. Beat eggs in a mixing bowl until light. Add sugar, oil, vanilla and zucchini. Mix well.
3. Sift flour, baking powder, baking soda and add to batter. Add cinnamon and nuts. Pour into a greased and floured loaf pan. Bake in a 325°F oven for 1 hour. Don't overbake.

Preparation and Cooking Time: 1¼ hour

The Best Sugar-Free Applesauce Cupcakes

Sybil Kaplan
Overland Park, Kansas

Yield: 28 Applesauce or
20 Banana Cupcakes

I adapted from a recipe found in the newspaper.

2 cups flour
7 teaspoons sugar substitute
  plus ¼ cup sugar
1 teaspoon salt
2 teaspoons baking soda

1¾ teaspoons cinnamon
4 eggs or "egg beaters"
1¼ cups vegetable oil
2 cups applesauce

1. Preheat oven to 350°F.
2. In a mixing bowl, combine flour, sugar substitute, sugar, salt, baking soda and cinnamon.
3. Add eggs or "egg beaters", oil and applesauce.
4. Spoon batter into greased muffin cups. Bake in a 350°F oven for 20 to 25 minutes.

If you wish banana cupcakes instead of applesauce, substitute three ripe mashed bananas for the applesauce.

If you want the cupcakes larger, then fill just 24.

Preparation and Cooking Time: 35 minutes

Eggnog Cupcakes

Sybil Kaplan
Overland Park, Kansas

Yield: 12 Cupcakes

1¾ cups flour	¼ cup water
¾ cup sugar	2 eggs
1¾ teaspoons baking powder	½ teaspoon nutmeg
½ teaspoon salt	⅛ teaspoon ginger
¼ cup unsalted margarine, soft	¾ teaspoon rum extract
½ cup orange juice	¼ teaspoon vanilla

1. Preheat oven to 350°F.
2. In a mixing bowl, combine flour, sugar, baking powder and salt.
3. Add margarine, orange juice, water and eggs and mix.
4. Stir in nutmeg, ginger, rum and vanilla extracts. Fill greased cupcake cups one-half to three-quarters full. Bake in a 350°F oven for 35 minutes.

Preparation and Cooking Time: 45 minutes

Cookies
&
Sweet Rolls

Kossuth Crescents

Ruth Gluck
Phoenix, Arizona

Hungary
Yield: 40 Crescents

Linda Radke explains that she got this recipe from Ruth, her mother's sister, who was born in Hungary.

½ pound butter
1 cup sugar
Juice of 1 lemon
6 eggs, separated
2 cups flour

1 teaspoon baking powder
¼ teaspoon salt
½ pound walnut meats, ground
½ cup sugar

1. Preheat oven to 350°F.
2. With electric mixer at medium speed, cream butter and sugar. Add lemon juice and egg yolks.
3 In another bowl, sift flour, baking powder and salt together. Add to creamed mixture and mix for about 3 minutes.
4. In another bowl, beat egg whites until stiff. Slowly fold by hand into the dough. Pour batter into a greased oblong pan.
5. Mix walnuts with ½ cup sugar. Spread on dough. Bake in a 350°F oven for 15 to 20 minutes. Cut into moon shapes while warm.

Preparation and Cooking Time: 30 to 35 minutes

Note: From **That Hungarian's In My Kitchen** by Linda F. Radke, Five Star Publications.

Apple Streusel Bars

Margarete Jacoby
Kansas City, Missouri

Poland
Yield: 20 Bars

I came from Schlessia (on the Polish border with Germany). I remember how my mother used to make these bars, so I tried to recreate it and developed my own recipe.

Streusel
1½ sticks butter or
  margarine
½ cup sugar
1 cup flour
½ cup walnuts or
  pecans, chopped

Dough
1 stick butter or
  margarine
½ cup sugar
2 eggs

Filling
4 apples, peeled and grated
¾ cup sugar
1 tablespoon cinnamon
⅛ teaspoon ground cloves
⅛ teaspoon ground
  coriander (optional)
½ cup raisins
⅓ cup plus 2 tablespoons
  milk
1 tablespoon vanilla
2 cups flour

1. Preheat oven to 350° F.
2. In a bowl combine 1½ sticks butter or margarine, ½ cup sugar and 1 cup flour with walnuts. Work with your hands until crumbly. Set aside.
3. In a second bowl, cream 1 stick butter or margarine with ½ cup sugar. Add eggs and vanilla.
4. Mix baking powder with 2 cups flour. Alternate flour and milk into creamed mixture. Spread in a greased 9x15x1-inch baking pan.
5. In a bowl, mix apples, sugar, cinnamon, cloves, coriander, if used, and raisins. Mix and put on top of dough. Top with sugar/flour/margarine/nut streusel topping. Bake in a 350° F oven 1 hour.

Preparation and Cooking Time: 1¼ hours

Note: Streusel is the topping sprinkled on cakes or coffee cakes and comes from the German word for "sprinkle."

"And if thy offering be a meal-offering baked on a griddle, it shall be of fine flour unleavened, mingled with oil. Thou shalt break it in pieces and pour oil thereon." *(Leviticus 2:5-6)*

Butter Cookies
Vajas Pogacsa

Vera Cecilia Barnyanka Weiss   Hungary
Scottsdale, Arizona   Yield: 84 Cookies

Vera, who is from Transylvania, is married to Linda Radke's Uncle Irv, her mother's brother. Her background is Hungarian like this recipe.

3½ cups flour	8 ounces sour cream
½ pound butter	3 eggs
2 tablespoons baking powder	Pinch of salt
1 cup sugar	

1. Preheat oven to 350°F.
2. Place flour in a mixing bowl. Cut in butter. Add baking powder and sugar.
3. Add sour cream, eggs and salt. Mix together to form a soft dough.
4. Roll out dough on a floured surface to ½-inch thickness. Cut with a round cookie cutter. Place rounds on a greased cookie sheet and bake in a 350°F oven for 20 to 25 minutes.

Preparation and Cooking Time: 40 minutes

Butter Cookies
Vajas Pogacsa

Vera Cecilia Barnyanka Weiss and Zelma Fulop   Hungary
Scottsdale, Arizona   Yield: 12 Dozen Cookies

Vera, who is from Transylvania, is married to Linda Radke's Uncle Irv, her mother's brother, whose background is Hungarian like this recipe.

5 cups flour	1 pound butter or
2 teaspoons baking powder	margarine
1 cup sugar or 9 packets	3 eggs
artificial sweetener	1 tablespoon sour cream
Pinch salt	

1. Preheat oven to 350°F.
2. In a mixing bowl, mix together flour, baking powder, sugar and salt.
3. Cut in softened butter or margarine and mix together. Make a hole in the center and add eggs and sour cream. Mix together into a soft dough. Cut dough in two pieces.
4. Roll out each dough piece on a floured board to about ¼-inch thickness. Cut with a small round cookie cutter.
5. Place cookies on a greased cookie sheet and bake in a 350°F oven for 20 to 22 minutes until light beige.

Preparation and Cooking Time: 35 minutes

Butter Circles
Putter-Gebeks

The Aleph-Bet of Jewish Cooking   Russia
                                                   Yield: 72 Pieces

3 cups flour	2 eggs
3 tablespoons butter,	2 tablespoons sugar
cut in small pieces	3 tablespoons sugar
2 tablespoons sour cream	Water
1 teaspoon salt	Cinnamon

1. Preheat oven to 350° F.
2. In a mixing bowl, sift flour. Add butter pieces, sour cream, salt, eggs, and 2 tablespoons sugar. Knead dough to avoid lumps. Cool for 30 minutes.
3. In a saucepan, make syrup by adding a little water to the 3 tablespoons sugar. Heat, stirring continuously until sugar is completely dissolved.
4. Roll out dough thin on a floured surface. Cut out circles 10 centimeters (4 inches) in diameter.
5. Pour syrup over circles, sprinkle on cinnamon. Fold each circle in half, pinching ends to seal. Place on a greased cookie sheet. Pierce here and there. Bake in a 350° F oven until brown.

Jam or sugar may be substituted for syrup.

Preparation and Cooking Time: 45 minutes to 1 hour

Note: Reprinted with permission from Shvut Ami, the International Center for Soviet Jews, Jerusalem, Israel.

Cheese Cake Cookies

Sybil Kaplan
Overland Park, Kansas   Yield: 60 Cookies

I got this recipe from my mother, Rae Horowtiz.

⅔ **cup margarine, melted**   **2 eggs**
⅔ **cup sugar**   **2 teaspoons vanilla**
2 cups flour   **½ cup sugar**
1 cup nuts, chopped   **2 tablespoons lemon juice**
1 8-ounce package cream   **4 tablespoons milk**
   cheese, softened

1. Preheat oven to 350°F.
2. Place margarine in a mixing bowl. Add sugar, flour and nuts and stir until crumbly. Reserve 1 cup for topping. Press the rest into a well-buttered 9x13-inch greased baking pan. Bake in a 350°F oven 10 minutes or until golden brown.
3. Meantime, mix in a bowl, cream cheese, eggs, vanilla, sugar, lemon juice and milk. Pour over baked crust and top with reserved crumbs. Bake in a 350°F oven for 25 minutes. Cook and cut into squares.

Preparation and Cooking Time: 45 minutes

Crispy Crullers
Csorge

Ruth Gluck   Hungary
Phoenix, Arizona   Yield: 30 Crullers

Linda Radke explains that Ruth is her mother's sister, born in Hungary.

6 egg yolks	**1 teaspoon brandy**
½ cup sour cream	**1 tablespoon white vinegar**
2½ cups flour	**Vegetable oil**
1 teaspoon salt	**Powdered sugar**
¼ cup sugar	

1. Place egg yolks and sour cream in a mixing bowl. Add all or enough of the flour to make a soft dough.
2. Add salt, sugar, brandy and vinegar. Knead until smooth.
3. Roll out dough very thin on a floured surface. Cut into diamond shapes. Make a slit in the center and pull one end through the slit.
4. Heat oil in a pot and fry the crullers until light brown. Drain on paper toweling. Sprinkle generously with powdered sugar

Preparation and Cooking Time: 25 minutes

Note: From **That Hungarian's In My Kitchen** by Linda F. Radke, Five Star Publications.

Pecan Rolls

Sybil Kaplan
Overland Park, Kansas   Yield: 48 Rolls

This was my mother's recipe which she says she found once in a Jewish cookbook.

2 cakes or packages yeast	**½ cup sour cream**
½ cup lukewarm milk (use water with dry yeast)	**½ cup brown sugar**
1 teaspoon sugar	**3 tablespoons shortening, melted**
4½ cups sifted flour	**¼ cup nuts, chopped**
¾ teaspoon salt	**1 teaspoon cinnamon**
½ cup sugar	**¼ cup raisins**
½ pound shortening	**Shortening, melted**
3 eggs, well beaten	**Pecan halves**

1. Dissolve yeast in a cup with lukewarm water and 1 teaspoon sugar. Let stand while other preparations are made.
2. In a mixing bowl, combine flour, salt, ½ cup sugar. Cut in shortening. Add eggs, sour cream, then yeast mixture.
3. Knead until dough comes away from the bowl. Cover and set in refrigerator overnight. (This can actually be stored in the refrigerator for up to one week.)
4. Next day: Preheat oven to 375°F. Grease muffin tins. Remove dough from refrigerator and roll out ⅛-inch thick on a floured board. Brush with melted shortening. Sprinkle with sugar, cinnamon, nuts and raisins.
5. Roll up dough like a jelly roll. Cut in 1-inch slices. In each muffin cup, place 2 teaspoons melted shortening, 1 tablespoon brown sugar and 3 pecan halves.
6. Place each slice in prepared muffin cup. Let rise 1 to 2 hours in a warm place until double in bulk. Bake in a 375°F oven for 20 to 30 minutes until brown. Remove from pan immediately.

Preparation and Cooking Time: 15 hours

Rugelach

Sybil Kaplan
Overland Park, Kansas   Yield: 32 Pieces

I got this recipe from my mother, Rae Horowitz.

½ **pound cream cheese at**	**Cinnamon**
room temperature	**Sugar**
2 sticks unsalted margarine	**Raisins**
2 cups flour	**Chopped nuts**
1 teaspoon vanilla	
Margarine, melted	

1. Preheat oven to 350° F.
2. Place cream cheese, margarine and flour in a mixing bowl and cream. Add vanilla. Knead well. Place in refrigerator overnight or at least a few hours.
3. Divide dough into quarters. Roll out one quarter at a time on a floured board to a round circle shape. Cut into eight wedges. Spread each wedge with melted margarine. Sprinkle with cinnamon, sugar, raisins and nuts. Jam may also be used as a filling. Roll up from the wide side. Sprinkle with more sugar and cinnamon. Place on a greased cookie sheet. Bake in a 350° F oven for 20 minutes.

Preparation and Cooking Time: 3 to 4 hours

Scottish Oat Breads

Hilda Meth

Richmond, Virginia

New Glasgow, Nova Scotia

Yield: 72 Pieces

This recipe was given to me by Mrs. Kathleen Ferguson from New Glasgow, Nova Scotia. She is the granddaughter of the lighthouse keeper at Caribou, Nova Scotia, and this was her mother's recipe. I have tried other recipes for Scottish Oat Breads, but in my opinion, this is the best. It is an easy one to do with children of all ages.

3 cups rolled oats
  (big ones, not instant)
3 cups white flour
1½ cups brown sugar
½ teaspoon salt

½ teaspoon baking soda
2 cups butter or unsalted
  pareve margarine
¼ to ½ cup water

1. Preheat oven to 350° F.
2. Combine oats, flour, sugar, salt and baking soda in a mixing bowl. Mix well. Cut in softened butter or margarine or work it in with your hands. (This is the part the children love!)
3. Moisten with water until it has the consistency that you need to roll it out. If the dough is too soft, put in the refrigerator for a short time. Roll out dough on a floured surface. Cut into squares. Place squares on ungreased cookie sheet. Bake in a 350° F oven for 15 minutes or until cookies start browning at the edges. Let cool before you take them off the sheet.
   When cold, "cookies" should be crisp. If not, bake 2 to 3 minutes longer. Keep in airtight container up to six months.

Preparation and Cooking Time: 30 minutes

Pareve

Bourbon Balls

Sybil Kaplan
Overland Park, Kansas   Yield: ⅓ Pound

I got this recipe from my mother, Rae Horowitz.

12 ounces vanilla wafers	½ cup bourbon
4 tablespoons carob powder	4 tablespoons syrup
1½ cups nuts, chopped	Confectioners' sugar
2 cups confectioners' sugar	

1. Pulverize vanilla wafers. Put in a bowl. Add carob powder and nuts.
2. Add sugar, bourbon and syrup. Mix well. Form into balls. Roll balls in confectioners' sugar.

Preparation and Cooking Time: 20 minutes

My Carob Brownies

Sybil Kaplan
Overland Park, Kansas   Yield: 16 Brownies

1 cup sugar	⅔ cup flour
2 eggs	½ teaspoon baking powder
⅓ cup unsalted margarine, soft	¼ teaspoon salt
3 tablespoons carob powder	½ cup nuts, chopped, or coconut
1 teaspoon vanilla	

1. Preheat oven to 350° F.
2. Combine in a mixing bowl, sugar, eggs, margarine, carob powder and vanilla. Blend well.
3. Add flour, baking powder and salt and mix well. Stir in nuts or coconut. Spread on a greased 8-inch square baking pan. Bake in a 350° F oven for 25 minutes.

Preparation and Cooking Time: 35 minutes

How do you make your own vanilla?

Combine 1 ounce or 6 whole vanilla beans, cut lengthwise in four pieces with 1 cup brandy. Shake and let age for 6 months.
Strain and store.

You can also break up one whole vanilla bean, place in jar with 3 ounces vodka and ⅓ teaspoon sugar and age one month in a sealed bottle. Shake often. Strain before using. When amount is depleted, add equivalent amount of vodka for each amount of extract used and keep using.

Mocha Bars

Marilyn Landes   Israel
Jerusalem, Israel   Yield: 16 Bars

Marilyn, who has lived in Israel since 1949 when she came on aliyah, is originally from Revere, Massachusetts. She told me she got this recipe from an American friend more than 20 years before, but she uses more chocolate because the bars taste better that way. She always makes them for special company and everyone who eats them says they're delicious!.

150 grams (5 ounces) **bittersweet chocolate or**	**¾ cup sugar (if using** **cocoa: use more if using**
¾ cup cocoa	**bitter-sweet chocolate)**
200 grams (1 cup) unsalted **margarine**	**1 cup flour** **2 tablespoons coffee**
4 eggs	**½ teaspoon salt**
	Chopped nuts

1. Preheat oven to 350° F.
2. Mix chocolate or cocoa with margarine in a mixing bowl. Add eggs, sugar, flour, coffee and salt.
3. Spoon into a greased baking pan. Sprinkle nuts on top. Bake in a 350° F oven for 30 to 45 minutes.

This can be used as Passover by substituting 1 cup matzah flour for the regular flour.

Preparation and Cooking Time: 1 hour

Taliques

Barbara Gorodetzky   Greece
Kansas City, Missouri   Yield: 96 Pieces

*My son-in-law, Eddie Newfouse, gave me this recipe. His parents
came from Salonica, Greece, but I'm not sure of the origin of these
cookies.*

3 eggs   1 teaspoon baking powder
1¼ cups sugar   ¾ cup oil
4 cups flour   Sesame seeds

1. Preheat oven to 375° F.
2. In a mixing bowl, combine eggs and sugar and blend.
3. Stir in flour, baking powder and oil. Blend until you have
    a smooth dough. Take a small piece of dough. Separate it
    into three parts, then braid together to make a tiny challah.
    Place on a greased cookie sheet. Continue making small
    cookie challot until all the dough is used.
4. Sprinkle each cookie with sesame seeds. Bake in a 375° F
    oven for 25 minutes.

    These cookies are hard and each looks like a miniature
    bread.

Preparation and Cooking Time: 45 minutes

Pareve

Sugar-Free Date Nut Cookies

Dora Levy
Kansas City, Missouri   Yield: 15 Cookies

A friend gave this recipe to me because I need gluten-free recipes.

3 eggs
8 ounces dates, chopped
8 ounces nuts, chopped

1. Preheat oven to 350°F.
2. Beat eggs in a bowl. Add dates and nuts.
3. Grease cookie sheet with no-stick cooking spray. Drop batter by teaspoon on sheet. Bake in a 350°F oven for 10 to 12 minutes.

Preparation and Cooking Time: 20 minutes

Note: Figs could also be used instead of dates.

Hermits

Sybil Kaplan
Overland Park, Kansas   Yield: 72 Cookies

I got this from my mother, Rae Horowitz.

1 cup shortening, or oil	3½ cups flour
2 cups brown sugar	1 teaspoon cinnamon
2 eggs, beaten	1 teaspoon nutmeg
½ cup cold coffee	½ cup raisins
1 teaspoon baking soda	½ cup nuts

1. Preheat oven to 400°F.
2. In a mixing bowl, cream shortening or oil, sugar and eggs.
3. In a second bowl, combine coffee and baking soda. Add to creamed mixture. Add flour, spices, raisins and nuts. Drop by tablespoon onto a greased cookie sheet. Bake in a 400°F oven for 10 to 12 minutes.

Preparation and Cooking Time: 20 minutes

Note: Hermits are said to have originated in New England in Colonial times and were named because they could be hidden away like a hermit and then eaten and then they tasted better!

Pareve

Polka Dot Macaroons

Sybil Kaplan
Overland Park, Kansas   Yield: 2½ Dozen Cookies

I got this from my mother, Rae Horowitz.

3 egg whites	**3 cups cornflakes**
½ teaspoon salt	**crushed**
¾ cup sugar	**6 ounces chocolate chips**
	1 teaspoon vanilla

1. Preheat oven to 350° F.
2. Beat egg whites to soft peaks in a bowl with salt. Add sugar and continue beating until stiff.
3. Fold in cornflakes, chocolate chips and vanilla. Drop by spoonfuls on a greased cookie sheet, 2 inches apart. Bake in a 350° F oven for 25 to 30 minutes.

Preparation and Cooking Time: 40 minutes

How do you tint coconut?

Place coconut in a jar or bowl. Sprinkle a few drops of food coloring, diluted with 1 teaspoon water, on top. Shake or toss until colored evenly.

No "Mandel" Mandel Bread

Reva Kaplan
Kansas City, Missouri

German Style
Yield: 40 Pieces

*My recipe came from an old dear friend who has passed away.
I changed the nuts from almonds to English walnuts.*

3 eggs
1 cup sugar
1 cup vegetable oil
1 teaspoon vanilla
Pinch of salt
1 teaspoon baking powder

4 cups flour
1 cup big pieces of
 English walnuts
Cinnamon
Sugar

1. Preheat oven to 350° F.
2. Beat eggs in a mixing bowl with sugar. Gradually pour in oil and beat well.
3. Add vanilla and salt.
4. Mix together baking powder and flour. Stir into egg mixture with a spoon. Add nuts.
5. Divide dough into 3 pieces. Roll out dough and place on a greased cookie sheet. Bake in a 350° F oven for 25 to 30 minutes until top cracks and bottom is brown.
6. Slice into pieces while hot. Sprinkle with cinnamon and sugar. Set pieces on one end, then return to oven for 15 minutes to brown.

Preparation and Cooking Time: 1 hour

Note: The real name of this cookie is mandelbrot from the German words mandel (meaning almond) and brot (bread)

Pareve

No-Flour Peanut Butter Cookies

Dora Levy
Kansas City, Missouri   Yield: 15 Cookies

1 egg
¾ cup brown sugar
1 cup peanut butter

1 teaspoon vanilla or
1 tablespoon orange juice
15 chocolate chips *

1. Preheat oven to 325°F.
2. Combine egg and sugar in a mixing bowl. Add peanut butter, vanilla or orange juice and mix well
3. Grease a cookie sheet with no-stick cooking spray. Drop batter on sheet with a teaspoon. Wet another teaspoon and flatten each cookie. Add a chocolate chip in the center of each cookie. Bake in a 325°F oven for 12 minutes.

* You can also use a nut instead of chocolate chips.
Preparation and Cooking Time: 20 minutes

Poppy Seed Tarts
Peris Kees

Reva Kaplan   Russia
Kansas City, Missouri   Yield: 40 Pieces

*This recipe came from my Grandmother Cohn, who came from
Russia in the late 19th or early 20th century. It was given to me by
an aunt (her sister-in-law) who wrote it down.*

4 cups flour	**1 teaspoon salt**
1 cup poppy seeds	**2 eggs**
1 cup sugar	**White or dark thick syrup**
1 cup oil	**Poppy seeds**
1 cup water	

1. Preheat oven to 400° F.
2. In a mixing bowl, combine flour, poppy seeds, sugar, oil,
   water, salt and eggs. Blend into a dough.
3. Roll out dough flat. Spread syrup over dough with a
   spatula. Roll up dough. Cut into one-inch pieces.
4. Grease a cookie sheet. Place "tarts" dough side down on
   sheet. Bake in a 400° F oven 30 minutes. Remove from
   cookie sheet to wax paper. Drizzle syrup on top and
   sprinkle with more poppy seeds.

Preparation and Cooking Time: 50 minutes

Desserts, Pastry, Candy & Ice Cream

Pineapple-Pistachio Salad

Susan Parrish
Overland Park, Kansas   Yield: 10 to 12 Servings

My in-laws gave this to me. They said they got it from a restaurant in Michigan and passed it on to me because they said it was so good.

1 15¼-ounce can crushed pineapple with juice	1 8-ounce container low-fat whipped topping
1 ⅜-ounce package instant pistachio pudding mix	1½ cups miniature marshmallows

1. Place crushed pineapple and juice in a mixing bowl.
2. Add pudding and mix well by hand.
3. Fold in whipped topping, then marshmallows. Chill before serving.

Preparation and Cooking Time: 10 minutes

Whipped Cheese Fruit Salad

Sybil Kaplan
Overland Park, Kansas   Yield: 6 to 8 Servings

I had this once at a luncheon and adapted it because it was so attractive with dairy meals and great to take for dairy pot-luck luncheons.

2 cups cottage cheese
1 ⅝ cup whipped topping
1 cup crushed pineapple with juice
1 cup mandarin oranges, drained
1 package dry lime gelatin

1. Mix all ingredients together in a bowl. Refrigerate.

Preparation and Cooking Time: 10 minutes

Bananas Foster

Sybil Kaplan
Overland Park, Kansas   Yield: 4 Servings

*A chef at a local country club gave me this recipe after preparing it
for our table.*

¼ cup butter or margarine	**¼ cup cinnamon sugar**
Juice of 1 small orange	**1 jigger banana liqueur**
Juice of 1 small lemon	**Brandy**
1½ cups brown sugar	**Vanilla ice cream**
3 bananas, sliced lengthwise	

1. Melt butter or margarine in a frying pan over a low heat.
2. Add orange juice and lemon juice and brown sugar. Stir
   until sugar dissolves.
3. Add bananas, half the cinnamon sugar and the banana
   liqueur. Add a little brandy and light the brandy. Continue
   stirring while the brandy flames exist until the pure caramel
   sauce is created.
   Serve over vanilla ice cream.

Preparation and Cooking Time: 15 minutes

Espresso Nut Mousse

Sybil Kaplan
Overland Park, Kansas   Yield: 6 Servings

1½ cups milk
2 tablespoons sugar
4½ teaspoons instant espresso
  coffee powder
1 envelope unflavored gelatin
⅓ cup nuts, finely ground

⅛ teaspoon salt
2 egg whites
2 tablespoons sugar
1¼ cups thawed whipped
  topping

1. Place milk, 2 tablespoons sugar and coffee in a saucepan. Sprinkle gelatin on top. Cook over low heat until gelatin dissolves.
2. Place gelatin mixture in a bowl with nuts and salt. Refrigerate 45 minutes.
3. Beat egg whites in a bowl until peaks form. Sprinkle in 2 tablespoons sugar. Continue beating until peaks are stiff.
4. Fold egg whites and 1 cup whipped topping into coffee mixture. Spoon into wine or dessert glasses or a mousse dish. Refrigerate 2½ hours. Garnish with ¼ cup whipped topping.

Preparation and Cooking Time: 3½ hours

"I went down to the garden of nuts..."
(Song of Solomon 6:11)

1. P
   Turn
2. Add ma
   Adjust amou
3. Mold into balls
   Refrigerate. Before
   confectioners' sugar.
For Passover, add matzah cru
baking pan and refrigerate. Cut
Preparation and Cooking Time: 3 hours

Ruchi's Neapolitan Windmill Cake

Sybil Kaplan   Israel
Overland Park, Kansas   Yield: 10 Servings

I first met Ruchi when she and her husband were sent to Chicago in the 1980s from kibbutz to work with the religious youth movement. She was Canadian born and had lived on kibbutz for some years; her husband was born on the kibbutz. She gave me this recipe.

2½ cups cookie crumbs	½ teaspoon extract*
4½ ounces unsalted margarine, melted	½ teaspoon extract*
12 ounces low-fat cream cheese	2 teaspoons chocolate syrup
1 cup sugar	½ teaspoon instant coffee
4 eggs, separated	Coconut
½ cup sugar	Chocolate sprinkles
Pink drink syrup	Nuts, chopped

1. Combine cookie crumbs and melted margarine and press into a greased pie plate. Set aside.
2. In a bowl, mix cream cheese with 1 cup sugar. Blend in egg yolks.
3. In another bowl, beat egg whites until stiff, adding ½ cup sugar near the end. Fold into main batter.
4. Place one-third of the batter in a bowl and add pink drink syrup and ½ teaspoon extract. Place one-third batter in another bowl and add ½ teaspoon extract, chocolate syrup and instant coffee. Leave third of batter in main bowl.
5. Pour each third of the batter onto ⅓ of the crust, windmill effect around the plate. Decorate top with coconut, chocolate sprinkles, nuts or any combination. Freeze until firm.

You can also place the crust in a deep loaf pan and place the filling on top in layers.
    * Use extracts of your choice which blend.

Preparation and Cooking Time: 3 hours

Grandma's Rice Pudding

Cindy Megiddo
Forest Hills, New York

Yield: 8 Servings

This recipe came from my grandmother, Fannie Sobiloff, who came from Russia, near Kiev. She lived her adult life in Fall River, Massachusetts. She was a fabulous cook, but this was the number one favorite of all of us grandchildren. The recipe was dictated to me by her in her own words.

1 tablespoon butter	1 cup raisins
Water	2 tablespoons brown sugar
1 cup raw rice	2 or 3 eggs
3 big apples, sliced	3 tablespoons butter
1 cup cranberries or	
1 package whole cranberries made according to package directions	

1. Preheat oven to 350°F. Grease baking dish with 1 tablespoon butter.
2. Place water in a saucepan, bring to a boil, add rice and cook rice until cooked but not too soggy. Drain and put in a bowl.
3. Add eggs to rice. Add apples, cranberries, raisins, brown sugar (omit if using canned cranberries which have sugar) and remaining 3 tablespoons butter. Blend well.
   Pour into greased baking dish. Bake in a 350°F oven 1 hour.

Preparation and Cooking Time: 1½ hours

Sugar-Free Rice Pudding

Sybil Kaplan
Overland Park, Kansas

Yield: 3 to 4 Servings

1 cup cooked rice	½ teaspoon vanilla
¾ cup milk	1 egg
½ cup diabetic brown sugar	¼ teaspoon lemon peel
1½ teaspoons unsalted	2½ tablespoons raisins
margarine, cut into pieces	for baking

1. Preheat oven to 325°F.
2. Place rice and milk in a mixing bowl. Add brown sugar, margarine pieces, vanilla, egg, lemon peel and raisins and blend.
3. Pour into a greased baking dish. Bake in a 325°F oven 50 minutes.

   Recipe can be doubled if you have more rice. It is best to use rice that has been made earlier in the day or leftover rice.

Preparation and Cooking Time: 1 hour

Safra's Chocolate Balls

Sybil Kaplan   Israel
Overland Park, Kansas

I first met Safra when she and her husband were sent to Chicago and he was director of the Israel Government Tourist office and later my boss. She was a great cook and entertainer and she gave me this recipe.

4 tablespoons cocoa	1 teaspoon rum extract
1 cup sugar	Leftover cookie or
1 cup milk	cake crumbs
5 ounces unsalted margarine	Coconut, nuts,
1 egg yolk	confectioners' sugar

1. Place cocoa, sugar and milk in saucepan. Cook until hot. Turn off heat.
2. Add margarine, egg and rum. Add some crumbs and stir. Adjust amount so mixture holds together.
3. Mold into balls and place on a tray on wax paper. Refrigerate. Before serving, roll in coconut, nuts or confectioners' sugar.

For Passover, add matzah crumbs. Pour into a greased baking pan and refrigerate. Cut into slices to serve.

Preparation and Cooking Time: 3 hours

Heavenly Hash

Cindy Megiddo
Forest Hills, New York   Yield: 16 Squares

*This is a chocoholic's dream! My mother, Sara Feinberg, from
Providence, Rhode Island, started making this in the 1960s. She
collected recipes from magazines, from her sister, from friends, and
then she would improvise. This was so popular, so sublime, that
when people ate it, they couldn't stop eating it. Every year I would
take some to a cousin in Israel and she would hide it from her
family!*

1 12-ounce package chocolate bits	1 teaspoon instant coffee
2 ounces unsweetened chocolate	1 teaspoon vanilla
1 teaspoon instant coffee	1 cup walnuts, chopped
1 lump butter, size of an egg	1 package large marshmallows, cut in half
1 14-ounce can sweetened condensed milk	

1. Place chocolate bits and unsweetened chocolate in a
   saucepan atop a second saucepan filled with water (double
   boiler style). Add coffee and butter and heat until
   chocolates melt. Remove from heat.
2. Add milk and vanilla. Add nuts and marshmallows. Pour
   into a greased 8-inch square baking dish. Refrigerate 2 to
   3 hours.
   To serve, cut into squares.

Preparation and Cooking Time: 2 to 3¼ hours

My Mother's Strudel

Cindy Megiddo
Forest Hills, New York

This recipe is from my mother, Sara Feinberg, who came from Providence, Rhode Island. I found the recipe in her handwriting which she wrote up for a presentation. My mother was a fabulous baker and this was so loved by my friends that she used to make little packages for special friends. The way Grandma used to travel to family dinners with her gefilte fish and knaidlach, my mother traveled with the pastry, chiefly her strudel and her Heavenly Hash. It was even transported to cousins in Israel who waited for us to bring it every year.

Dough	**Filling**
1 8-ounce package cream cheese, softened	Apricot preserves
½ pound butter, softened	Walnuts, chopped
2 cups flour	White raisins
2 tablespoons milk	Coconut (optional)
	Graham cracker crumbs

1. Place cream cheese and butter in a bowl of mixer or food processor and blend until creamy.
2. Add flour gradually, then add milk. If the dough is hard to handle, add more milk. Blend well to make dough and then remove from bowl and form into a nice size ball. Wrap in foil or plastic wrap. Refrigerate overnight.

Next day:
3. Preheat oven to 350° F.

4. Place dough on a floured board. Split dough into five pieces. Roll out each. Spread preserves on each thinly; sprinkle walnuts, raisins and coconut, if using, on each. Sprinkle graham cracker crumbs around the open ends to prevent leakage. Roll up each like a jelly roll. Place on a greased cookie sheet. Bake in a 350° F oven 30 to 45 minutes and check after 30 minutes to see if it is beige or tan in color. Cool on wax paper, then slice. If you want to freeze this, freeze before slicing.

Preparation and Cooking Time: 25 hours

"And Abigail made haste and took...a hundred clusters of raisins..." *(I Samuel 25:18)*

Crepes--Hungarian Style
Palachinta

Ethel Quarnstrom/Ann Foster　　　　　　　　　Hungary

Yield: 12 Servings

Linda Radke says, this is my all-time favorite. It comes from Ann Foster who is my mother, born in Hungary and Ethel Quarnstrom, my mother's sister.

4 cups flour	**4 tablespoons unsalted**
4 eggs	**butter, melted**
4 cups milk	**2 tablespoons vanilla**
½ cup sugar	**Filling of preference**

1. In an electric mixer bowl, place flour, eggs, milk, sugar, melted butter and vanilla. Beat well. The batter should be thin.
2. Butter a frying pan. Pour about 2 ounces of mixture at a time from measuring cup into pan to make thin pancake. Brown and turn to do the other side. Remove to a counter top or plate or towel to cool and repeat until all batter is used.

 Fill with favorite filling such as cheese, cherry or apple, and roll up.

Preparation and Cooking Time: 20 minutes

Note: From **That Hungarian's In My Kitchen**
by Linda F. Radke, Five Star Publications.

Strawberry Ice Cream

Marly Rein
Kibbutz Yavne, Israel

Israel
Yield: 3 Quarts

  2 cups sour cream
  6 large eggs
  2 cups sugar
  1 teaspoon vanilla
  3 to 3½ cups fresh strawberries, crushed

1. Separate eggs with yolks into a small bowl and whites into a medium bowl.
2. Add sour cream to a large bowl.
3. Beat egg whites and add ⅔ cup sugar very gradually. The whites should stand in soft peaks.
4. Transfer beater to sour cream bowl and beat with ⅔ cup sugar added gradually while beating.
5. Transfer beater to yolks and beat with ⅔ cup sugar, vanilla and strawberries. When smooth, add yolks to sour cream mixture, continue to beat until well blended.
6. Fold in egg white mixture to sour cream until well blended. Pour into plastic container, seal well and freeze.

Preparation and Cooking Time: 3 to 4 hours

Note: This recipe is best doubled or tripled because it doesn't pay to make too little.   The texture is a little bit icier because of the water content but tastes great!

Coffee Ice Cream

Marly Rein   Israel
Kibbutz Yavne, Israel   Yield: 3 Quarts

*My father came from Germany, my mother from Czechoslovakia; they
met and married in Palestine but got stuck when they went back to
Europe before the War. I was born in France, then the family
immigrated to the United States. My family and my husband, Marty,
and I moved to Israel in 1968 with our infant son. We have lived in
Kibbutz Yavne ever since. We have a 27½-year-old son who is on
the kibbutz; our second son, 26, also works on the kibbutz; our
youngest son, 22, is an officer in the army. I've been working in the
diet kitchen for the last 12½ years; my husband washes all the
clothes for the whole kibbutz. My oldest son loves this ice cream and
claims it's the best ice cream in the world.*

2 cups sour cream   **1 teaspoon vanilla**
6 large eggs   **8 teaspoons instant coffee**
2 cups sugar   **powder**

1. Separate eggs with yolks into a small bowl and whites into
   a medium bowl.
2. Add sour cream to a large bowl.
3. Beat egg whites and add ⅔ cup sugar very gradually.
   Alternately add 4 teaspoons coffee powder, 1 teaspoon at a
   time. The whites should stand in soft peaks and be smooth
   with no sugar or coffee granules apparent.
4. Transfer beater to sour cream bowl and beat with ⅔ cup
   sugar added gradually while beating.
5. Transfer beater to yolks and beat with ⅔ cup sugar, vanilla
   and 4 teaspoons coffee powder, added gradually while
   beating all the time. When smooth, add yolks to sour
   cream mixture, continue to beat until well blended.

6. Fold in egg white mixture to sour cream until well blended. Pour into plastic container, seal well and freeze.

   This recipe is best doubled or tripled because it doesn't pay to make too little.

Preparation and Cooking Time: 3 to 4 hours

Hana's Vanilla Pie

Sybil Kaplan

Overland Park, Kansas

Israel

Yield: 6 Servings

Hana and I became friends when she and her husband, Yehudah, were sent to Chicago and he was an aliyah shaliach (immigration emissary). She was a very good cook and I learned a lot from her. She gave me this recipe.

1 16-ounce package plain cookies	2 cups milk
½ cup unsalted margarine, melted	Whipped cream
1 package instant vanilla pudding	Sliced bananas (optional)
	Chocolate chips (optional
	Chopped nuts (optional)

1. Put cookies in blender and make into crumbs. Add margarine and mix. Place crumb mixture in a greased pie plate.
2. Make pudding with milk. Pour onto shell. Refrigerate 1 hour. Spread on whipped cream, bananas, chocolate chips, nuts or any combination before serving.

Preparation and Cooking Time: 1½ hours

Marshmallow Fruit Dumplings

Sybil Kaplan
Overland Park, Kansas   Yield: 4 Servings

I've had this recipe for years and have a faint recollection that it was one of those I learned in home ec class in junior high!

3 medium apples, pared, cored, cut into eighths
½ teaspoon salt
16 marshmallows
¼ cup cinnamon candies
1 cup flour

1 teaspoon baking powder
¼ teaspoon salt
2 tablespoons butter or margarine
½ cup milk or non-dairy creamer

1. Place apple pieces in a saucepan with salt and eight of the marshmallows. Cook and stir until marshmallows melt. Add cinnamon candies and set aside.
2. Combine in a bowl, flour, baking powder and salt. Cut in butter or margarine. Add milk or non-dairy creamer to make a dough.
3. Drop spoonfuls of dough on top of apple-marshmallow mixture. Bring to a boil. Place an additional marshmallow on top of each dumpling. Cover and steam for 15 minutes. Don't lift the cover.
Serve dumplings with hot sauce.

Preparation and Cooking Time: 30 to 40 minutes

Guacamole Ice Cream

Dalia Carmel
New York, New York

Mexican Style
Yield: 2 Servings

2 avocados
Juice of ½ lemon
2 garlic cloves

Hot sauce to taste
Salt to taste
1 cup whipped cream*

1. Peel avocados and puree flesh with lemon juice and garlic.
2. Place in a freezer container. Add hot sauce and salt, then fold in whipped cream. Freeze.

   * Use pareve whipped cream if planning to serve with meat meal.

Preparation and Cooking Time: 3 to 4 hours

Frozen Mocha Parfait

Sybil Kaplan
Overland Park, Kansas

Yield: 4 Servings

I created this recipe while living in Israel.

½ cup sugar	⅓ teaspoon vanilla
3 tablespoons coffee	1 cup whipping cream
3 egg yolks	(regular or pareve)
1 ounce chocolate, melted	Cinnamon

1. Place sugar and coffee in a saucepan and cook together over low heat for 5 minutes.
2. Beat egg yolks in a bowl, then add to coffee syrup. Stir in chocolate. Set aside to cool.
3. Add vanilla and whipping cream. Place bowl in freezer to freeze.
4. For serving, remove from freezer and spoon into parfait glasses. Sprinkle top with cinnamon.

Preparation and Cooking Time: 3 to 4 hours

Note: Originally the word mocha referred to coffee grown in Arabia and shipped from Mocha, Arabia. Today it has come to mean a coffee-chocolate combination. Parfait is French for "perfect," and refers to a dessert served in a tall, narrow, footed glass.

Couscous Dessert

Sybil Kaplan
Overland Park, Kansas

Middle East Style
Yield: 4 to 6 Servings

1 box couscous
Water
Margarine as required
½ cup unsalted margarine
¾ cup raisins
¾ cup dates, chopped
½ teaspoon nutmeg

½ teaspoon cinnamon
2 tablespoons slivered
  almonds
2 tablespoons
  confectioners' sugar
Whipped cream, pareve
or dairy

1. In a saucepan, bring water and margarine to boil as directed
   on the box of couscous and then add couscous and stir.
   Remove from heat and let stand.
2. Melt margarine in another saucepan. Stir in raisins, dates,
   nutmeg, cinnamon and almonds. Simmer for 5 minutes.
   Stir in confectioners' sugar.
3. Fluff couscous with a fork. Pour into serving dishes. Pour
   fruit spice sauce on top. Garnish with whipped cream.

Preparation and Cooking Time: 20 minutes

Note: Couscous is a major item in North African diets and is
a form of semolina. Couscous is most popular in Algeria,
Morocco and Tunisia, and this form as a desert is also a
variation.

Fruit Pudding Dessert

Sybil Kaplan
Overland Park, Kansas

Yield: 4 Servings

1 cup pareve whipping cream
1¾ cup milk or
   non-dairy creamer
1 tablespoon chocolate-orange
   liqueur or orange juice
1 package instant vanilla
   pudding

4 to 6 cups melon,
   bananas, peaches,
   plums, grapes, or any
   combination you like.

1. In a mixing bowl, whip whipping cream until stiff. Set aside.
2. In a second bowl, combine milk or non-dairy creamer with liqueur or orange juice and pudding. Beat for 1 minute. Add whipping cream. Beat 1 minute more.
3. Place fruit in serving dishes. Pour pudding over fruit.

Preparation and Cooking Time: 10 minutes

"And ye shall take you on the first day the fruits of goodly trees..." *(Leviticus 23:40)*

Plum Clafouti

Sybil Kaplan
Overland Park, Kansas

French Style
Yield: 4 Servings

¾ pound small purple plums,
    halved and pitted
Sugar
1½ tablespoons sugar
¼ teaspoon cinnamon
1¼ cups milk or
    non-dairy creamer

3 eggs
⅓ cup flour
3 tablespoons sugar
⅛ teaspoon salt
1 teaspoon vanilla

1. Preheat oven to 375° F.
2. Butter a 9-inch pie plate. Sprinkle with sugar. Combine
   1½ tablespoons sugar and ¼ teaspoon cinnamon. Arrange
   plums, skin side down. Sprinkle with cinnamon sugar.
3. Blend milk or non-dairy creamer with eggs, flour, sugar,
   salt and vanilla in a blender until smooth. Pour batter over
   the fruit. Bake in a 375° F oven for 40 to 45 minutes.
   Serve warm.

Preparation and Cooking Time: 1 hour

Note: Clafouti is a French dessert served hot and can be used
for cherries, peaches or pears.

Peach Kuchen

Sybil Kaplan
Overland Park, Kansas

Yield: 4 to 6 Servings

1 pound ripe peaches, sliced
1 tablespoon lemon juice
¾ cup sifted flour
¼ cup sugar
1 teaspoon baking powder
¼ teaspoon salt
1 egg
1 tablespoon non-dairy
   creamer or pareve
   whipped cream

¾ teaspoon lemon peel,
   grated
2 tablespoons unsalted
   margarine, melted
2 tablespoons sugar
¼ teaspoon cinnamon
1 egg yolk
1½ tablespoons non-dairy
   creamer or pareve
   whipped cream

1. Preheat oven to 400° F.
2. Slice peaches in a bowl. Add lemon juice. Set aside.
3. Sift flour, sugar, baking powder and salt. Set aside.
4. In another bowl, combine egg, non-dairy creamer or pareve
   whipped cream, lemon peel and melted margarine. Butter a
   springform or tube pan. Combine dry and creamed
   mixture. Spread in the bottom of the pan.
5. Place peaches on top of batter. Combine 2 tablespoons
   sugar and ¼ teaspoon cinnamon. Sprinkle with cinnamon
   sugar. Bake in a 400° F oven 25 minutes.
6. Beat egg yolk with non-dairy creamer or whipped cream.
   Spread on top of cake. Bake 10 minutes more.

Preparation and Cooking Time: 1 hour

Note: Kuchen originated in Germany as a fruit-filled cake
served for breakfast or dessert.

Pareve

Old Israeli Fruit 'n Flan

Sybil Kaplan   Israel
Overland Park, Kansas   Yield: 8 Servings

I received this recipe from Carmel wine while living in Israel.

1 cup sugar
3 tablespoons cornstarch
½ teaspoon salt
1 cup white dry wine
1 egg, beaten
⅔ cup orange juice

2 tablespoons unsalted
  margarine
1 cup seedless grapes
1 cup strawberries, sliced
2 peaches, sliced

1. In a saucepan, combine sugar, cornstarch and salt. Mix in
   wine, stirring constantly and bring mixture to a boil. Cook
   for 5 minutes or until clear and thick. Remove from heat.
2. Blend in beaten egg. Return to heat and cook 1 minute
   more. Add orange juice and margarine. Cool.
3. Arrange fruits in layers in serving dishes. Pour wine sauce
   over fruits.

Preparation and Cooking Time: 20 minutes

"They cut down a branch with one cluster of grapes..."
(Numbers 13:23)

Apple Enchantment

Sybil Kaplan
Overland Park, Kansas

Israel
Yield: 4 Servings

I received this recipe from Carmel wine while living in Israel.

¼ cup sugar	4 large, firm apples
¼ cup Amaretto	peeled, cored,
Peel of 1 orange	thickly sliced
Juice of 1 orange	Coconut (optional)
	Whipped cream (optional)

1. Combine sugar, Amaretto, orange peel and orange juice in a saucepan. Heat slowly until bubbly.
2. Add apple slices. Simmer until apples are tender and all liquid has evaporated. Chill.

Serve plain, with coconut or with whipped cream.

If whipped cream is dairy, this becomes a dairy recipe.

Preparation and Cooking Time: 25 minutes

Henrietta's Baked Pears in Wine

Sybil Kaplan
Overland Park, Kansas

Yield: 6 Servings

Henrietta and I became acquainted when I lived in Israel. She was an American and loved to entertain. She gave me this recipe.

6 pears	4 teaspoons sugar
6 whole cloves	½ teaspoon cinnamon
⅔ cup red wine	¼ teaspoon ginger
⅓ cup water	1 teaspoon lemon juice

1. Preheat oven to 375°F.
2. Stick 1 clove in the bottom of each pear. Place in a casserole.
3. In a bowl, mix wine, water, sugar, cinnamon and ginger. Pour over pears. Bake in a 375°F oven 1 hour. Add lemon juice. Heat a few minutes.

Preparation and Cooking Time: 1¼ hours

Annette's Chocolate Covered Strawberries

Sybil Kaplan
Overland Park, Kansas   Yield: 6 to 8 Servings

*I met Annette, an American chef, living in Jerusalem, at an
International Jewish Culinary Conference held in Israel where she
won a medal for vegetable sculptures. I was invited to a reception at
her home and she made this dessert for the first time.*

3½ ounces cooking chocolate
1 tablespoon vegetable oil
20 to 25 large, perfectly shaped strawberries

1. Melt chocolate in a pot set in a pot of boiling water (double
   boiler style).
2. Place washed strawberries on paper towels to dry. Dip
   each strawberry in the chocolate, one at a time. Set on wax
   paper or a glass plate to set. If chocolate doesn't harden,
   place in refrigerator.

Preparation and Cooking Time: 30 minutes

Pareve

Pavlova

Susan Arons   New Zealand
Wellington, New Zealand   Yield: 8 Servings

*This recipe is a typical dessert we make here in New Zealand. I
never had it until I came to live here 26 years ago. It can be used
after meat or fish meals. It can also be used for afternoon tea. If
used after meat, serve with gelatin and fruit. In New Zealand, the
three fruits used the most are strawberries, kiwi and passion fruit.
This Pavlova is slightly crispy on the outside but like marshmallow
inside. If one wants more of a meringue, cook a little longer in the
oven.*

6 eggs, separated	**1 teaspoon vanilla**
1½ cups sugar	**1 teaspoon malt vinegar**
1 heaping teaspoon cornstarch	**Food coloring (optional)**

1. Preheat oven to 200° F.
2. Place egg whites in an electric mixer bowl and beat until
   fluffy and form peaks. Gradually add sugar while beating,
   then at the end, add cornstarch and continue beating.
3. Add vanilla and vinegar and beat. If you want to make this
   in color, add green, pink, yellow or blue food coloring
   before cornstarch.
4. Place baking paper on a cookie sheet. Pour mixture on
   paper in a circle the size of a dinner plate. Bake in a 200° F
   oven 1½ hours. Open oven door and leave 15 minutes
   before removing Pavlova.
   The Pavlova will rise during cooking, but will drop slightly
   after cooking. Decorate with whipped cream and
   strawberries if using after a fish or dairy meal. Use
   appropriate colored fruit for colored Pavlova, e.g., kiwi for
   green Pavlova.

Preparation and Cooking Time: 2 hours

Note: Pavlova is originally from Australia and was named
after the Russian ballerina, Anna Pavlova.

Custard
Phus

Solomon Michael Daniel   India
Bombay, Maharashtra   Yield: 6 To 8 Servings

250 to 300 grams
(9 to 12 ounces) poppy seeds
4 eggs (duck eggs preferred)
2 coconuts, cracked, removed
from shell, grated and
blended fine, reserve milk
350 to 400 grams
(12 to 14 ounces) sugar

50 grams (2 tablespoons)
cardamon
50 grams (2 tablespoons)
almonds
50 grams (2 tablespoons)
Pistachio nuts, finely cut

1. Preheat oven to 350° F.
2. Clean poppy seeds and soak in a bowl for 1 hour. Grind to
   a very fine paste.
3. Beat eggs in another bowl.
4. Mix poppy seed paste with eggs, sugar and coconut milk
   with a large spoon in a saucepan. Mix thoroughly.
5. Place pan on stove on very low heat and cook for ½ hour,
   stirring continuously.
6. Add cardamon, almonds, pistachios. Cook over low heat
   until it forms like a jelly (thick). Remove from heat. Put
   in oven at 350° F for 30 minutes.
7. Chill or cool to room temperature. Serve in small dishes.

Preparation and Cooking Time: 1¾ hours

Bread Pudding

Susan Arons
Wellington, New Zealand

New Zealand
Yield: 8 to 12 Servings

This has been used in my family for years; I have no idea its origin. My grandmother used it and passed it to my mother who then gave it to me. I have been making it for 30-plus years. It can be used after meat or milk meals. It can be used as a dessert served hot or cold. If served cold, one can put custard, ice cream or cream on it. It can also be used as a cake. You can also freeze this dish.

750 grams (26½ ounces) bread
  (white, brown or mixed
  with crusts)
2 eggs
2 tablespoons syrup
1 apple, grated with skin on
250 grams (9 ounces) dried fruit
50 grams (¼ cup) candied peel
  (optional)
4 tablespoons margarine,
  melted

2 teaspoons allspice
2 to 3 teaspoons cinnamon
2 tablespoons sweet or
  cream sherry or red
  kosher wine (optional)
½ teaspoon almond or
  orange extract
2 tablespoons marmalade,
  red
150 grams (4¼ ounces
  brown sugar

1. Preheat oven to 350° F.
2. In a large bowl, soak bread in cold water and then squeeze dry, using your hands or put through a sieve. Bread will be sloppy soft.
3. Add eggs, syrup, apple, dried fruit, candied peel and mix. Add margarine, spices, sherry or wine and extracts. Mix thoroughly.
4. Grease a 14x10-inch baking dish. Pour half the mixture in the dish. Spread marmalade on top. Add the rest of the mixture. Sprinkle with brown sugar. Bake in oven 1½ to 1¾ hours until top is brown. This may vary depending on oven.

5. Allow to cool slightly, then cut into squares or whatever size you want.

Preparation and Cooking Time: 2 hours

Pareve

Carob-Date Candy

Sybil Kaplan
Overland Park, Kansas   Yield: 6 Servings

    24 pitted, pureed dates
    4 teaspoons carob powder
    Honey
    1 cup nuts, chopped

1. Blend dates, carob powder and honey so mixture is sticky.
2. Add nuts and mold into a roll. Roll in more nuts.
   Refrigerate until cold. Slice to serve.

Preparation and Cooking Time: 1 hour

Sugar-Free Chocolate Nut Noodles

Sybil Kaplan
Overland Park, Kansas   Yield: 12 Small Candies

I adapted this from an old recipe I found.

   3 ounces diabetic chocolate candy bar
   ⅜ cup Chinese chow mein noodles
   ¼ cup salt-free peanuts
   3 teaspoons sugar substitute

1. Melt or microwave chocolate. Stir in noodles, peanuts and
   sugar substitute.
2. Spoon into a wax paper covered tray or cookie sheet.
   Refrigerate several hours.

   This recipe can easily be doubled for larger quantities.

Preparation and Cooking Time: 15 minutes

Pareve

Hana's Marzipan

Sybil Kaplan   Israel
Overland Park, Kansas   Yield: 40 tiny Candies

This is one of the many recipes Hana gave me when she was living in Chicago. She and her husband came from Israel so he could serve as the aliyah shaliach (immigration emissary).

9 ounces almonds, ground	**Juice of ½ lemon**
½ teaspoon vanilla	**5 ounces semi-sweet**
½ teaspoon almond extract	**chocolate**
9 ounces confectioners' sugar	**1 tablespoon water**
1 egg	

1. In a mixing bowl, combine almonds, vanilla, almond extract, confectioners' sugar, egg and lemon juice. Blend, then make into little balls.
2. Melt chocolate and water in a saucepan over low heat or in a double boiler. Drop in balls to coat. Remove with a slotted spoon to wax paper. Refrigerate at least two hours. Place in small papers to serve.

Preparation and Cooking Time: 2½ hours

Note: Real marzipan is made of almond paste, sugar and egg whites, and is European in origin.

Short-Cut Turkish Delight Candy

Sybil Kaplan
Overland Park, Kansas

Middle East Style
Yield: 32 Pieces

3 3-ounce packages lemon or
  orange gelatin
Dash salt
½ cup boiling water

1½ teaspoons fresh lemon
  or orange juice
½ teaspoon lemon or
  orange peel, grated
Confectioners' sugar

1. Place gelatin in a saucepan. Add salt and boiling water.
   Stir to mix. Simmer over low heat 5 minutes.
2. Stir in lemon or orange juice and grated peel. Pour into a
   square cake pan that has been sprayed with no-stick
   cooking spray. Cool and chill until firm.
   Cut into 1-inch squares. Toss in confectioners' sugar.

Preparation and Cooking Time: 2 hours

Note: Turkish delight is a candy which is popular in the
Middle East and has a rubbery texture.

Shabbat & Holidays

SHABBAT
Barley and Mushroom Casserole

Tania Horn
Teaneck, New Jersey   Yield: 4 to 6 Servings

This recipe came from my days in Boston when the children were very small and they loved this. Now I make it for the grandchildren for Shabbat.

4 tablespoons butter or margarine	**1 medium onion, chopped**
1 cup soup barley	**2 cups bouillon, boiling**
1 small can sliced mushrooms, drained	**½ teaspoon salt**

1. Preheat oven to 350° F.
2. Melt butter or margarine in a heavy pan. Add barley, mushrooms and onion and start to brown.
3. Add bouillon and salt. Cook until barley is brown and has a nutty flavor.
   Place in a greased casserole, cover and bake 50 to 60 minutes in a 350° F oven.

Preparation and Cooking Time: 1¼ hours

"For the Lord thy G-d bringeth thee into a good land..a land of wheat and barley" *(Deuteronomy 8:7,8)*

Pareve

SHABBAT
A Honey of a Challah

Richard deSola Mendes
Pound Ridge, New York   Yield: 4 Loaves

*A long time ago, probably 20 years, I started with **The Jewish Catalog** recipe. Then I started substituting and introducing and somewhere along the line I tried more and more new things with this recipe until it's entirely mine now.*

1 cup vegetable oil	1 egg
1½ cups honey	Poppy seeds or
1 cup golden raisins	sesame seeds
2 cups lukewarm water	Chopped walnuts or
1 block fresh yeast or	dried black currants
3 packages dry yeast	Nutmeg
1½ cups whole wheat flour	Cinnamon
4 eggs	
1½ teaspoons salt	
6½ cups high gluten	
bread flour	

1. Preheat oven to 350° F.
2. Put the oil, then honey and raisins in a large mixing bowl. Put the warm water in a measuring cup and crumble the yeast in it. Add to mixing bowl. Then stir in whole wheat flour.
3. Add 4 eggs and salt. Add flour, one cup at a time, and stir with wooden spoon. When the mixture becomes too thick to mix with the wooden spoon, transfer it to a heavily floured board. Keep adding flour and knead the dough until it is smooth and elastic. When the dough stops trying to adhere to the board, your hands, or anything else within reach, you have added enough flour. Kneading is an important step in coming up with a good bread. Take your time and work out all your aggressions.

4. When you are kneading, fold the dough in half, then in half again until it is pretty much in a ball. While the dough is still sticky, sprinkle flour heavily on the board and on top of the dough. To spare yourself aches and pains, place the heels of your hands on the bread, keep your arms straight, and lean your full weight on the dough. Keep moving around the dough and leaning until it is pretty much flattened out, then repeat the process. Once the dough is of the proper consistency and no longer sticks, give it up to another 5 minutes of kneading.

5. Put the dough back in the bowl, cover it with plastic wrap and put it in a warm place away from drafts. Let the dough rise for 1½ to 2 hours, until doubled. Punch it down. Take it out of the bowl and knead it lightly for a minute or two to get out any large gas bubbles.

6. Use a kitchen scale and divide the dough into four equal parts. (a) <u>For rectangular loves:</u> for each loaf, take the dough and divide it into three equal pieces. Roll out the pieces on the board into "snakes" about 1½ inches in diameter. Pinch the three strands together at one end and begin braiding. (Lift the strand on the left over the middle strand, then lift the one on the right over the new middle strand which used to be the left strand.) Keep alternating between the outer strands until you run out of dough, then pinch the strands together at the end. Oil 4 bread loaf pans and lightly sprinkle with cornmeal to keep the bread from sticking. Put a braided loaf into each pan.

(b) Put the four loaves back in the warm place for their second rising. The longer you let the dough rise, the lighter your loaves will be so leave them three, four or even five hours. Once the second rising is on, set the oven to 350°F and turn it on. Beat the fifth egg and brush the tops of the loaves with it. Then sprinkle sesame seeds or poppy seeds on top. Bake for 30 to 35 minutes.

(c) When the loaves are done, remove from pans and place
them on a wire rack to cool. After they have cooled,
loaves can be wrapped in plastic bags and frozen.
To use, let them thaw for a few hours and pop into a
300° F oven for half an hour to give that fresh-baked
taste.

7. For round loaves: instead of braiding the loaves, you can
take the dough for a loaf and roll it into a single, long
strand. Flatten it slightly and lightly oil the top surface.
Sprinkle lightly with nutmeg, then sprinkle generously with
ground cinnamon. Cover with black currants and chopped
walnuts. Then roll it up from one end (snailwise) and
pinch the other end. Stand it on end (when you look from
the top, you see the spiral pattern) in a round pan with high
sides, such as a fluted bobeche pan (oiled and cornmealed
as above). Bake in 350° F oven 30 to 35 minutes.

Preparation and Cooking Time: 3 hours

SHABBAT
Gefilte Fish Loaf

Lil Spungen
Kansas City, Missouri   Yield: 10 to 12 Servings

The recipe was given to me by a cousin in California. It's wonderful for Shabbos and excellent for Pesach.

1 large onion	¾ cup water
2 carrots, peeled	2 teaspoons dill
¼ cup oil	2 tablespoons sugar
2 pounds ground fish	½ to 1 teaspoon
(½ whitefish, ½ pike or carp)	white pepper
3 eggs, separated	3 tablespoons matzah meal

1. Preheat oven to 350°F.
2. Grate onion and carrots. Put in a pot with oil. Cover and cook 10 minutes on a very low heat. Remove from heat and cool a few minutes.
3. Combine ground fish, egg yolks, water, dill, sugar, white pepper and matzah meal in a food processor, mixer or by hand. Remove to a bowl.
4. Beat egg whites in a bowl until stiff. Fold into fish mixture.
5. Pour into a well-greased 9x5-inch loaf pan. Bake in a 350°F oven 1¼ hours.
   Cool 15 minutes in pan; turn out onto a rack to continue cooling. Refrigerate.

This can be kept five days and can also be served cold for a luncheon entree.

Serve cold with horseradish.

Preparation and Cooking Time: 2 hours

SHABBAT
Overnight Meat-Bean Stew
Cholent

Tania Horn   Lithuania
Teaneck, New Jersey   Yield: 10 Servings

This is the recipe of my mother, Dora Rabinovitch. This was served at traditional Shabbat lunch, and was started to cook before Shabbat began on Friday afternoon. My mother is a Holocaust survivor from the Kovno Ghetto in Lithuania who now lives in Montreal. In the town in Lithuania where she grew up, in the winter they would take their cholent pot to the baker in town on Friday, early afternoon, and pick it up Saturday after Shul at about 12:30 p.m. (You had to be sure to remember which pot was yours!)

1 package white beans (2 cups)	**Salt and pepper to taste**
½ package barley (1 cup)	**½ teaspoon paprika**
3 onions, sliced	**3 pounds flanken and**
6 potatoes, pared and	**meat bones**
quartered	**A little onion powder**

1. Preheat oven to 300°F.
2. Rinse beans and barley very well.
3. Place onions on bottom of a soup pot, usable in oven. Add potatoes. Sprinkle salt, pepper, paprika and onion powder on top. Add barley and beans.
4. Rub meat with salt, pepper and paprika. Add to pot. Add bones. Repeat all the layers. Cover with cold water. Bring to a boil. Cover pot very tightly by placing aluminum foil on top before putting on lid.
Place in 300°F oven for 2 to 3 hours. Then lower temperature to 200°F and cook in oven overnight until noon the next day.

Preparation and Cooking Time: 21 hours

Note: Cholent was a universal dish among Eastern European Jews. Each group of townspeople had variations on the ingredients, but it was cooked overnight Friday night to eat Saturday lunch. The word cholent is Yiddish and goes back to the 13th century.

SHABBAT
Hana's Kubaneh

Sybil Kaplan   Yemen/Middle East
Overland Park, Kansas

Hana and I met in Chicago where she lived. For fun, we organized cooking classes for Israelis, in English, but somehow I received this recipe from her. Hana's family was Yemenite and she had come from Israel.

1 package dry yeast	3½ cups flour
1 cup warm water	1 teaspoon salt
1 teaspoon salt	4 tablespoons sugar
1 teaspoon sugar	2 tablespoons oil

Friday:
1. Preheat oven to 350°F.
2. In a measuring cup, combine yeast, warm water, 1 teaspoon salt and 1 teaspoon sugar. Let sit 5 minutes to foam.
3. In a mixing bowl, combine flour with 1 teaspoon salt and 4 tablespoons sugar. Add yeast mixture. Knead dough by hand or transfer to a food processor to mix. Add oil.
4. Turn dough into an oiled pot 4½ inches deep, 7 inches in diameter. Cover and let rise.
5. Place in 350°F oven and bake 1 hour. Reduce heat to the lowest and cook 4 hours. *

Preparation and Cooking Time: 5 to 21 hours

Note: Traditionally, Yemenites put this bread in the oven at the lowest temperature Friday evening, just before Shabbat begins, and let it cook overnight so they can eat it Shabbat breakfast.

ANY HOLIDAY
Sweet 'n Sour Salmon

Lil Spungen
Kansas City, Missouri   Yield: 6 to 8 Servings

*I got this recipe from my mother-in-law, Anna Spungen of
Philadelphia. My mother-in-law kept this recipe a secret from her
family and friends all her life. She finally gave it to me after 10
years of marriage with the promise that I'd give it to no one. I've
kept that promise until today--48 years. This dish is delicious after
Shul, on a holiday, with cold beet borscht, a salad and cold
watermelon.*

3 onions, sliced	**Water**
Cracked pepper	**3 pounds fresh, sliced**
Juice of 3 lemons	**salmon steaks**
1 teaspoon whole juniper	**3 eggs, beaten**
Sugar	

1. Place onions in a saucepan. Add pepper, lemon juice,
   juniper and sugar and water to make a sweet and sour
   marinade. Bring to a boil. Add fish to marinade.
2. Cook just until steaks lose their redness and are medium
   soft. Remove steaks and onions to a casserole dish. Let
   fish soup stay in pan to cook.
3. Add beaten eggs to soup and cook over a low heat, stirring
   constantly so eggs don't curdle. Cook until broth thickens.
   Pour custard over the fish and onions.
4. Refrigerate, covered, until fish is icy cold and sauce is
   congealed.

Preparation and Cooking Time: 30 to 40 minutes

ROSH HASHANAH
Tzimmes

Sybil Kaplan
Overland Park, Kansas   Yield: 5 to 6 Servings

My mother told me she learned this recipe from my grandmother who was born in New Jersey. She probably learned it from her mother who came from Russia.

2 pounds brisket or short ribs	5 sweet potatoes, peeled
1 quart water	5 carrots, peeled
1 onion, sliced	5 white potatoes, peeled
1 rib celery	1 cup prunes
1 teaspoon salt	2 tablespoons flour
1/8 teaspoon pepper	1/4 cup brown sugar
	1/4 teaspoon citric acid

1. Preheat oven to 350°F.
2. Place brisket or short ribs in a large pot. Add water, onion, celery, salt and pepper. Bring to a boil. Reduce heat and simmer until meat is tender.
3. Add sweet potatoes, carrots and white potatoes. Cook until they are tender. Place in a greased baking dish. Add prunes. Make a paste of some of the liquid with flour, brown sugar and citric acid. Pour over tzimmes and bake in 350°F oven 1 hour.

Preparation and Cooking Time: 1½ hours

Note: Carrot tzimmes originated in the late medieval time among Ashkenazic Jews and was a favorite for Rosh Hashanah and Sukkot. By the late 1800s, it was customarily served in Eastern European Jewish homes on Friday night. The word tzimmes comes from the German word zummus meaning a compote or spicy concoction. Sometimes the dish contains meat with sweet potatoes and white potatoes and carrots. Other versions have fruits such as dried fruits and apples added.

ROSH HASHANAH
Carrot Ring

Sybil Kaplan
Overland Park, Kansas   Yield: 4 to 6 Servings

This recipe is from my mother, Rae Horowitz.

¾ cup shortening or oil   1¼ cups flour
½ cup brown sugar   1 teaspoon baking powder
1 egg   1 tablespoon baking soda
Juice of 1 orange   ½ teaspoon salt
2 cups raw carrots, grated

1. Preheat oven to 350°F.
2. Combine shortening or oil with brown sugar and egg. Add
   orange juice and carrots.
3. In a second bowl, combine flour, baking powder, baking
   soda and salt. Add to carrot mixture. Pour in a greased
   ring mold and bake in 350°F oven 1 hour.

Preparation and Cooking Time: 1¼ hours

ROSH HASHANAH/YOM KIPPUR
Honey Cake for a Crowd

Helen D. Hiller
Shorewood, Wisconsin   Yield: 16 Servings

2½ cups flour	1 pound honey
1 teaspoon baking soda	2 eggs, beaten
1¼ cups sugar	¾ cup warm water
1 teaspoon cinnamon	¼ cup oil
½ teaspoon ginger	2 heaping tablespoons
½ teaspoon nutmeg	orange marmalade
½ teaspoon cloves	Slivered almonds

1. Preheat oven to 325°F.
2. Sift together in a large bowl, flour and baking soda. Add sugar, cinnamon, ginger, nutmeg and cloves.
3. Make a well in the center and add honey, beaten eggs, warm water, oil and orange marmalade. Mix well. Pour into a greased and floured rectangular 9x12-inch baking pan. Sprinkle slivered almonds on top. Bake in 325°F oven 1 hour or until a toothpick inserted in the center comes out clean.
Cut into squares when cool.

This honey cake is great for a crowd at a Bar Mitzvah, bris or for the High Holy Days.

Preparation and Cooking Time: 1¼ hours

"a little honey, spices, and myrrh, pistachio nuts and almonds." (Genesis 43:11)

ROSH HASHANAH
Honey Loaf Cake

Sybil Kaplan
Overland Park, Kansas   Yield: 8 Servings

My mother, Rae Horowitz, created this as an alternative to Rosh Hashanah honey cake.

3½ cups flour	4 eggs
¼ teaspoon salt	¾ cup sugar
1½ teaspoons baking powder	4 tablespoons oil
1 teaspoon baking soda	2 cups honey
½ teaspoon cinnamon	½ cup strong coffee
⅛ teaspoon cloves	½ cup raisins
½ teaspoon ginger	½ cup nuts, chopped
¼ teaspoon nutmeg	

1. Preheat oven to 325°F.
2. Combine flour, salt, baking powder, baking soda, cinnamon, cloves, ginger and nutmeg in a mixing bowl.
3. In a second bowl, beat eggs and sugar until fluffy.
4. Stir in oil, honey and coffee to creamed mixture. Then add flour mixture to creamy batter. Add raisins and nuts. Pour into a greased loaf pan or two smaller loaf pans. Bake in 325°F oven 1½ hours.

Preparation and Cooking Time: 2 hours

ROSH HASHANAH
Steamed Rice Cakes
Sandan

Solomon Michael Daniel   India
Bombay, Maharashtra

This recipe comes from the Jews of India called Bene-Israel.

2 cups water
Two pinches of salt
500 grams (17½ ounces)
  rice flour
2 cups coconut water
½ cup full rice flour,
  ground coarsely
1 onion, small, peeled
2 cups coconut milk

75 to 100 grams (2 to 3½)
  ounces sugar
50 grams (2 tablespoons)
  cardamon
100 grams (¼ cup)
  almonds
100 grams (¼ cup)
  pistachios
100 grams (¼ cup)
  transparent, seedless
  raisins

1. Boil 2 cups boiling water with salt. Add coarse rice flour and let cook 5 minutes. This is called khalla.
2. Add coconut water to fine rice flour which is finely ground. Mix and knead well both flour mixtures. If dough is too dry, add a little hot water to get dough consistency. Knead well. Put dough in container with tight-fitting lid. Place hole deep in middle of dough. Insert 1 small peeled whole onion. Cover onion with dough. Keep container covered for 2 hours.
3. Extract two cups of coconut milk from coconut.
4. Open container with dough, remove onion, pour in coconut milk and sugar. Do not mix or stir dough. Close container overnight or for about 9 hours.
5. Open container and see if contents have mixed and risen. Mix with big spoon.
6. Add cardamon, almonds and pistachios and raisins. Pour mixture into small dishes.

7. Boil water in a steamer. Place filled dishes in it on a sieve. Cover and steam 15 to 20 minutes. Touch and test if done. Remove from steamer. Repeat until all the flour batter is used.

Preparation and Cooking Time: 2½ hours

"Take of the choice fruits of the land in your vessels...nuts and almonds" *(Genesis 43:11)*

ROSH HASHANAH
Wheat Halva

Solomon Michael Daniel   India
Bombay, Maharashtra

This recipe is from Bene-Israel Jews.

1 kilo (2 pounds) wheat (P.C. or khandva wheat) or
1 kilo (2 pounds) nishista made from wheat milk
2 coconuts
Dash saffron
Milk
450 grams (2 cups) sugar
50 grams (¼ cup) cardamon

100 grams (3½ ounces) almonds
100 grams (3½ ounces) pistachios
100 grams (3½ ounces) raisins

Night before:
1. Soak the wheat.
Next day:
2. Grind the wheat. Mix water and strain through muslin cloth. Keep overnight. Drain out water from the top.
3. Scrape the coconuts and take out the juice three times with hot water.
4. Dissolve the saffron in a little milk and then mix the coconut milk with the wheat milk, sugar and the saffron milk. Put in a large pot and heat, stirring all the time until thick and mixture sits on a plate when tested.
5. When nearly done, add cardamon powder, half of the almonds, pistachios and raisins.
6. When done, pour into plates. Sprinkle almonds, pistachios and raisins on top. Cool, then cut into diamond shaped pieces

Preparation and Cooking Time: 2 days

ROSH HASHANAH
Taiglach

Ruth deSola Mendes
Pound Ridge, New York   Yield: 3 Dozen Pieces

About 28 years ago I got this recipe from someone on a New Year card; I changed it a little and one year sent it to Sybil. She told me when she was looking for recipes for this cookbook, she found the recipe, called me for permission and that's how we got in touch more recently, since we've known each other probably close to 40 years.

4 cups sifted flour	**¾ pound honey**
1 teaspoon baking powder	**½ cup sugar**
3 tablespoons oil	**½ cup filberts, chopped**
4 eggs	**Pinch ginger**

1. Preheat oven to 375°F.
2. Mix and knead flour, baking powder, oil and eggs in a mixing bowl until smooth.
3. Form into rolls ⅓-inch thick and cut into ½-inch pieces.
4. Boil honey and sugar in a large pot. Add dough pieces. Cook about 10 minutes.
5. Place pieces on a greased cookie sheet in a 375°F oven. Do not stir until dough is well puffed and is just beginning to brown. Add nuts. Let bake until brown, occasionally stirring.
6. Take from oven, turn out on a wet board and cool slightly. Pat until flat, with hands dipped in cold water. Sprinkle with ginger and refrigerate.

Preparation and Cooking Time: 30 minutes

Note: Taiglach probably came from Eastern European Jews who had some leftover dough pieces and made a syrup of honey to dip them in, then they let them harden.

SUCCOT
Cabbage Strudel

Joan Nathan   Israel
Washington, D.C.   Yield: 8 To 12 Pieces

I first tasted the recipe with caraway seeds in Jerusalem at the enchanting home of Josef Tal, the famous Israeli composer. This is one of my favorite recipes

1 2-pound head cabbage	1 tablespoon sugar
1 teaspoon salt	1 teaspoon cinnamon
4 tablespoons vegetable oil	8 fillo leaves
1 medium onion,	6 tablespoons butter or
coarsely chopped	pareve margarine,
Freshly ground black pepper	melted
1 teaspoon caraway seeds	½ cup fine bread crumbs
(optional)	1 egg white

1. Remove the core and shred the cabbage, using a food processor or grater.
2. Sprinkle with salt and let stand about 15 minutes. Squeeze out the excess water.
3. Place about 4 tablespoons oil in a heavy frying pan. Brown the onion until golden. Remove, and begin sautéing the cabbage (you will probably have to do this in 2 batches), cooking carefully until wilted.
4. Combine the cabbage and the onions. Sprinkle with pepper, caraway seeds, if using, sugar and cinnamon. Adjust seasoning to taste.
5. Preheat oven to 350°F.
6. Cover a pastry board with a cloth. Taking 1 fillo leaf at a time, lay it on the board and brush with melted butter or margarine, 1 tablespoon bread crumbs, and pepper. Lay the next fillo leaf on top and brush with the identical combination. Continue until you have 4 layers of fillo leaves and topping. Along the longer side of the fillo, spoon out half the cabbage filling about 4 inches from the edge of the dough. Fold the edge over the cabbage.

Then, using both hands, lift the dough and let the cabbage roll fall over and over itself, jelly-roll fashion, until the filling is completely enclosed in the pastry sheet. Place, seam down, in a greased jelly-roll pan. If the roll is too long, cut with a serrated knife to fit your pan.

7. Repeat the above process with remaining 4 fillo leaves, bread crumbs, cabbage and pepper.
8. Brush the crust with additional melted butter or margarine. Then brush with egg white which has been lightly stirred.
9. Bake 45 minutes or until golden. Slice thin and serve immediately. Or serve lukewarm, sprinkled with confectioners' sugar, as a dessert.

Note: After the rolls have been formed, you can freeze them on cookie sheets and then remove them to plastic containers for freezer storage.

This scrumptious dish can be served as an elegant hors d' oeuvre, a vegetable accompaniment to goose, chicken or pot roast, or sprinkled with confectioners' sugar as a dessert.

Preparation and Cooking Time: 1½ hours

Note: Cabbage, one of the oldest known vegetables, was highly regarded by Jews for both nutritive and medicinal purposes. Because the grapevine and the cabbage plant were said to loathe one another, cabbage came to be thought of as a prevention against intoxication. If a man ate cabbage while drinking, he would not become inebriated. It was also a cure for hangovers. It is no wonder, then, that Hungarians traditionally prepare cabbage strudel for Simchat Torah and Purim, the two holidays when drinking and revelry take place.

From: **Jewish Holiday Kitchen** by Joan Nathan, 1988 (Schocken Books).

Edda Servi Machlin was born in Pitigliano, Italy, the descendant of Italian-Jewish families who lived in Italy for almost 2,000 years.

From: **The Classic Cuisine of the Italian Jews I**, Giro Press, P.O. Box 203, Croton-on-Hudson, New York 10520.

How do you prevent the odor of cabbage when cooking?

Place a slice of bread on top the cabbage while cooking.

SUCCOT
Succot Cookies
Ginetti Di Sukkot

Edda Servi Machlin   Italy
Croton-on-Hudson, New York   Yield: 4 Dozen Cookies

Ginetti is an ancient recipe. Like most old recipes, their appearance leaves much to be desired. Nevertheless, their taste and texture are really fine, and for the sake of authenticity the recipe is given in its original form.

1 cup sugar	1 teaspoon cinnamon
⅓ cup olive oil	1 teaspoon orange or
¼ teaspoon salt	lemon rind, grated
2 eggs	1 teaspoon vanilla extract
1 cup blanched almonds,	½ teaspoon almond extract
ground	2 cups unbleached flour
2 teaspoons anise seeds	

1. Preheat oven to 350°F.
2. Cream together sugar, oil and salt in a mixing bowl. Add one egg at a time, beating after each addition.
3. Add ground almonds, anise seeds, cinnamon, grated lemon or orange rind, vanilla and almond extracts.
4. Add enough flour to form a rather stiff dough. Turn out on a floured working surface, knead for 1 minute, then roll into a rope 1 inch wide. With a sharp knife, cut diagonally into 2-inch pieces.
5. Place on a well-floured baking sheet and bake in preheated 350°F oven for 15 minutes. Remove from oven and transfer to a wire rack to cool.
   Store in a tin box, at room temperature, where ginetti keep fresh at least 8 days, the duration of Succot.

Preparation and Cooking Time: 30 minutes

CHANUKAH
Chanukah Rice Pancakes
Frittelle Di Riso per Chanukah

Edda Servi Machlin   Italy
Croton-on-Hudson, New York   Yield: 6 Servings

*Although rice pancakes are traditionally made for Chanukah, I like
to serve them throughout the year. They are a delightful alternative
to plain rice as a side dish. (Try them with Pollastriani alla Griglia,
broiled young roosters; and they make a delicious breakfast,
luncheon or snack.) Rolled in sugar or sugar and cinnamon, they
can be served as a dessert.*

1 cup Italian rice
2½ cups water
1 teaspoon salt
1 cup dark, seedless raisins
½ cup pinoli (pine nuts) or
  slivered almonds

2 teaspoons lemon rind,
  freshly grated
6 eggs, slightly beaten
1 cup olive oil or other
  vegetable oil
Granulated sugar and
  cinnamon (optional)

1. Place the rice in a saucepan with 2½ cups of water and the
   salt. Bring to a boil. Lower the heat to simmer, cover and
   cook, without stirring, for 30 minutes, or until the rice is
   well done and quite dry. Remove from heat.
2. Add raisins, nuts and lemon rind and stir. Cool for at least
   half an hour.
3. Add eggs and mix well.
4. Heat half the oil in a large frying pan. Drop the rice
   mixture into the hot oil by rounded tablespoonfuls. Fry 2
   to 3 minutes, turn and fry another 2 minutes or until
   frittelle are golden brown on both sides. Transfer to a
   serving plate lined with paper towels. Place another piece
   of paper over them.

5. Keep on stacking frittelle with paper between layers. Add remaining oil as necessary until mixture is used up.
   When you're through with frying, remove the paper towels and serve frittelle hot, plain or rolled in sugar and cinnamon.

Preparation and Cooking Time: 1 hour

Edda Servi Machlin was born in Pitigliano, Italy, the descendant of Italian-Jewish families who had lived in Italy for almost 2,000 years.

Note: From: **The Classic Cuisine of the Italian Jews II**, Giro Press, P.O. Box 203, Croton-on-Hudson, New York 10520.

Meat

SUCCOT
Unstuffed Cabbage

Tania Horn
Teaneck, New Jersey

Lithuania Style
Yield: 4 Servings

This recipe came from my mother, who was born in Lithuania and adapted her original stuffed cabbage recipe to make it faster. This is a good dish for Succot.

1 head cabbage, cut in chunks	1½ cups water
1 16-ounce can tomatoes	1 pound chopped meat
1 8-ounce can tomato sauce	1 egg
¼ cup vinegar	¼ teaspoon salt
¾ cup brown sugar	¼ cup raw rice
2 tablespoons lemon juice	White raisins (optional)

1. Preheat oven to 325°F.
2. Put cabbage in a large roaster pan.
3. In a saucepan, put tomatoes, tomato sauce, vinegar, brown sugar, lemon juice and water. Cover and cook over medium heat briefly.
4. Meantime, combine chopped meat, egg, salt and raw rice in a bowl. Form into meat balls. Place on top of the cabbage. Pour the sauce on top. Cover and bake in a 325°F oven 2 hours. Add raisins if using and cook 30 minutes more.

Preparation and Cooking Time: 3 hours

CHANUKAH
American Potato Latkes

Dave Blackman
Overland Park, Kansas

Yield: 60 Latkes

I made this up and have been making it this way for more than 20 years--maybe longer! The key thing is to hand grate the potatoes.

5 pounds potatoes, peeled	**2 teaspoons salt**
½ onion, grated	**1 cup flour**
4 eggs	**Oil**

1. Hand grate potatoes into a mixing bowl. Drain well to remove potato starch.
2. Add onion. Add more if you like a more onion taste. Add eggs and salt. Add flour and mix well.
3. Heat oil in a frying pan. Drop by spoonfuls around pan according to the size pancake you want. Fry until brown on both sides. Drain on paper towels.

If you are serving the latkes soon, place on a cookie sheet in single layers in 200°F oven to keep warm.
If you plan to serve later, cool, then place in air-tight plastic bag in freezer. When ready to serve, place on cookie sheet in 450°F oven and bake about 10 minutes. Check to make sure they are crisp but not burned.

Preparation and Cooking Time: 30 minutes

CHANUKAH
Sweet Potato Latke Pizza

Jackye Goldberg
Overland Park, Kansas

Yield: 8 Servings

I saw this recipe in the newspaper and decided to make it, with variations, because it was a different kind of Chanukah latke.

2 pounds sweet potatoes, peeled and coarsely grated	1 teaspoon salt
¼ cup flour	½ teaspoon pepper
4 eggs	¼ teaspoon pumpkin pie spice
1 teaspoon fresh ginger root, grated	¾ cup ginger snap crumbs

1. Preheat oven to 450°F.
2. Grate sweet potatoes into a mixing bowl. Add flour and eggs and blend.
3. Add ginger, salt, pepper and pumpkin pie spice.
4. Spray a pizza pan with no-stick cooking spray. Sprinkle ginger snap crumbs all around pan. Spread batter on top. Bake in 450°F oven 45 minutes. Cut into wedges.

Preparation and Cooking Time: 1 hour

CHANUKAH
Yaffa's Zingole

Sybil Kaplan
Overland Park, Kansas

Middle East
Yield: 4 to 6 Servings

While living in Israel, I wrote a food column for Israel's only English language daily, The Jerusalem Post. One Chanukah I wanted some unusual recipes, so I went to all my neighbors and this is one I received from my neighbor who had learned it from her mother, Yaffa, who came from Syria..

½ ounce yeast
Few spoons warm water
2 cups flour
1 to 2 cups water

Oil
1 cup sugar
1 cup water
1½ tablespoons lemon
    juice

1. Dissolve yeast in a bowl with warm water. Add to flour and add enough water to make a liquid batter.
2. Heat oil in a frying pan. Spoon batter around pan like pancakes. Fry until brown on both sides. Drain on paper towels.
3. In a saucepan, combine sugar, water and lemon juice. Cook until sugar dissolves.
4. To serve, dip each pancake in sauce, then place on serving platter.

Preparation and Cooking Time: 20 to 30 minutes

CHANUKAH
Chanukah Balls

Rochel Mark
Milwaukee, Wisconsin

Yield: 6 Dozen Balls

1 cup dates, cut up
1 cup candied red and
 green cherries, cut up
1 cup walnuts, chopped

¼ cup shredded coconut
1 can sweet condensed
 milk

1. Preheat oven to 350°F.
2. In a large bowl, combine dates, red and green cherries, walnuts, coconut and milk.
3. Wet hands. Shape mixture into 1-inch balls. Spray cookie sheet with no-stick cooking spray. Arrange cookie balls on sheet. Bake in 350°F oven 12 to 20 minutes or until firm to the touch.

Preparation and Cooking Time: 30 minutes

PURIM
Grandma's Prune Filled Hamantashen

Sybil Kaplan
Overland Park, Kansas   Yield: 36 Small Hamantashen

2 cakes dry yeast
½ cup lukewarm milk
2 eggs
½ cup sugar
½ cup butter or margarine
1 teaspoon salt

1 cup sour cream
4 to 5 cups flour
  Filling
1½ cups prunes, pitted and
  cut up
¼ cup sugar
2 teaspoons lemon juice

Day before:
1. Dissolve yeast in a bowl with warm milk. Let stand a few minutes.
3. Beat eggs and sugar in a mixing bowl. Add yeast, butter or margarine, salt and sour cream and beat.
4. Add 4 cups flour. Mix thoroughly. Gradually add the rest of the flour then turn out dough to a floured board and knead until it is smooth and does not stick to your hands. Place dough in a greased bowl. Turn dough until it is covered with the oil. Cover with a cloth and refrigerate overnight.

Next day:
5. Preheat oven to 350°F.
6. Roll out dough ¼-inch thick, on a lightly floured board. Cut into 16 squares.
7. In a small bowl, combine prunes, sugar and lemon juice. Place 1 spoon of filling on each square. Fold to form triangles. Place on a greased cookie sheet. Let rise 1 hour until double in size. Bake in 350°F oven 20 minutes or until brown.

Preparation and Cooking Time: 25½ hours

PURIM
Marathi Puran Polis

Solomon Michael Daniel   India
Bombay, Maharashtra

300 grams (10½ ounces) refined flour (maida)	**500 grams (10½ ounces) chana dal (Bengal gram)**
200 grams (7 ounces) wheat flour (atta)	**400 grams (14 ounces) sugar**
½ teaspoon salt	**½ teaspoon nutmeg**
30 ml (1 ounce) oil	

1. Place the maida and atta flours and salt in a bowl. Add half the oil and knead a soft, elastic dough, sprinkling water on the dough in the process. Set aside for 2 to 3 hours.
2. Meanwhile, place the chana dal in a pan and cook until tender with just enough water to cook. Add sugar and cook until mixture becomes thick and moisture evaporates. Cook until the mixture is soft and neither too liquid or too dry.
3. Add nutmeg to the mixture. Grind on the grinding stone (a very sticky and tedious process) to a smooth paste. The idea is to make the flour so soft and elastic that a lump pulled out of it will trail behind a tail of dough.
4. Use a large, flat tawa to bake the chapatis. Take a lump of dough the size of a medium-size lemon. Put a dot of oil in the palm of your hand and mold this ball into a hollow katori shape. Take 2½ times as much stuffing as dough. Form it into a neat ball and place it in the katori of dough.

5. Gently mold the dough around the stuffing to close at the top. Sprinkle the rolling board liberally with flour and roll out the ball into a fine thin chapati. This is a very delicate operation. You cannot lift the chapati and turn it over as you would an ordinary chapati. The plentiful flour keeps the chapati moving on the board. An expert can work this size of ball into a chapati about 27.5 cm (11 inches), but a thicker, smaller chapati could be made to start with. Once rolled, the chapati has to be put on the tawa* very carefully.

The traditional way to do this is to roll it around the rolling pin and then unroll it on the tawa. Let it bake well on one side, then carefully turn it over. When the second side is done, apply ghee** or dalda*** on both sides and remove from the tawa.

Preparation and Cooking Time: 4 hours

Note: * Tawa is a flat, iron grid for baking chapaties. A non-stick frying pan can also be used.
Chapati is an unleavened pancake like bread from India where the dough is rolled into thin rounds and baked on a griddle.
** Ghee is butter which is slowly melted to separate the milk solids from the golden liquid on the surface.

PURIM
Grandma's Poppy Seed Filling
for Hamantashen

Sybil Kaplan
Overland Park, Kansas

My mother told me that my grandmother always made her hamantashen with <u>mohn</u> (poppy seeds) and a yeast dough. My mother said when she was a child, she could remember her mother boiling the poppy seeds, draining them, and then she and her brothers took turns chopping them in the pestle which her father had gotten from Europe.

1 cup poppy seeds	**2 tablespoons honey**
¾ cup milk	**½ cup raisins**
2 tablespoons butter or margarine	**½ cup nuts, chopped**
	1 teaspoon vanilla

1. Place poppy seeds, milk, butter or margarine, honey, raisins and nuts in a saucepan. Bring to a boil.
2. Reduce heat and simmer until milk is absorbed. Stir in vanilla. Let cool before using in recipe for hamantashen.

Preparation and Cooking Time: 15 minutes

PASSOVER
"Sabra" Haroset

Sybil Kaplan   Israel
Overland Park, Kansas

*I found this in **The Jerusalem Post** more years ago than I can remember.*

2 apples, peeled and cored	1 cup unsalted nuts
6 bananas, peeled	1 cup dry red wine
Juice and peel of 1 lemon	Matzah meal
Juice and peel of 1 orange	2 teaspoons cinnamon
20 dates, pitted	Sugar to taste

1. Blend or puree apples, bananas, lemon, orange and dates and place in a bowl.
2. Add wine and matzah meal to the consistency you like. Mix in cinnamon and sugar to taste.

Preparation and Cooking Time: 15 minutes

"the trees of the field shall yield their fruit"
(Leviticus 26:4)

PASSOVER
Spinach-Mushroom "Mina"

Dalia Carmel   Turkey
New York, New York   Yield: 6 to 8 Servings

The original recipe was given to me by Edmond Feinstein who was manager of the catering company that provides in-flight meals for El Al Israel Airlines. This was his mother's layered Matzot pie, a Sephardic recipe from Izmir, Turkey, traditionally served during Passover week. I adapted the recipe and made some changes and this is the result.

1 tablespoon olive oil
1 cup onions, chopped
1 teaspoon garlic, minced
½ pound mushrooms, trimmed
  and finely chopped
2 10-ounce packages frozen
  spinach, thawed and squeezed
  between 2 plates to release
  excess liquid
6 ounces feta cheese,
  crumbled
¾ teaspoon salt

⅛ teaspoon black pepper
  freshly ground
6 squares matzot
Water
1 teaspoon margarine
3 large eggs, beaten
1 sweet red pepper, cut
  into thin strips
2 tablespoons parsley,
  finely minced
Black olives

1. Preheat oven to 375°F.
2. Heat oil in a large skillet. Add onions and garlic and sauté 3 minutes, stirring frequently. Add mushrooms and cook over medium heat, stirring frequently, until most of the liquid released by mushrooms has evaporated, 3 to 5 minutes longer.
3. Remove from heat and stir in spinach, feta, salt and pepper.
4. Place matzot in a 7x12-inch baking dish. Pour over ample water to cover. Gently press matzot down into water just long enough to moisten surfaces, about 30 seconds. Remove matzot. Pour out water and dry the baking dish. Grease dish with margarine.

5. Beat eggs in large, flat dish with sides. Soak each matzah in beaten eggs about 1 minute on each side. Set 2 egg-dipped matzot, side by side, in bottom of prepared baking dish, overlapping slightly. Evenly distribute half of filling on top.

6. Add second layer of egg-dipped matzot and then remainder of filling. Top with remaining egg-dipped matzot. Reserve any remaining beaten egg.

7. Tightly cover with foil. Bake in 375°F oven 20 minutes. Remove oil. Brush top with remaining egg. Continue to bake until top is lightly browned, 5 to 10 minutes longer. Arrange red pepper strips on top. Sprinkle with parsley and dot with olives.

   To serve, cut like lasagna.

Preparation and Cooking Time: 40 minutes

Note: This recipe previously appeared in an interview of Dalia Carmel by Lorna Sass in *The Los Angeles Times* (undated).

PASSOVER
Yemenite Haroset

Sybil Kaplan   Middle East
Overland Park, Kansas

I found this in **The Jerusalem Post** *and I have no idea when.*

30 dates, pitted and chopped	**2 teaspoons hot ginger**
20 dry figs, chopped	**powder**
2 tablespoons sesame seeds	**Matzah meal**
	Dry red wine

1. Place chopped fruit in a bowl. Add sesame seeds, ginger, matzah meal and wine to make a firm paste.

Preparation and Cooking Time: 15 minutes

"And the trees said to the fig tree, come you, and reign over us" *(Judges 9:10)*

PASSOVER
Turkish Charoseth

Ruth deSola Mendes
Pound Ridge, New York

Middle East Style
Yield: 2 cups

When we were first married, a coworker of my husband's brought back a cookbook from a Los Angeles Sephardic congregation and a recipe like this was in it. Over the years I have adapted it.

⅔ cup golden raisins
Wine
1 pound dates, pitted
1 orange, cut up with peel

1 Granny Smith apple,
peeled and cored
⅓ cup almonds (optional)

1. Place raisins in a bowl. Add wine and soak for 2 hours.
2. Grind dates, raisins, apple and almonds, if using, in a food processor. This will have the consistency of thick jam.

It is delicious throughout Pesach on matzah.

Preparation and Cooking Time: 15 minutes

Pareve

PASSOVER
Passover Bagels

Lisa Goldman
Chandler, Arizona

Yield: 12 Bagels

½ cup oil
1½ cups water
1 teaspoon salt

1 teaspoon sugar
2½ cups matzah meal
4 eggs

1. Preheat oven to 350°F.
2. Place oil, water, salt and sugar in a saucepan. Bring to a full boil. Remove from the heat.
3. Add matzah meal all at once and stir with a wooden spoon until well blended.
4. Add eggs, one at a time, beating well after each addition. Let stand 15 minutes. If batter is too soft to form into bagels, refrigerate until easy to handle.
5. Drop by tablespoonfuls onto a greased cookie sheet two inches apart. You can also form into balls with greased hands. Wet the forefinger and place a hole in the center of each ball. Bake in 350°F oven 50 to 60 minutes.

Variations: roll dough into balls and bake as dinner rolls. Add onion powder or garlic powder (1 teaspoon) for flavored bagels.

Preparation and Cooking Time: 1½ hours

PASSOVER
Passover Rolls

Hilda Meth
Richmond, Virginia   Yield: 12 Rolls

I believe this recipe came from Jo Milgrom, the rabbi's wife.

2 cups matzah meal	**1 cup water**
1 teaspoon salt	**½ cup oil**
1 teaspoon sugar	**4 eggs**

1. Preheat oven to 375° F.
2. Combine matzah meal, salt and sugar in a bowl.
3. Bring oil and water to a boil in a saucepan. Add to matzah meal mixture and mix well.
4. Beat in eggs, one at a time. Allow to stand 15 minutes.
5. With oiled hands, shape into rolls and put on a well-greased cookie sheet. Bake in 375° F oven for 50 minutes or until golden brown

Preparation and Cooking Time: 1½ hours

PASSOVER
My Grandma's Fluffy Kneidel (matzah balls)

Sybil Kaplan
Overland Park, Kansas   Yield: 8 to 12 Balls

My Grandma, Sade Lyon, was a great cook. She was born in New Jersey and I imagine she learned to cook from her mother whom I am told was a great cook also. This was her special recipe for matzah balls for Pesach. My mother told me Grandma got the recipe from a relative who had gotten it from a woman who had a Jewish restaurant many years before that.

2 eggs	**2 tablespoons cold water**
2 tablespoons chicken fat	**Water**
½ cup matzah meal	**1 teaspoon salt**
⅓ teaspoon salt or salt to taste	

1. Beat eggs in a bowl until light in color. Add chicken fat and beat together.
2. Add matzah meal, salt and cold water. Mix together until smooth. Form into 8 to 12 small balls.
3. Heat a soup pot with water to which 1 teaspoon salt has been added. When water is boiling, drop in matzah balls. Cover and cook 30 minutes. Drain off water and add to soup.

Preparation and Cooking Time: 1 hours

PASSOVER
Orange Basted Chicken
with Matzah Nut Stuffing

Sybil Kaplan
Overland Park, Kansas   Yield: 4 to 6 Servings

2½ tablespoons oil or
  chicken fat
3 tablespoons onions, minced
3 tablespoons celery, chopped
3 tablespoons nuts, chopped
2 matzah sheets, broken or
  1¼ cup farfel
1 egg
¼ teaspoon salt
Dash pepper

⅔ cup chicken soup
1½ teaspoons orange peel
  grated
2-to 2¼-pound chicken
½ cup orange juice
1 teaspoon orange peel,
  grated
⅛ cup honey or
  brown sugar
⅛ cup oil

1. Preheat oven to 325°F.
2. Melt chicken fat or heat oil in frying pan. Sauté onion, celery and nuts until vegetables are tender.
3. Add matzah meal or farfel and mix well.
4. In a bowl, combine egg, salt, pepper, chicken soup and 1½ teaspoon orange peel. Add matzah-vegetable mixture and blend. Stuff inside chicken. Place chicken on a rack in a roasting pan.
5. In a bowl, combine orange juice, 1 teaspoon grated peel, honey or brown sugar and oil. Place chicken in a 325°F oven. Pour basing sauce on top. Turn and baste every 15 minutes for an hour. Continue roasting until brown or as done as you like it, basting frequently.

Preparation and Cooking Time: 1½ hours

PASSOVER
Passover Tzimmes

Sybil Kaplan
Overland Park, Kansas

Yield: 10 to 12 Servings

This recipe came from my mother, Rae Horowitz.

1-to 4-pound brisket	**¾ cup prunes**
2 onions, sliced	**8 carrots, sliced**
1¼ cups water	**4 sweet potatoes,**
1½ tablespoons brown sugar	**peeled and sliced**
¼ teaspoon nutmeg	**4 white potatoes,**
¾ cup apricots	**peeled and sliced**

1. Preheat oven to 300°F.
2. Pierce meat with fork. Place in a roaster. Add onions and brown on top of the stove.
3. Add water, sugar and nutmeg. Place in 300°F oven. Allow 45 minutes per pound. One hour before done, add apricots, prunes, carrots and potatoes.

Preparation and Cooking Time: 1 to 3 hours

PASSOVER
Vermicelli or Pasta
Kremzlach

The Aleph-Bet of Jewish Cooking   Russia

Yield: 12 Pieces

2 eggs, separated	**2 teaspoons potato starch**
½ teaspoon salt	**Pinch pepper**
¼ cup matzah meal	**Butter or margarine**

1. Place egg whites in a bowl with salt and beat.
2. Place egg yolks in another bowl and beat. Add to whites very carefully.
3. Add matzah meal, potato starch and pepper. Mix thoroughly.
4. Heat butter or margarine in a frying pan. Drop in teaspoonfuls of dough and fry on both sides until brown. Drain on paper towels.

Preparation and Cooking Time: 20 minutes

Reprinted with permission from Shvut Ami, the International Center for Soviet Jews, Jerusalem, Israel.

Note: Kremzlach is Yiddish for vermicelli and was eaten traditionally on Friday evening after kiddush.

Pareve

PASSOVER
Spinach Fritada

Ruth deSola Mendes
Pound Ridge, New York   Yield: 8 Servings

*I found this recipe in Rica deSola Mendes' handwritten cookbook.
She was my husband's grandmother, and her father was the first
rabbi in Canada, the London-born Abraham deSola of the Spanish-
Portuguese synagogue in Montreal.*

3 matzot	**Salt and pepper to taste**
Hot water	**Cooking parchment**
7 large eggs	**(optional)**
3 packages frozen, chopped	**⅓ cup olive oil**
spinach, thawed and	
squeezed dry	

1. Preheat oven to 350° F.
2. Place hot water in a shallow plate. Soak matzot for a
   minute. Drain and squeeze out excess water.
3. Beat eggs in a large bowl. Add spinach and matzot, salt
   and pepper. Stir until it is well blended.
4. If using cooking parchment, lightly oil a 9x13-inch pan or
   glass baking dish and place parchment in dish. Pour in oil.
5. If not using parchment, pour oil in baking dish. Add
   mixture and spread evenly. Sprinkle about 1 teaspoon oil
   on top. Bake in 350° F oven 1 hour. Cut into squares.

This is good hot, at room temperature or even cold. For a
dairy meal, blend in 1 cup ricotta cheese to spinach mixture
before making.

Preparation and Cooking Time: 1¼ hours

Note: The purpose of the parchment is to enable removal of
the fritada one piece at a time if you choose to make this
ahead of time.

PASSOVER
Yemenite Sweet Avocado Dessert

Ruth deSola Mendes
Pound Ridge, New York

Middle East Style
Yield: 6 Servings

This was passed on to me by an Ashkenazi girl friend who married a Bukharian Jew and started cooking Sephardic recipes.

3 small avocados	**2 tablespoons lemon juice**
½ cup walnuts, ground	**2 tablespoons honey**
⅓ cup orange juice	**6 walnut halves, shelled**

1. Split avocados in half. Carefully remove pits and flesh and place flesh in a bowl. Reserve scooped-out shells.
2. Mash avocado flesh with a fork and stir in ground walnuts, orange juice, lemon juice and honey. Blend well with a fork.
3. Spoon mixture back into shells. Place a walnut half on each top and chill until ready to serve.

Preparation and Cooking Time: 15 minutes

PASSOVER
Matzah Fruit Kugel

Sonia Golad
Kansas City, Missouri   Yield: 10 to 12 Servings

This recipe came from my daughter, Kacey Kahn, who lived in Los Angeles. Usually for Passover I did the cooking, but one year she said she wanted to do something and she made this for us. It was outstanding! I really cherish this because now my daughter is gone, but I have this recipe.

5 matzot	1 tablespoon lemon juice
6 large eggs	1 teaspoon cinnamon
2 red apples, shredded	2 teaspoons vanilla
with peels	2 tablespoons margarine,
1 small pear, shredded	unsalted
with peel	2 tablespoons sugar mixed
¾ cup golden raisins	with ½ teaspoon
3 tablespoons sugar	cinnamon
Grated peel of 1 lemon	2 tablespoons currant jelly

1. Preheat oven to 325°F.
2. Break matzot into pieces in a bowl and cover with water. Soak 2 minutes and drain.
3. Beat eggs until fluffy in a second bowl. Stir in apples, pear, raisins, sugar, lemon peel, lemon juice, cinnamon and vanilla. Mix together. Add matzot and blend.
4. Place margarine in a 9x13-inch casserole and heat in a 325°F oven until melted. Swish margarine around in pan so it is coated well. Pour excess margarine into matzot-fruit mixture. Stir, then pour into casserole, spreading evenly.

5. Mix sugar and cinnamon in a bowl and sprinkle on top of casserole. Top with jelly. Bake in 325°F oven for 45 minutes.

Preparation and Cooking Time: 1½ hours

Note: Kugel is Yiddish for baked pudding, usually served at Sabbath lunch. Kugel came from the German word for ball or sphere and people from each country had variations in the kinds they made. Matzah kugel was particularly Polish.

"take of the best fruits in the land in your vessel and carry down the man a little honey" (Genesis 43:11)

Pareve

PASSOVER
Matzah Cake

Sybil Kaplan
Overland Park, Kansas   Yield: 8 to 12 Servings

*An Israeli friend of an Israeli friend brought this cake to dinner
during Pesach at my friend's and since it was unusual, I asked for
the recipe.*

2 sticks unsalted margarine	3½ tablespoons
12 sheets matzah	unsweetened cocoa
Water	Chopped nuts (optional
Wine	Sliced bananas (optional
1 egg	Sliced strawberries
¼ cup sugar	(optional)

1. Place margarine in a saucepan and melt.
2. Meanwhile, place matzah in a colander, wet slightly.
   Sprinkle with wine.
3. Place margarine in a bowl. Add egg, sugar and cocoa.
   Spread mixture on one piece of matzah placed on a plate.
   Sprinkle nuts or add banana slices or strawberry slices on
   top. Continue layering until you have six .
4. Start over and repeat process until you have six layers.

This recipe makes two six-layer cakes.

Preparation and Cooking Time: 20 minutes

PASSOVER
Wine and Nut Cake

Helen D. Hiller
Shorewood, Wisconsin   Yield: 12 to 14 Servings

8 eggs	4 ounces sweet red wine
2 cups sugar	Pinch salt
Juice of one orange	1 cup matzah cake flour
Peel of one lemon	1 cup nuts, finely chopped

1. Preheat oven to 325°F.
2. Separate eggs into two bowls. Beat yolks. Add 1 cup sugar. Beat again. Set aside.
3. Beat whites until stiff, adding 1 cup sugar when whites are almost stiff.
4. Add orange juice, lemon rind and wine to yolks and beat again. Add yolks to whites very slowly.
5. Add salt, flour and nuts. Fold mixture gently until whites are not seen. Pour into a ungreased tube pan. Bake in 325°F oven 55 minutes to 1 hour or until a toothpick inserted into the center comes out clean.
6. Turn over baked cake pan to cool on the prongs of the cake pan or over the neck of a bottle.

Preparation and Cooking Time: 1¼ hours

PASSOVER
Signy's Macaroons

Ruth deSola Mendes
Pound Ridge, New York   Yield: 60 Macaroons

Ted Spiegel is a photographer. His wife, Signy, is a friend and Swedish. This is her recipe passed on and adapted slightly.

4 egg whites
1 cup sugar
½ teaspoon vanilla sugar
3 cups shredded coconut

1. Preheat oven to 375° F.
2. Beat egg whites in a mixing bowl until stiff, adding sugar.
3. Blend in vanilla sugar and coconut. Drop on ungreased cookie sheet by tablespoonfuls. Bake in a 375° F oven 10 to 15 minutes until light golden brown. Remove immediately and cool on a rack.

Preparation and Cooking Time: 30 minutes

PASSOVER
Matzah Meal Cookie
Zavarnoye Testoiz Matzovoy Muki

The Aleph-Bet of Jewish Cooking   Russia

Yield: 48 Cookies

1 cup water	4 eggs
1 teaspoon salt	Jam, sweet filling or
½ cup olive oil	powdered sugar
1 cup matzah meal	(optional)

1. Preheat oven to 375°F.
2. Mix water, salt and oil in a saucepan and bring to a boil. Remove from the heat.
3. Add matzah meal and return pot to low heat, continually stirring until the dough stops sticking to the sides of the pan. Remove from heat and let cool 10 to 15 minutes.
4. Add eggs, one at a time, stirring after each.
5. Oil a cookie sheet. Drop the dough by teaspoonfuls, leaving room between each piece for the dough to rise.
6. Bake in 375°F oven until golden brown. Let cool. Fill with jam or sweet filling or sprinkle powdered sugar on top.

Preparation and Cooking Time: 30 to 40 minutes

Note: Reprinted with permission by Shvut Ami, the International Center for Soviet Jews, Jerusalem, Israel.

Pareve

PASSOVER
Cocoa Coconut Matzah Balls

Marilyn Landes
Jerusalem, Israel

Israel
Yield: 20 Large Balls

Marilyn has lived in Israel since 1949, an American originally from Revere, Massachusetts. She teaches college, is active in a variety of organizations, does folk dancing, enjoys her grandchildren and has authored several books.

⅓ cup oil
1 egg
¼ cup water or coffee or
   orange juice
½ cup sugar
½ cup matzah meal

¼ cup nuts, ground
¼ cup cocoa
2 tablespoons cognac, wine
   or cherry brandy
1 tablespoon coconut

1. Place oil, egg, water or coffee or orange juice, sugar, matzo meal, nuts, cocoa, cognac, wine or brandy in a bowl. Mix until you can shape the ingredients into a ball. Add more matzah meal to make the dough stick together.
2. Place coconut on wax paper. Shape dough into balls, then roll in coconut. Place on a flat sheet and refrigerate.

Preparation and Cooking Time: 15 to 20 minutes

PASSOVER
Ginger Candy

Esther Goldman   Russia
Overland Park, Kansas   Yield: 40 Pieces

I got this from my mother, Doris Rainen, who came from Russia. This was something we all enjoyed and looked forward to for Passover.

1 pound farfel
2 eggs
1 pound honey
½ cup sugar
1 cup walnuts, broken up

1. Preheat oven to 350°F.
2. Place farfel in a bowl. Beat in eggs gently and rub the farfel with your hands.
3. Place on a baking plate in the 350°F oven to dry. When golden brown, remove. Pour into saucepan. Add honey and sugar and bring to a boil. Cook 5 minutes and add nuts. Continue cooking until mixture turns a light brown. Keep mixing with a wooden spoon about 15 minutes.
4. Turn onto a large wet wooden board. Keep wetting your hands as you pat dough to a thickness of about ⅜ inch. Sprinkle with ginger. The more ginger you add, the "hotter" it becomes.
5. Cut into diamond shapes as it cools. If you allow it to cool too much, it is impossible to cut.

Preparation and Cooking Time: 30 minutes

Note: The other name for this is ingberlach from the Yiddish word for ginger, ingber. Farfel are small toasted bits of noodle dough.

SHAVUOT
Blintzes

Sybil Kaplan
Overland Park, Kansas

Yield: 12 Blintzes

This recipe came to me from my mother, Rae Horowitz, who got it from my grandmother, Sade Lyon, who used it for may years.

Batter	Filling
1 cup flour	2 cups dry white cheese
1 teaspoon baking powder	½ cup cream cheese
1 teaspoon salt	1 egg
1 cup water	2 tablespoons sugar
2 eggs	½ teaspoon cinnamon
Butter, margarine or oil	Sour cream, sugar, honey cinnamon or preserves

1. Place flour, baking powder and salt in a mixing bowl. Blend.
2. Add water and eggs and mix batter until smooth.
3. Heat butter, margarine or oil in a small, 6 to 7-inch diameter frying pan. Spoon 1 large tablespoon of batter into pan, tip quickly to spread evenly and thinly to coat bottom of pan. Fry until edges look cooked (about 1 minute). Turn onto a dry dish towel on a table.
4. Continue until all batter is used.
5. Combine dry white cheese, cream cheese, egg, sugar and cinnamon in a bowl. Stir until smooth.
6. Place about 1½ tablespoons filling on each pancake. Tuck in sides and roll up. * Heat butter, margarine or oil in a frying pan. Fry each blintz open side down, then turn and fry on other side until brown.
Serve with sour cream, sugar, honey, cinnamon or preserves.

Preparation and Cooking Time: 20 to 30 minutes

Note: Blintzes probably came from the Ukraine and were a cousin to the Russian filled pancakes.

They have also been called "Jewish crepes."

* These can be wrapped and frozen at this stage and fried later on.

To make home-made yogurt cheese, place yogurt and a little salt in a clean piece of cloth over your sink overnight or at least 4 to 6 hours. Place bag in colander set in a drip pan. Cover and refrigerate overnight. Turn cheese out of cloth into covered bowl.

SHAVUOT
Israeli No-Bake Cheese Cake

Sybil Kaplan
Overland Park, Kansas

Israel Style
Yield: 4 to 6 Servings

I learned this while living in Israel.

1 package instant
  vanilla pudding
2 cups low-fat milk
2 cups low-fat white cheese
½ cup raisins
Milk

64 lightly sweetened
  plain cookies
Coconut (optional)
Pineapple slices (optional)
Strawberries, sliced
  (optional)

1. Mix pudding in a bowl with milk according to package directions. Add cheese and raisins. Set aside.
2. Place some milk in a shallow dish. Dip 16 to 20 cookies in milk. In a deeper square or rectangular baking dish, arrange 4 to 5 rows of 4 to 5 cookies each. Spread one-third pudding-cheese mixture on top.
3. Add another layer of 16 to 20 cookies, which have first been dipped in milk, on top of first layer. Spread second third of pudding-cheese on top mixture. Add final layer of cookies on top. Refrigerate until ready to serve.

For decoration, sprinkle coconut on top or arrange pineapple slices or strawberry slices on top.

Preparation and Cooking Time: 20 to 30 minutes

SHAVUOT
Low-Fat, Sugar-Free, Crustless Cheese Cake

Sybil Kaplan
Overland Park, Kansas   Yield: 4 to 6 Servings

2 eggs
2 tablespoons sugar
1½ teaspoons sugar substitute
1 teaspoon vanilla
1½ cups low-fat creamed
   cottage cheese

8 ounces low-fat cream
   cheese
1 cup low-fat or imitation
   sour cream

1. Preheat oven to 350°F.
2. Blend eggs, sugar, sugar substitute, vanilla, cottage cheese and cream cheese.
3. Pour into a 9-inch round floured and greased cake pan. Bake in 350°F oven 35 to 40 minutes or until center is firm.
4. Remove from oven. Spread with sour cream while cake is hot. Cool, then refrigerate.

Preparation and Cooking Time: 50 minutes

"He shall eat curd; for curd and honey shall every one eat" *(Isaiach 7:22)*

SHAVUOT
⌐ Rich Cheese Cake

Sybil Kaplan
Overland Park, Kansas
Yield: 8 Servings

This recipe came from my mother, Rae Horowitz. She said it was her favorite cheese cake recipe and it is absolutely tops! She got it from my Grandma's sister, Aunt Esther Simon.

Crust	Filling
2 cups plain cookies, crushed	**1½ cups cream cheese**
½ cup butter or margarine, softened	**2 eggs**
¼ cup sugar	**½ cup sugar**
Dash cinnamon	**½ teaspoon vanilla**
	½ teaspoon salt

Topping	
2 cups sour cream	**Crushed pineapple,**
2 tablespoons sugar	**Fresh strawberries,**
½ teaspoon vanilla	**Canned cherries or**
⅛ teaspoon salt	**yogurt**

1. Preheat oven to 350°F.
2. Combine crushed cookies, butter or margarine, sugar and cinnamon for crust in a mixing bowl. Place in a spring-form pan. Bake in 350°F oven 10 minutes. Remove.
3. Place cream cheese in a bowl and whip with mixer. Add eggs, sugar, vanilla and salt. Continue beating until fluffy. Pour into baked crust and bake 30 minutes more. Remove from oven.
4. Combine and blend in a mixing bowl, sour cream, sugar, vanilla and salt. Spread on top of cake. Return to oven and bake 10 minutes.
   Top with crushed pineapple, fresh strawberries, canned fruit or yogurt.

Preparation and Cooking Time: 1 hour

SHAVUOT
Mom's Noodle Kugel

Sybil Kaplan
Overland Park, Kansas

Yield: 4 to 5 Servings

This was a recipe which came from my mother, Rae Horowitz. She told me it was my Grandma Sade Lyon's recipe and she learned to make it from her.

Water
1 teaspoon salt
1½ cup wide noodles
1 egg
3 tablespoons sugar
1 tablespoon butter or
   margarine

¼ teaspoon cinnamon
½ cup raisins
⅛ teaspoon salt
1⅛ cups cottage cheese
   (optional)
⅜ cup sour cream
   (optional)

1. Preheat oven to 350° F.
2. Place water in a saucepan with salt and bring to a boil. Add noodles and cook for 10 minutes. Drain and place in mixing bowl.
3. Add egg, sugar, butter or margarine, cinnamon, raisins and salt. If you wish, add cottage cheese and sour cream. Blend well. Pour into a greased casserole. Bake in 350° F oven 30 minutes.

Preparation and Cooking Time: 1 hour

Pareve/Dairy

POST TISHA b'AV
Marathi Birda

Solomon Michael Daniel   India
Bombay, Maharashtra

This dish is prepared by the Bene-Israel Jews in India particularly on the 9th day of Av to be eaten after Tisha b'Av. The beans called "vals" are first cleaned, sorted out and put in the sun for 4 to 5 days. Then they are preserved in an air-tight jar with leaves of the neem tree. If the vals are soaked in water even after a year or two, they sprout. The beans are just as the Jews, even though they have been persecuted, ill treated and harassed, they again grow in numbers. That is the reason the Bene-Israel have this traditional dish.

2 cups val (beans)	6 green chilies
½ inch turmeric	10 garlic cloves
1 teaspoon salt	1 inch ginger
2 onions, chopped	1 teaspoon cumin seeds
2 tablespoons oil	Milk of 1 coconut
½ bunch coriander leaves (cilantro)	1 teaspoon garam masala powder*

1. Soak the val overnight in water. Then place them in a muslin cloth bag and hang it, taking care to keep it damp all the time.
2. After 24 hours when the beans have sprouted, put them in water and remove the peel. Soak the peeled val in hot water for a few minutes then drain the water.
3. In a frying pan, heat oil and brown onions. Add spices and fry. Add peeled val and a little water and cook. When the water is absorbed, add coconut milk. Continue until cooked.

- 430 -

4. Add salt. Remove from heat when gravy thickens.
   Serve with puris (deep fried, round, flat, unleavened whole wheat bread) or chapatis (unleavened pancake-like bread made of whole wheat flour) and lime.

Preparation and Cooking Time: 25 hours

Note: Garam masala powder is a blend of ground spices. This version contains cardamon, cinnamon, cloves and pepper.

Wine

Not Just For Kiddush

**"Blessed art Thou, O Lord our G-d,
King of the universe, who created the fruit of the vine."**

Most of us are familiar with that traditional <u>kiddush</u>, the blessing over the wine, and we tend to associate kosher wine with--something sweet, dark red, syrupy or Passover.

Today, a new trend is growing in the kosher wine industry. One might say, a revolution has taken place and the words associated with it are Sauvignon, Emerald Riesling, Zinfandel and Chardonnay.

While a segment of the Jewish population today still drinks only the sweet wines for Shabbat and other ritual occasions, others are changing the stereotype and discovering that kosher wine can be a high-quality beverage to have with meals. Many people have refined their tastes in food, they enjoy wine as a complement, and they are actively seeking these wines to drink.

Take our community of 22,000 Jews with one kosher butcher who also has a bakery and grocery section as part of the store. One wall is now filled with fine kosher table wines from numerous countries and the United States and Israel.

Wine drinking has had an interesting historical evolution. Eastern European Jews who immigrated to the United States in the late 1800s and early 1900s took the grapes available, added lots of sugar and made their own wine. When the first kosher wines were produced commercially, they too were sweet and used for rituals.

The first winemaker was actually Noah, so they say, and when Moses sent spies to explore the land of Israel, they returned with a cluster of grapes upon a pole. Wine is frequently mentioned in the Bible and viticulture has become a real science and art in modern-day Israel.

Not only are kosher wines produced in Israel, they are also produced in Spain, France, Italy, Denmark, the United States and other countries.

What makes a wine kosher? Wines are considered kosher only if Sabbath-observant Jews are involved in the process from harvesting to fermentation to processing and production. Ingredients such as gelatin, lactose, glycerines, corn products, non-wine yeast or most chemical additives are not added during the processing, lest they render the wine non kosher for year-round use, including Passover.

All of the American producers of kosher wines have long histories. All have added to the traditional sweet wine other varieties such as creams, champagnes, cooking wines and California varietals.

Articles even appear from time to time in gourmet food magazines discussing kosher wines today and the changes which have taken place especially during the 1970s.

Wine can make a difference in cooking as well. At the end of this chapter is a list of more than 60 recipes in this cookbook using wines, liqueurs or cordials which we hope you will enjoy.

The following recipes come from staff members or the chef from two of the well-known American producers of kosher wines: Hagafen Cellars in California and Kedem Royal Wine Corporation in New York State. We have also included some brief synopses of these two wine producers and some of their recommended recipes.

Next time you think of kosher wine, remember,
"A feast is made for laughter,
And wine maketh glad the life" (Ecl. 10:19)

Sybil Kaplan

Hagafen Cellars, Napa Valley, California

Hagafen ("the vine" in Hebrew) crushed and bottled its first wines in 1980 and became Napa Valley's only producer of premium table wines that are also kosher. The winery was founded by Ernie Weir in 1979 and annually produces Cabernet Sauvignon, Chardonnay, Johannesberg Riesling, Pinot Noir, Harmonia Red, White and Blush tables wines. All are either dry or off-dry. Hagafen wines are produced under strict kosher guidelines. They have won many awards and have been served on several occasions at the White House.

Kedem Royal Wine Corporation

Through eight generations and more than 140 years, from 19th century Czechoslovakia through Nazi-occupied Europe to modern-day America, the Herzog family has operated the Royal Wine Corporation, the world's largest importer/producer of kosher wines, foods and beverages. Often referred to as "Kedem," the company traveled a bumpy road before finding the path to success in America under the then family leader, Eugene Herzog. The name, Kedem, is derived from the Hebrew words, *chadaish yamanu cakedem*, "renew our days as before."

Beef Stew

Hagafen Cellars
Napa, California

Yield: 4 Servings

This recipe was submitted by Nancy Levenberg, Sales and Marketing.

2 pounds stew meat,
  well trimmed, cut into
  2-inch pieces
2 bay leaves
2 cups Hagafen Pinot Noir
3 tablespoons oil
2 medium red onions,
  peeled and quartered
1 to 3 garlic cloves, peeled
  and flattened
6 potatoes, scrubbed and
  cut into 2-inch chunks

6 carrots, peeled and cut
  into 2-inch lengths
1 16-ounce can pureed
  tomatoes
2 strips fresh orange peel
2 teaspoons thyme
Salt and pepper to taste
Mushrooms (optional)
Turnips (optional)
Peas (optional)

Day before serving:

1. Place stew meat and bay leaves in a large porcelain bowl.
   Cover with wine. Cover with plastic wrap and place in
   refrigerator to marinate at least 12 hours and preferably 24
   hours.
   Next day:
2. Remove meat and marinade from refrigerator at least one
   half hour before you plan to cook it. Let it come to room
   temperature. Remove meat from marinade, reserve
   marinade and pat meat dry.
3. Place oil in a large and heavy stew pot. Warm over
   medium heat. Brown meat cubes in small batches until all
   meat has been browned, removing from the pot as pieces
   are done.

4. To pan juices, add onions and garlic and stir briefly before adding meat, potatoes, carrots, pureed tomatoes, orange peel, thyme, salt, pepper and reserved wine. Add other vegetables here if using. If the liquid does not cover the mixture, add more wine. Cover the pot and bring the liquid to a boil. Reduce heat to barely simmer and cook until meat is tender, 1 to 2 hours. The stew should be thick and flavorful when served.

If you like a very thick gravy, remove the meat and vegetables, increase the heat to high, reduce the gravy by boiling it down, stirring continually.

You may also thicken the mixture by adding cornstarch and water.

The high acidity of the Hagafen Pinot Noir makes for a very tender and succulent stew because the acid helps break down the fat in the stew meat as it marinates and cooks.

Preparation and Cooking Time: 24 hours

For a cheaper cut of meat for making stew, use strong tea instead of water when cooking.

Veal Shanks in a Wine Sauce

Hagafen Cellars
Napa, California

Yield: 12 Servings

Judy Zeidler, television chef, created this recipe for Hagafen.

12 pieces veal shanks, cut 2 inches thick	6 celery ribs
Salt and pepper to taste	6 fresh thyme or rosemary sprigs
½ cup oil	6 ounces dried prunes
6 garlic cloves	6 ounces dried apricots
2 large onions, chopped fine	½ to ¾ cup Johannesberg Riesling
2 to 3 carrots, scraped and chopped	¼ cup parsley, chopped

1. Wash and dry veal shanks. Lightly sprinkle with salt and pepper.
2. Heat oil in a large, heavy frying pan over medium heat. Brown shanks on all sides (about 5 minutes) then remove to a platter.
3. Add to skillet garlic, onions, carrots, celery, thyme or rosemary and sauté until lightly browned. Place veal on top of onion mixture.
4. Plump prunes and apricots in wine in a bowl. Drain and place wine in frying pan. Cook until reduced by half (3 to 4 minutes).
5. Add prunes and apricots. Continue cooking 30 minutes to 1 hour until meat is tender enough to fall away from the bones. Garnish with parsley.

Preparation and Cooking Time: 1¼ hours

Note: Serve with Hagafen Pinot Noir or Cabernet Sauvignon.

Pears Poached in Red Wine

Hagafen Cellars
Napa, California

Yield: 4 Servings

This recipe was submitted by Nancy Levenberg, Sales and Marketing.

2 cups Hagafen red wine
1 cinnamon stick
⅓ cup sugar
2 strips lemon peel
2 whole cloves

4 ripe pears, D'Anjou or
Bosc, peeled with pith
and seeds removed
Freshly whipped cream
with 1 teaspoon vanilla
and 1 teaspoon sugar
added

1. Place wine, cinnamon stick, sugar, lemon peel and cloves in a heavy saucepan. Warm over medium heat until sugar is dissolved.
2. Add the pears so they are covered by the liquid. If not, add water. Cook the pears on medium-low heat for 30 to 45 minutes, stirring periodically and turning the fruit. The pears are done when they are easily pierced by a sharp knife.
3. Remove pears from the pan and set in a bowl. Increase the heat to high and reduce the liquid by one half by boiling. Add vanilla and sugar to whipped cream.

For each serving, place two pear halves on a plate, pour reduced wine sauce on top. Garnish with a dollop of whipped cream.

Preparation and Cooking Time: 1¼ hours

Fresh Lake Trout Baked in White Wine

Hagafen Cellars
Napa, California

Yield: 6 Servings

Zell Schulman, cookbook author, created this dish for Hagafen.

3 pounds trout, boned and
butterflied
¼ cup lemon juice
Cold water
1 tablespoon shallots,
chopped
Salt and pepper to taste
½ teaspoon thyme

½ cup Hagafen white wine
¼ cup oil
¼ cup skim milk
1 tablespoon margarine
½ teaspoon potato starch
1 tablespoon cheese,
grated (optional)

1. Preheat oven to 325° F.
2. Dip fish in a dish into which lemon juice has been mixed with cold water. Dry well with paper towel. Place in a baking dish, skin side down. Sprinkle with shallots, salt, pepper and thyme.
3. Add wine and oil. Cover fish with foil. Bake in a 325° F oven 15 to 20 minutes, or until fish flakes and feels firm to the touch. Remove from oven. Pour liquid in pan into a 1-cup measuring cup. Add milk.
4. Melt margarine in a saucepan. Add potato starch and stir well with wire whisk. When mixture begins to bubble, add milk mixture and cheese if using. Continue stirring until it thickens.
5. Pour sauce over fish and serve. For a little more color, place fish under boiler a few minutes. Serve with Johannesberg Riesling or Chardonnay.

Preparation and Cooking Time: ½ hour

Raspberry Balsamic Vinaigrette

Kedem Royal Wine Corporation
Brooklyn, New York

Yield: 1⅓ Cups

Chef Bare created this for Kedem.

> 3 ounces Bartenura Balsamic Vinegar
> 3 ounces Kedem Raspberry Syrup
> Salt and pepper to taste
> 1 tablespoon dry herbs
> 8 ounces extra virgin olive oil

1. Blend vinegar, syrup, salt, pepper and herbs.
2. Slowly drizzle in olive oil, beating until emulsified. Taste and adjust if necessary.

Preparation and Cooking Time: 10 minutes

What do you do with leftover wine that is beginning to sour?

Measure the wine. Add 2 tablespoons red-wine vinegar for red wine or 2 tablespoons white-wine vinegar for white wine for every cup. Let sit without a lid for 36 hours then store with tight-fitting cover.

Barbecue Sauce

Kedem Royal Wine Corporation
Brooklyn, New York

Yield: 1 Cup

Chef Bare created this for Kedem.

2 tablespoons oil
1 large onion, chopped
3 garlic cloves, chopped
4 ounces Baron Herzog
  Cabernet Sauvignon
3 ounces Bartenura Balsamic
  vinegar
1 8-ounce can tomato sauce

2 ounces tomato paste
4 tablespoons brown sugar
1 ounce soy sauce
2 tablespoons horseradish
1 teaspoon ginger
1 teaspoon celery seed
1 teaspoon dry mustard

1. Heat oil in a frying pan. Sauté onion until soft but not brown.
2. Add garlic, wine and vinegar and cook to reduce to half.
3. Add tomato sauce, tomato paste, sugar, soy sauce, horseradish, ginger, celery seed and dry mustard. Simmer until thick, about one half hour.

This can be used right away or kept in the refrigerator and used within a week.

Preparation and Cooking Time: 1 hour

Poached Salmon

Kedem Royal Wine Corporation
Brooklyn, New York

Yield: 6 Servings

Chef Bare created this for Kedem.

6 6-ounce salmon steaks
2 cups water
6 ounces Baron Herzog
  Chardonnay
4 ounces margarine

1 lemon, sliced
2 bay leaves
4 whole peppercorns
Salt to taste

1. Rinse salmon.
2. Place water, Chardonnay, margarine, lemon, bay leaves, peppercorns and salt in a poaching pan or shallow pot. Bring to a boil.
3. Add salmon. Bring to a boil. Reduce heat and simmer 15 to 20 minutes. Serve hot or cold.

Preparation and Cooking Time: 30 to 40 minutes

Chicken in Chardonnay
Poulet en Chardonnay

Kedem Royal Wine Corporation
Brooklyn, New York

French Style
Yield: 6 to 8 Servings

Chef Bare created this for Kedem.

1 3-4 pound chicken
2 garlic cloves
1 teaspoon garlic powder
1 teaspoon onion powder
1 teaspoon chili powder

½ teaspoon paprika
1 teaspoon dry herbs
4 ounces Baron Herzog
   Chardonnay

1. Preheat oven to 350° F.
2. Rinse chicken in cold water and let drain. Rub chicken inside and out with garlic.
3. Mix spices with 2 ounces wine to form a paste. Spread on chicken.
4. Place chicken in roasting pan, breast side down. Pour 1 ounce wine on top. Cover and roast in 350° F oven for half an hour.
5. Uncover and pour remaining 1 ounce wine to top. Continue cooking 30 minutes, basting every 10 minutes.

Preparation and Cooking Time: 1¼ hours

Chicken Cacciatore

Kedem Royal Wine Corporation
Brooklyn, New York

Italian Style
Yield: 6 To 8 Servings

Chef Bare created this for Kedem.

1 cup flour
Salt and pepper to taste
2 3½-pound chickens,
  cut in quarters
4 ounces oil
1 large onion, sliced
2 medium red peppers,
  sliced
2 medium green peppers,
  sliced

3 cloves garlic, crushed
4 ounces Baron Herzog
  Sauvignon Blanc
6 ounces chicken stock
12 ounces tomato sauce
6 ounces mushrooms,
  sliced
1 teaspoon lemon juice

1. Preheat oven to 350°F.
2. Place flour in a plastic bag; season with salt and pepper. Toss in chicken and coat.
3. Heat oil in a frying pan. Sauté chicken until brown. Place on a plate.
4. Sauté onion until brown in the same oil. Add peppers and garlic. Add wine and cook until liquid is reduced by half. Add chicken stock and reduce again by half.
5. Add tomato sauce, mushrooms and lemon juice. Taste to season. Add chicken to a casserole which has been sprayed with no-stick vegetable spray. Cover with sauce. Cover and bake in a 350°F oven for 45 minutes to 1 hour.

Preparation and Cooking Time: 1½ to 2 hours

French Roast with Sundried Tomatoes

Kedem Royal Wine Corporation
Brooklyn, New York

French Style
Yield: 6 to 8 Servings

Chef Bare created this for Kedem.

1 4-pound French roast
1 garlic clove
Salt and pepper to taste
1 large onion, sliced
4 ounces button mushrooms,
    quartered

1 bottle French dressing
    with sundried tomatoes
4 ounces Herzog French
    Merlot

1. Preheat oven to 350°F.
2. Rub meat with garlic and sprinkle with salt and pepper.
3. Place onion and mushrooms in roasting pan sprayed with no-stick vegetable spray. Place meat on top.
4. Mix dressing and wine and pour over meat. Roast, uncovered, in 350°F oven until desired doneness is reached.

Preparation and Cooking Time: 1½ to 2 hours

Brisket in Red Wine

Kedem Royal Wine Corporation
Brooklyn, New York

Yield: 8 To 10 Servings

Chef Bare created this for Kedem.

2 large onions, sliced
2 cloves garlic, crushed
1 4 to 5 pound brisket
Salt and pepper to taste
3 carrots, sliced
4 ribs celery, sliced
½ basket mushrooms,
  quartered

1 sweet potato, cubed
4 ounces Baron Herzog
  Cabernet Sauvignon
3 ounces Bartenura
  Balsamic vinegar
1 8-ounce can tomato
  sauce

1. Preheat oven to 350°F.
2. Spray a frying pan with no-stick vegetable spray. Sweat onions and garlic.
3. Season brisket and sear on both sides. Remove to a plate.
4. Add carrots, celery, mushrooms and sweet potato to pan and brown. Spray a roasting pan with non-stick vegetable spray. Place half of vegetables in bottom of roasting pan. Place brisket on top. Cover with remaining vegetables.
5. Pour wine and vinegar in frying pan. Deglaze and let reduce by half. Add tomato sauce and bring to a boil. Season and pour over brisket. Cover and cook in 350°F oven 1½ hours. Uncover and cook another ½ hour.

Preparation and Cooking Time: 2½ hours

"the vine with the tender grapes give a good smell."
(Song of Solomon 2:13)

Israeli Coffee

Royal Wine Corporation
Brooklyn, New York

Israeli Style
Yield: 4 Servings

2 cups strong coffee
½ **cup orange juice**
¾ **cup Sabra liqueur**

½ **cup dark rum**
½ **cup whipped cream**
Sugar

1. Half fill large stemmed glasses with coffee poured down the stem of a spoon.
2. Add orange juice, Sabra and rum to each in equal proportions, reserving 1 tablespoon rum.
3. Top with whipped cream. It is better if cream is not stiff. Sprinkle lightly with sugar.
4. Heat the tablespoon of rum and flame, pouring flaming rum on top of each glass.

Preparation and Cooking Time: 10 to 15 minutes

Crepes Sabra Style

Royal Wine Corporation
Brooklyn, New York

Israeli Style
Yield: 4 To 6 Servings

Crepes
3 tablespoons flour
2 tablespoons sugar
3 eggs, beaten
Dash salt
3 drops vanilla
⅔ cup milk

Sabra Sauce
3 tablespoons butter
2 tablespoons sugar
3 tablespoons orange juice
1 teaspoon orange peel,
   grated
¼ cup brandy
¼ cup Sabra liqueur

1. In a bowl, mix flour and sugar for crepes. Add beaten eggs, salt, vanilla and milk. Beat until smooth.
2. Butter a small frying pan over medium heat. Add enough batter to thinly cover the bottom (tilt the pan to get it covered). Loosen edges of crepe as it cooks. Turn over when brown. Remove to a heated plate.
3. Continue frying and piling crepes on top of one another but keep covered while each new crepe is being fried.
4. Fold crepes in quarters.
5. Melt butter in a hot larger frying pan. Add sugar, orange juice and orange peel and mix. Add crepes and sprinkle lightly with sugar.
6. Add 3 tablespoons brandy, reserving about 1 tablespoon, and Sabra, allowing them to heat until bubbling. Heat a little brandy in a large spoon and light it, then spread the flaming brandy over the mixture. Stir while flaming. When flame dies out, serve.

Preparation and Cooking Time: 45 minutes to 1 hour

PURIM
Sabra Hamantaschen

Royal Wine Corporation
Brooklyn, New York

Israeli Style
Yield: 24 Hamantaschen

1 cup prunes, pitted
¼ cup golden raisins
½ orange, sliced
½ lemon sliced
½ cup Sabra liqueur
¼ cup blanched almonds
  or walnuts, chopped

1 8-ounce package crescent
  roll dough or preferred
  packaged kosher dough
  or home-made biscuit
  type pastry
Churned honey
Rind of ½ orange, grated

1. Preheat oven to 375°F.
2. Place prunes, raisins, orange and lemon in a saucepan. Pour Sabra over fruit, bring to a boil, reduce heat and simmer, covered 5 to 10 minutes until prunes are slightly plumped and some of the liqueur is absorbed. Remove from heat and cool.
3. Put cooked fruit, except for half of the raisins, and liquid in blender and blend. Remove to a bowl.
4. Add reserved raisins and ½ chopped nuts. Stir with spoon or fork to mix.
5. Slightly overlap cut roll dough and flatten with rolling pin to form rectangle about 6 x 16 inches; or prepare your own pastry to form this size.
6. Cut into 24 2-inch squares, then fold each square in half to form 48 triangles. Spread half the triangles with honey, not quite to the edge and sprinkle with grated orange rind. Cover with plain triangles, seal edges and flatten with rolling pin.
7. Sprinkle with reserved chopped nuts. Place on ungreased cookie sheet and bake in a 375°F oven 10 minutes until pastry is golden. Cool and eat.

Preparation and Cooking Time: 30 to 40 minutes

Recipes in Kosher Kettle Using
Wines, Liqueurs, Cordials, Etc.

Apple enchantment (Amaretto)
Apple punch (Sabra, cognac or brandy)
Apple-squash soup (wine or vermouth)
Bananas Foster (banana liqueur)
Barbecue sauce (wine)
Beef stew (wine)
Beef ribs (wine)
Bourbon balls (bourbon)
Brandied peach butter (brandy)
Brandy banana bread (brandy)
Bread pudding (wine or sherry)
Brisket (wine)
Cappuccino (brandy)
Carbonades Flamandes (beer)
Cherry soup, cold (wine)
Chicken Baja California (sherry)
Chicken cacciatore (wine)
Chicken casserole, Chinese (sherry)
Chicken in chardonnay (wine)
Chicken kebab (wine)
Chicken, lemon (wine, sherry or vermouth)
Chicken and linguine (wine)
Chicken marbella (wine)
Chicken with mushrooms and wine (wine)
Chicken á la Sabra (wine)
Chicken schnitzel, Italian (wine)
Coffee cordial (vodka)
Creme de menthe cordial (vodka)
Crepes, Sabra style (liqueur)
Crullers (brandy)
Fish appetizer, Chinese (vermouth)
French roast with sundried tomatoes (wine)
Fruit n'flan (wine)
Fruit pudding dessert (liqueur)
Hot and sour soup (sherry)

Israeli coffee (liqueur)
Lamb riblets (wine)
Liver in wine sauce (sherry or wine)
London broil (wine)
Mulled wine (wine)
Macaroni-meat pie (wine)
Orange punch (liqueur, cognac or brandy)
Pears, baked (wine)
Pears, poached (wine)
Poached salmon (wine)
Pumpkin soup (sherry)
Roast beef (wine)
Sabra hamantaschen (liqueur)
Sabra orange cake (liqueur)
Sangria (wine)
Scrambled-ahead eggs (sherry)
Seafood marinade (wine)
Sherry cake (sherry)
St. Peter's fish soup (sherry or brandy)
Three mushroom pilaf (sherry)
Trout (wine)
Tuna crepes (sherry)
Turnips (rum)
Veal stiffado (wine)
Veal shanks (wine)
Vegetarian "shrimp" balls (wine or vermouth)

About Sybil Kaplan

Sybil Ruth Kaplan was born in Kansas City, Missouri. She graduated from the University of Missouri at Kansas City where she received a bachelor's degree in English and Secondary Education. She did graduate work at New York University in English and dramatic criticism.

For eight years, she worked in the editorial departments of Doubleday Publishing in New York, then, in 1970, she moved to Israel where she worked as a foreign correspondent. She also was the first public relations director of the Encyclopedia Judaica when it was first published; she taught English as a second language; lectured on Israeli foods and cooking; and was a feature writer for a number of Israeli magazines and press services. For four years she wrote a cooking column in *The Jerusalem Post*, Israel's only English-language daily.

While in Israel, she wrote three cookbooks on Israeli cooking--all in English. She returned to the United States, to Chicago in 1980 where she did free-lance writing, public relations, consulting, lecturing for the speakers' bureau of the Consulate General of Israel and was public relations consultant to the Israel Government Tourist Office in Chicago.

In 1988 she moved to Kansas City, Missouri, and became a feature writer for the *Kansas City Jewish Chronicle*. She also continued book reviewing which she had begun while in Israel by syndicating reviews to Anglo-Jewish newspapers around the United States.

Since 1991 she has been librarian at a traditional synagogue and a substitute teacher for middle and high schools. She is active in her synagogue and Jewish community activities. She also has served Hadassah at the regional level, and is the 1996-97 president of the Greater Kansas City Chapter of Hadassah.

She is the compiler/editor of all editions of a guidebook for those planning aliyah, **Coming Home**, which were published between 1969 and 1980. She is author of two published cookbooks, **The Wonders of a Wonder Pot or Cooking in Israel Without an Oven**; **Israeli Cooking on a Budget** (published by the Jerusalem Post and in print 12 years); and the unpublished, **From My Jerusalem Kitchen**.

She also edited **Alphabet Soup, Jewish Family Cooking from A to Z**, published by the Solomon Schechter Day Schools of Northbrook and Skokie, Illinois; and compiled and edited **Inspirations, From the Kitchen of Rena Hadassah**, published by the Hadassah group of Mount Vernon, New York.

She is wife to Barry, vice president and national sales manager of a large importer and distributor of headware; and mother to Shara and Elissa. Sybil lives in Overland Park, Kansas.

Five Star Publications

Perception of need plus imaginative ways to fill the needs can create success. It has done more than that for Linda Radke, a young professional business owner in Arizona who has more than proven the maxim. In her firm, **Five Star Publications**, and its offshoot, **Publishers Support Services**, she combines business and education experience into a career of matching human needs and human help, sometimes within usual patterns, sometimes in new procedures. In **Publishers Support Services**, she specializes in helping writers and publishers prepare and market books and, perhaps more important, she guides their promotional efforts.

Ms. Radke graduated from Arizona State University in 1976, with a degree in Special Education and Elementary Education. From there, she stepped into a position as an instructor of special education at ASU, working on a federally funded program of Parallel Alternative Curriculum aimed at guiding high school students into the mainstream of education. Continuing in education, Ms. Radke was a sixth-grade teacher for two years. Then, becoming aware of the need to bring together employers and employees in the domestic help arena, Ms. Radke owned and operated a household employment agency in Scottsdale, Arizona for five years. Her publishing venture began with the writing and publishing of supplementary materials in the domestic employment field. Her first title, **The Domestic Screening Kit**, was followed by **Options: A Directory of Child and Senior Services**, then **Nannies, Maids & More: The Complete Guide for Hiring Household Help**, and the other side of that coin, **Household Careers: Nannies, Butlers, Maids & More**. The last received the 1994 AACE Citation for Career Education Initiatives; first place in Arizona Press Women, Inc.'s 1994 Communications Contest, Non-Fiction Books; and honorable mention in the National Federation of Press Women's 1994 Communication Contest. A human touch and keen awareness of the reader's needs carried these books on to success. Other books from **Five Star Publications** also reflect lively links between the subject and the approach. These have included: three titles by Cass Foster, **Shakespeare for Children: The Story of Romeo** and Juliet; **The Sixty-Minute Shakespeare** and **Shakespeare: To Teach or Not To Teach**; and a cookbook, by Ms. Radke, **That Hungarian's in My Kitchen**, a predecessor to **Kosher Kettle: International Adventures in Jewish Cooking**. **Kosher Kettle** features recipes from around the world, bound together by a common religion.

In early 1996 came **The Economical Guide to Self-Publishing: How to Produce and Market Your Book on a Budget** in which Linda instills her experiences as an author, publisher, and publicist, in a step-by-step process from writing to marketing a book and with all the accompanying activities of personal interviews and promotion efforts. Dan Poynter calls it "A . . . road map to economical self-publishing." **Economical Guide to Self-Publishing** was recently selected as a 1996 Writer's Digest Book Club selection and first place, instructional book category winner in the 1996 Arizona Press Women, Inc. communications contest. Ms. Radke also received first place in newsletter, educational catalog, and news release and second place in brochures.

Her firm's name, **Five Star Publications**, has its own history. "My mother grew up in a family of nine brothers and sisters," Ms. Radke explains. "Five of the family, including my mother, served in World War II. During the war, parents who had sons or daughters in the war displayed stars in the windows -- one for each child in the service. It was a patriotic gesture and also expressed the deep hope that each would return home safely. Five stars became the symbol of my mom's family. One of my mother's brothers was captured and held as a prisoner of war. Fortunately, all eventually returned home."

One of my uncles used the name "Five Star" after the war when he opened his first grocery store in Indiana. The name continues with my publishing company.

Linda and her husband, Lowell, and children Gradey and Daniel, live in Arizona.

In MAZON's Own Words

In America, hungry children take turns eating breakfast. Millions of elderly people choose each month between paying their heating bill or buying groceries. This is the problem. The rest of the story follows. It is about our Jewish tradition — and you.

Among the greatest and most rewarding of Jewish traditions is to mark the days of our celebrations, large and small, by sharing our abundance with family and friends.

Woven into the tradition is the concept of inviting the poor to the table. In simpler terms it was much more than a concept. In days of old, the rabbis would not allow the celebration to begin until the poor of the community were seated among other guests, and fed.

Today, times have changed. We do not literally invite the poor to our table. But we can continue the tradition of sharing our abundance with the poor and hungry by symbolically inviting them to the table through MAZON: A Jewish Response to Hunger.

A teacher in Minnesota asked his class: "How many of you ate breakfast this morning?" As he expected, only a few of them raised their hands. So he continued, "How many of you skipped your breakfast this morning because you didn't like your breakfast?" Lots of hands went up. "And how many of you skipped breakfast because you didn't have time for it?" Many other hands went up. He was pretty sure by then why the remaining children hadn't eaten, but he didn't want to ask them about poverty, so he asked, "How many of you skipped breakfast because your family doesn't usually eat breakfast?" A few more hands were raised. Then he noticed a small boy in the middle of the classroom, whose hand had not gone up. Thinking the boy hadn't understood, he asked, "And why didn't you eat breakfast this morning?" The boy replied, his face serious: "It wasn't my turn."

No one should have to go to bed hungry or wake up hungry.

By the end of 1995, MAZON will have granted more than $10.3 million to organizations confronting hunger, principally in the United States.

For more information and ideas for how to help, write to MAZON: A Jewish Response to Hunger, 2940 Westwood Blvd., Suite 7, Los Angeles, CA 90064-4120. Tel: 470-7769.

FOREIGN COUNTRY/AREA INDEX

Balkan Peninsula
(Yugoslavia, Romania, Bulgaria, Albania)
Ghivetch

Belgium
Carbonades Flamandes

Chinese/Oriental
Chicken casserole
Chicken "spare ribs"
Egg foo yung
Fish appetizer
Gelatin
Hot and sour soup
Jerusalem Chinese salad dressing
Sate and dipping sauce
Sweet rice cakes
Thai style fried chicken
Vegetable salad
Vegetarian "shrimp" balls

England
Rolled cabbage

France
Chicken in Chardonnay
Fish with mushroom sauce
Onion soup
Plum clafouti
Roast with sundried tomatoes
Three mushroom pilaf

Germany

Brisket soup
Cucumber salad
Cherry soup, cold
Mandel bread
Red cabbage with apples

Greece

Borrekas, Sephardic
Borrekas, Greek
Chicken avgolemono with orzo pilaf
Chicken lemon soup
Green peppers, stuffed
Lentil soup
Macaroni-meat pie
Moussaka, dairy
Moussaka, meat
Orzo pilaf
Spinach and rice
Taliques
Tarama (roe dip)
Tuna-avocado spread
Veal stiffado

Hungary

Butter cookies
Chicken and dumplings
Crepes
Crispy crullers
Fish soup
Golden butter puff
Goulash
Kossuth crescents
Lecho
Letcho with meat
Roast beef
Stuffed cabbage

India

Banana peanut fish
Beans, Tisha b'Av
Chicken
Custard
Marathi Birda
Mint chutney
Mutton Alveress
Mutton Vindaloo
Pulao (rice)
Puran polis
Steamed rice cakes
Wheat halva

Israel

Apple enchantment
Avocado salad
Barbecued ribs of beef
Cabbage strudel
Carrot pie-cake
Cheese cake, no-bake
Cheese spread
Chicken á la Sabra
Chocolate balls
Chopped liver, mock
Chopped liver, pareve
Cocoa coconut matzah balls
Coffee
Coffee ice cream
Cream of spinach-potato soup
Crepes
Eggplant salad
Eggplant slices, pickled
Egg salad
Eggs, baked in tomatoes
English cake
Fruit n'flan
Hamantaschen

Haroset
Jerusalem pudding
Marinated schnitzel
Marzipan
Matzah cake
Melon shake
Mocha bars
Mousaka
Neapolitan windmill cake
Okra au gratin
Orange chiffon cake
Punch, hot apple
Punch, orange
Sabra orange cake
Spaghetti kugel
Spinach, creamed
Spinach soup, cold
Squash appetizer/salad
Squash-potato pancakes
Squash, stuffed
St. Peter's fish cocktail
St. Peter's fish pizza
St. Peter's fish in rice
St. Peter's fish soup
Strawberry ice cream
Tomato pizza
Tomatoes printannieres
Tomatoes stuffed with hearts of palm
Vanilla pie
Vegetable souffle

Italy/Sicily

Breast of veal, stuffed
Broccoli salad
Cappuccino, mocha
Cappuccino, quick
Cappuccino, quicker

Italy/Sicily

Chicken cacciatore
Chicken and linguine
Crushed olives and vegetables
Fettucini verdi
Pasta with eggs
Rice pancakes
Rice salad
Rice salad primavera
Schnitzel
Steak, olives and potatoes
Succot cookies
Tomatoes, baked

Korea

Chicken with vegetables
Potatoes

Lithuania

Cholent
Unstuffed cabbage

Mexico

Guacamole ice cream

Middle East/North Africa

Avocado dessert, Yemenite
Beets
Boulette, Tunisian
Bread salad, Syrian
Broad beans, Egyptian
Bulgur salad
Chicken kebab, Turkish style
Chicken stew with couscous, Moroccan
Coffee, Turkish
Cooked olive salad, Moroccan
Couscous dessert
Couscous, Turnisian

Middle East/North Africa

Cream cheese and celery salad
Eggplant and vegetables, Turkish
Grape leaves, stuffed
Haroset, Turkish
Kubaneh, Yemenite
Kubbeh, Kibbeh or Kibbee
Lamb riblets with eggplant
Lentils and rice, Egyptian
Lemon potatoes, Moroccan
Olive salad
Pita
Saloufa or Mithani, Yemenite
Shakshouka
Spinach mushroom mina, Turkish
Stuffed cauliflower
Stuffed green peppers
Stuffed squash
Tahina dressing
Turkey steaks
Turkish delight candy
Turkish salad
Vegetarian falafel loaf
Zingole, Syrian

New Zealand

Bread pudding
Pavlova

Poland

Apple streusel bars
Lentil soup
Rouladen, potato dumplings and sauerkraut

Romania

Mamaliga
Eggplant relish

Russia

Baked cheese sandwiches
Borscht, cold
Butter cookies
Chicken stuffed with potato
Egg garlic sandwiches
Fluden
Gefilte fish with fried onions
Ginger candy
Herring, baked
Kremzlach
Mashed potato knaidlach (dumplings)
Matzah meal cookies
Poppy seed tarts
Stuffed tomatoes
Tea
Walnut chocolate chip cake

Scandinavia

Fish chowder

Scotland

Oat breads

South Africa

Boston bread

South America

Liver in wine sauce
Peruvian chicken salad

<u>Spain</u>

Mushroom salad tapas
Sangria

<u>Thailand</u>

Fried chicken

<u>Turkey</u>

Chicken kebab
Eggplant and vegetables
Spinach mushroom mina

INDEX

★ Five Star Publications ★
A Learning Experience

Economical Guide to Self-Publishing: How to Produce and Market Your Book on a Budget by Linda F. Radke offers practical, easy-to-follow advice. The author steers the self-publisher through the maze of both the publishing and marketing worlds, offering money-saving tips at every turn. This award-winning self-publisher has helped numerous authors publish and market their books. A 1996 Writer's Digest Book Club Selection.

(Paper, $19.95, ISBN 1-877749-16-8)

Household Careers: Nannies, Butlers, Maids & More: The Complete Guide for Finding Household Employment by Linda F. Radke shows that there are professional positions available in the child care and home help arenas if you just know where and how to look. Learn how to earn up to $60,000 per year and cultivate a respected career. "Provides succinct and comprehensive information on a wide range of 'hidden careers' on the home front..."—Vann T. Atwater, Director of Professional Nanny Training, University of New Mexico/Los Alamos.

(Paper, $14.95, ISBN 1-877749-05-2)

Nannies, Maids & More: The Complete Guide for Hiring Household Help by Linda F. Radke takes the reader step-by-step through the process of hiring and keeping household help. Complete with sample ads, interview questions, and sample employment forms. It can help you find the right addition to your household.

(Paper, $14.95, ISBN 0-9619853-2-1)

That Hungarian's in My Kitchen by Linda F. Radke is filled with recipes for traditional foods, spiced with the warmth of family traditions. This book will appeal to both the novice cook and the sophisticated chef. The ingredients are easy to find and the directions make preparation simple. Every kitchen should have a copy.

(Spiral/Paper, $12.50, ISBN 1-877749-02-8)

Shakespeare for Children: The Story of Romeo & Juliet by Cass Foster makes this play enjoyable for the young reader without destroying Shakespeare's words. Fully illustrated. Nominated for the Benjamin Franklin Children's Storybooks Awards.

(Paper, $9.95, ISBN 0-9619853-3-X)

Order additional copies as gifts...You might be invited to dinner!

Name _____ Address _____
City _____ State _____ Zip _____ Country _____
Phone (____) _____ Fax (____) _____

If this a gift, please indicate to whom the book should be sent (a gift card will be enclosed):

Name _____ Address _____
City _____ State _____ Zip _____ Country _____

Gift from:

☐ Check enclosed (U.S. funds only)   ☐ Money order enclosed
☐ Visa   ☐ Mastercard   ☐ American Express   Expiration date: _____
Name as it appears on card: _____
Authorized signature: _____

_____ Number of copies Kosher Kettle @ $24.95 each $ _____
_____ Number of copies That Hungarian @ $12.50 each $ _____

Shipping/Handling ($4.00 for the first copy and $.50 for each additional $ _____
(Please add $4.00 for each separate gift address)

Order 3 or more copies shipped to the same address
and the shipping and handling costs are Five Star Publications gift to you!

Total Enclosed $ _____

☐ Yes, please send me a free catalog of other books published by Five Star Publications
Do you have comments about **Kosher Kettle?** We'd love to hear them: _____

Mail to: **FIVE STAR PUBLICATIONS**, 4696 W. Tyson St., Chandler, AZ 85226
Or for faster service order toll-free: **(800) 545-STAR, ext. 54** (have your credit card handy when you call)
Phone **(602) 940-8182** • Fax **(602) 940-8787** or e-mail us at fivestar@ix.netcom.com

ISBN 1-877749-19-2
Easy lay-flat binding
$24.95

ISBN 1-877749-02-8
Spiral bound, soft cover
$12.50

Five Star Publications
4696 West Tyson Street
Chandler, AZ   85226-2903

Place
Stamp
Here